Ulster-American Religion

Episodes in the History
of a Cultural Connection

DAVID N. LIVINGSTONE

RONALD A. WELLS

D1091669

University of Notre Dame Press

NOTRE DAME, INDIANA

Copyright 1999 by
University of Notre Dame Press
Notre Dame, IN 46556
All Rights Reserved
Manufactured in the United States of America

Library of Congress Cataloging-in-Publication Data

Livingstone, David N., 1953–
    Ulster-American religion : episodes in the history of a cultural
connection / David N. Livingstone, Ronald A. Wells.
        p.   cm. — (The Irish in America)
    Includes bibliographical references and index.
    ISBN 0–268–04303–5 (alk. paper). — ISBN 0–268–04304–3 (pbk.: alk. paper)
    1. Ulster (Northern Ireland and Ireland)—Church history.
    2. United States—Church history.   3. Presbyterian Church—Ulster
(Northern Ireland and Ireland)—History.   4. Presbyterian Church—
United States—History.   I. Wells, Ronald, 1941–   .   II. Title.   III. Series.
BR797.U57L58   1999
285′.2416—dc21   99–22331

For
Mark A. Noll
scholar and friend

Contents

Acknowledgments

This book is no exception to the general rule that when a worthwhile book appears it is a product of a community of scholars and not merely the people with the byline. We are aware of our debts, financial, logistical, intellectual, and human. We are glad to acknowledge them here.

First, we are grateful that Calvin College, through the Calvin Center for Christian Scholarship (CCCS), provided the funding that made this project possible. Donna Romanowski, Administrative Assistant to the Director of the CCCS, was particularly helpful. Since both authors worked on both sides of the ocean we had to travel to consult libraries and archives as well as each other. Second, we are grateful for the help of various archivists and librarians at the following institutions: Calvin College, Queen's University, Biola University, Bob Jones University, Princeton Theological Seminary (especially William Harris), and the City of Belfast Central Library. Third, there are a number of scholars who have taken time to read and comment on this work. While they are not responsible for any remaining errors in fact or interpretation, we know that this is a stronger book because of the comments of Sir Gordon Beveridge, Joel Carpenter, Darryl Hart, David Hempton, Alvin Jackson, George Marsden, Mark Noll, and the unnamed readers at the University of Notre Dame Press. We particularly thank Mark Noll for providing inspiration, both humanly and scholarly, to this and other projects. In recognition of that, we dedicate this volume to him. We also thank Peter Wallace, now a graduate student at Notre Dame, for providing the appendix about Irish students at Princeton. This is work he began as an undergraduate at Wheaton College, under Mark Noll. Finally, we do not merely follow convention in thanking our spouses; in this case the love and support of Frances Livingstone and Barbara Wells were vital to our successful collaboration in Belfast and Grand Rapids. They traveled with us to both places and were unfailingly graceful in giving intellectual and human support.

D. N. L., Belfast
R. A. W., Grand Rapids

Introduction

This book is a work in transatlantic religious and cultural history, exploring the connection between Northern Ireland and the United States during the past century and a half, especially the period 1860–1940. This is mainly a story of Presbyterianism. The Presbyterian culture in Ulster and America was a dominant culture, or so was the self-understanding of leaders and people alike. But the nature of that hoped-for dominion ought to be seen as the desire (some would say calling) to give society moral leadership. As we will suggest in several ways, the leadership offered by Presbyterians was, over time, accorded increasingly less welcome by other people and organizations in the two societies. Conservative and evangelical Presbyterians more and more came to believe that the tide of history in the modern world was against them and their moral vision. Whether in education, science, theology, or politics, those who saw themselves as naturally appointed leaders were puzzled, even saddened, by the challenges to that leadership. For them, it was essential to maintain the boundaries of the mind, the spirit, and the nation. Religion was their self-chosen ground on which to contend for societal leadership.

This account of evangelical and Presbyterian history in Ulster and America is our attempt to paint the picture of this transatlantic connection on a larger canvas. We identify religious ideologies and practices in their various forms and situate them culturally, observing that context shapes and interprets religion and culture in a variety of ways. The episodes we examine reveal the way in which the intellectual and cultural meanings of religious belief change over time, especially when applied to such divergent contexts as scientific discussions at premier universities or the legitimating of populist politics. The themes discussed here offer salient observations on the history of the cultural connection between Ulster and America.

Transatlantic history resembles comparative history. The latter can be defined in several ways, but most people see immediately the intent of it, i.e., that national mentalities be transcended in an attempt to compare similar cultural forms (e.g., education, family, ethnicity, etc.). Americans have not always been interested in comparative analysis. As the historian C. Vann Woodward observed, (and Ian Tyrrel has echoed) in an era of global consciousness and international history, the relative lack of interest in comparative analysis invites the accusation of American parochialism.

> They are said to lay excessive claims to distinctiveness and uniqueness in their national experience, to plead immunity from the influences of historical forces that have swept most other nations, to shun or deprecate comparisons between their history and that of other people, and to seek within their own borders all the significant forces that have shaped their history.[1]

Woodward's comment appeared in his introduction, almost thirty years ago, to a book about the comparative approach to American history. Since that time, perhaps stimulated by Woodward and his colleagues, a great deal of comparative historical analysis has been published. A few examples will perhaps suffice. First, during the American Bicentennial some interesting comparative studies appeared that provided a nice counterpoint to the hoopla and myopia of the period. The careful analyses by British scholars, led by Harry Allen, helped markedly in this respect.[2] Second, on the vital American subject of race, important comparative studies have appeared in recent years. In particular, a whole new conversation on race was launched when comparative analysis was introduced, as the work of Davis, Degler, and Fredrickson attest.[3] Third, the anniversary of the 1492 Columbus event brought to the fore studies that looked anew—often askance—at the cultural connections between "old" and "new" worlds. The work of Axtell and Nash, for example, changed our minds about the meaning of "discovery" when looked at from the viewpoints of Native Americans and African Americans.[4] Fourth, comparative analysis about politics and culture is as old as the work of Tocqueville and Bryce and has been augmented in recent years by studies as numerous as they are sophisticated. In this area, the work of Greene, Morgan, and Bailyn has raised the level of analysis to rare and satisfying heights.[5] Finally, while the conservative Protestantism that is the concern of this book has not received as much treatment as politics, there have been several extremely valuable studies, for example, by George Rawlyk, Mark Noll, Harry Stout, and George Marsden.[6]

This brief review of comparative scholarship suggests an important tendency. On the one hand, the day has now largely passed when studies undertaken within a single state or cultural group could not be enriched by comparative analysis. On the other hand, the notion of "comparison" invites the perpetuation of supposed national differences. While one cannot reduce a wide range of historical literature to a single generalization, we suggest that something has emerged from a generation of attempts to do comparative history: a new idea—perhaps a re-cycling of an old idea—is to see the essential unity of the North Atlantic culture. Rather than national differences, emanating perhaps from "national character," we now see interesting continuities and discontinuities across putative political and cultural boundaries, which appear as regional differences within a larger cultural whole. We offer two examples of what we mean. In one of David Livingstone's chapters we note that James McCosh could move from Brechin to Belfast to Princeton and not skip a beat in the conversation. Similarly, in Ronald Wells's discussion of W. P. Nicholson, we see that the evangelist can move from southern California to Northern Ireland while being led by the same cultural light. In any case, this notion is not the invention of historians, but the self-understanding of the people we study. In the Victorian crisis of faith, and its aftermath in society and politics, a remarkable convergence of ideologies and practices emerged in Ulster and America. Within the Presbyterian network of institutions there was a considerable knowledge of, and concern about, what was happening on either side of the water. If a deep and abiding sense of cultural connection between Ulster and America had developed, religion was the tie that bound.

We are two scholars interested in the cultural and social location of ideas. We bring the different perspectives of our respective disciplines—cultural geography and social history—to this common effort, in the belief that each will enrich the other. A question that might be asked of us is why we chose these particular episodes to study. The answer is both simple and complex. Simply stated, these cases reflect our historical interests. With greater complexity, we note that we had been working independently as scholars, in different disciplinary contexts and networks. When we discovered that our interests converged in disclosing the inter-working of a transatlantic culture in which Presbyterians were important players, we decided to collaborate, in the hope that our contribution would offer some fresh insights. In the beginning chapters David Livingstone concentrates on transatlantic Presbyterian intellectual life in general and scientific culture in particular. He locates the debates engaged in by members of the intellectual elite in their respective social, political, and cognitive frameworks. Ronald Wells's succeeding chapters dwell largely, though not exclusively, on issues of theology and politics, and he likewise places controversy and contention within a broader conservative Ulster-American mentality.

While these subjects are seemingly discrete arenas of engagement, they are complementary in that they are concerned with placing intellectual and social history within a cultural matrix spanning the Atlantic ocean. While distant in physical space, we might say that Ulster and American Presbyterians were next-door neighbors in social space. In fact, we try in the following pages to make mental maps for those constructions of reality that are the patterns of perceptions made by the actors described. Peter Gould and Rodney White were the first scholars of human geography to use the term "mental maps," in their book of the same title.[7] Most people have seen, for example, a New Yorker's idea of the United States (with the Mississippi three-quarters of the way across, Hollywood and Las Vegas as states, and Texas on the Pacific Ocean near California). The map is, of course, a distortion, but it is a revealing index of how some New Yorkers perceive the rest of the United States, or how they hope the rest of the country might look. Perceptions are vital because they guide the world pictures and worldviews people actually have. Marking boundaries for one's own world—national, ethnic, moral, theological, scientific—is a profoundly human activity and the subject of much study in the social sciences. As the anthropologist Anthony P. Cohen and his colleagues have demonstrated, marking the boundaries of one's own group gives one a sense of belonging to something more permanent than the contingent relationships of modern culture.[8] Indeed, if the essential character of the modern person is a "homeless mind," then deep within our humanness there is a desire to protest this decline into a cosmopolitanism that robs us of our particularity in terms of gender, ethnicity, religion, and nationality; in short, it would be a world in which all are "New Age" adherents and speakers of Esperanto. The yearly ritual of villagers in colonial New England, carrying on the tradition brought from rural, premodern Britain, was to "beat the boundaries" of the village, that is, to see again—and reaffirm—the permissible borders of life.

In this work we suggest that in order to analyze Princeton University's self-understanding of "holding the line" for religion in higher education (and therefore for cultural leadership in America) we need to look again at James McCosh's decision to bring George Macloskie to take the new chair of natural history in 1875; in trying to reconstruct the educational consequences of McCosh's articulation of "the Scottish philosophy" at Princeton, we need to look again at his experiences at Queen's University, Belfast; and to identify the causes and consequences of the secessions in the Presbyterian churches in Ireland and America, we must re-examine the mentalities and institutional imperatives that impelled James Hunter and J. Gresham Machen to take the uncompromising stands they did. Furthermore, in constructing the mental map of the evangelical conjunction of religion and politics, the academic understanding of "the troubles" in Northern Ireland must first be deconstructed to see in both Ireland and America the common roots of a conservative Protestant disinclination to behave in a modern way in politics (i.e., to disjoin it from religion); and in order to see the power of revivalism to legitimate the state we must look again into the Irish and American influences on W. P. Nicholson whose evangelistic work played an important role in the foundation of an Ulster Unionist identity.

These instances vary enormously but an important common theme emerges. In our hope to write a cultural history of these various connections between Ulster and America, we pose the questions that arise from the self-understanding of the principle actors. In various ways the same question is being asked: are there no boundaries? These chapters in comparative, transatlantic history rise above the parochialism of a national focus, but they are rooted in the particularity of Protestantism (mostly Presbyterianism) in Ulster and America. If the episodes described here have salience, it is because these experiences of Ulster-America have resonance with all those people of faith who have tried, and are trying, to keep the faith of their fathers and mothers in the confusing and complex modern world.

One Culture and Curriculum

The Belfast-Princeton Connection

In 1844 Archibald Alexander—doyen of American Presbyterians who molded the shape of theology at Princeton for over a century[1]—drew attention to a cultural connection too frequently ignored within the ranks of his own American Presbyterian community. Writing that year in *The Biblical Repertory and Princeton Review*, he told his readers: "It is common to represent our church as having derived its origin from the Church of Scotland; and remotely this was the fact; but its immediate origin was from the Presbyterian Church of Ireland." This indeed was "a more intimate connection" than was shared with any other Presbyterian body, for— so Alexander mused—"not only did our first ministers come to us from Ireland, but the people who composed the first Presbyterian congregations were from the same country."[2] A decade and a half later these self-same sentiments were echoed by Archibald's third son, Joseph Addison Alexander, when, further reflecting on his father's earlier observations, he noted that these historical associations with Ulster, "together with a certain family likeness," afforded the strongest reason "for regarding that branch of the Presbyterian body with peculiar sympathy and friendly interest."[3] Indeed, in the interim Professor William Gibson, whose son was a student at the Princeton Seminary, returned from his 1858 visit to the United States determined to make the General Assembly's College (also known as the Presbyterian College) in Belfast into a transatlantic Princeton, which he regarded as "the headquarters of Presbyterianism in the world."[4]

These links were to remain both deep and lasting. For generations a considerable contingent of Ulster ministerial students crossed the Atlantic to study at Princeton, the publications of the Princeton theologians were staple diet for the Belfast students, and ties between key faculty in the two institutions were substantial.

Robert Watts, whose career will surface significantly in our next chapter, saw to it that generations of Belfast students for the Presbyterian ministry were well versed in Hodge's *Systematic Theology*, an "imperishable" work which he believed to be "without a peer in the whole history of theological exposition." Small wonder that, according to Robert Allen, Watts was also determined to make "Belfast another Princeton."[5] Moreover, subsequent research has revealed that the "Irish connection" was "the most significant" element in Princeton's international student clientele. "Over 340 Irish-born students," according to Wallace and Noll, "attended Princeton Seminary prior to 1929. Of these, 87 returned to Northern Ireland as their principal place of service, of whom at least four became moderators of the General Assembly of the Presbyterian Church in Ireland."[6] Thus during Princeton Theological Seminary's centennial celebrations, held in May 1921, one of the main addresses was delivered by Rev. John Macmillan who spoke about "Irish and American Presbyterianism." Here the moderator of the Presbyterian Church in Ireland reflected generally on the Ulster-Scots tradition in America but focused more particularly on links with Princeton. He could only speak of Princeton "with reverence and affection"; he recalled with evident warmth his own experience as a student of Charles Hodge and W. H. Green; he observed that the name of Warfield "is a household word among us"; and he reflected that Robert Watts revered his Princeton "preceptors as Saul of Tarsus revered Gamaliel."[7]

Besides these specifically ministerial connections, intellectual ties between Ireland and America were profound, and not least through the Scottish Common Sense philosophy which had its roots in the thinking of the Ulster-Scots philosopher and dissenter Francis Hutcheson, whose major works were published when he was still conducting his Dublin Academy prior to his appointment as professor of moral philosophy in the University of Glasgow.[8] For it was Hutcheson's moral and political thinking that profoundly conditioned the philosophical reasoning of John Witherspoon at Princeton, who used Hutcheson's *A System of Moral Philosophy* as the main source for his own lectures on the subject.[9] Nor was Witherspoon unique. Benjamin Franklin, James Madison, James Wilson, and John Adams were all influenced by the principles of civil and religious liberty which Hutcheson adumbrated. Indeed, as Norman Fiering puts it, "Hutcheson was probably the most influential and respected moral philosopher in eighteenth-century America." For the moral philosophy of the Scottish Enlightenment "was uniquely suited to the needs of an era still strongly committed to traditional religious values and yet searching for alternative modes of justification of those values."[10] This is scarcely surprising, since to Hutcheson popular consent was crucial to the exercise of all political authority, and he thus defended the right of the oppressed to defy the crown.[11]

Because the vast majority of Irish Presbyterian ministers in America had been trained in this philosophy in Glasgow and because of the personal influence of the Donegal-born Francis Alison (who emigrated to America, where he became vice provost of the College of Philadelphia in 1752), John Barkley could tellingly quip that this heady "philosophical polity was 'brewed in Scotland' . . . 'bottled in Ireland' . . . and 'uncorked in America.'"[12] Indeed, Ian McBride has noted that what were known as the "Scoto-Hiberni" students in Glasgow "not only sustained the intellectual life of Presbyterian Ulster, but as Scots-Irish emigrants to North America they became the chief exporters of enlightenment to the colonies."[13] Thereby they formed an informal transatlantic network that kept communication lines open between Enlightenment Scotland, Ulster, and America. The influence of their philosophical system, as the most acceptable of the various "Enlightenments" on offer, was thus profound in the New World and not least upon the domestic evangelical tradition there.[14]

Beyond the arenas of theological education and political philosophy, there remain other spheres of influence uniting transatlantic Presbyterianism, among which religious revivalism looms especially large. Throughout the North Atlantic world, Ulster-Scots Calvinist communities played a significant role in the nurturing of Protestant revivalism. In North America particularly these very Presbyterian immigrant communities exerted powerful influences on both the First and Second Great Awakenings during the mideighteenth and early nineteenth centuries.[15] Besides, it was news of revival outbreak in 1857, reaching Ireland from America, that encouraged Ulster Presbyterian clergymen—according to Stewart

J. Brown—to hope and seek for local revival "as a means of restoring a communal identity that was being threatened by rapid industrialization, urbanization and changing patterns of agriculture." [16] No doubt too it was for these reasons that the geography of the 1859 revival in Ulster very largely followed the contours of Presbyterian strength. [17] After all, the General Assembly, having received its commissioned report on the transatlantic awakening, prayed for revival at its annual meeting that same year. [18]

Many of the strands of Presbyterian culture—Scottish Common Sense philosophy, religious revivalism, ideals of learning, and scientific scholarship—connecting Ulster and America in general, and Belfast and Princeton in particular, manifest themselves in the remarkable transatlantic career of James McCosh, whose influence on both sides of the Atlantic was truly profound. By focusing on aspects of his life and thought we may thus catch a glimpse of a key moment in the history of the Ulster-American cultural connection, for McCosh's career channels many of the currents of cultural life flowing across the Irish Sea and on across the Atlantic Ocean.

EDUCATIONALIST: MOLDING A CORE CURRICULUM

In his remarkable and controversial diagnosis of *The Soul of the American University*, in which he charts the trajectory of American higher learning from "Protestant establishment to established nonbelief," George Marsden pauses to turn his attention to Princeton as "especially significant . . . because if a more traditionalist Protestant intellectual alternative to the emerging definitions of American academia was to survive at any major school, Princeton was the foremost candidate." [19] In large measure, along with the local influence of the seminary, this was on account of the towering presence of James McCosh, who arrived to take up the presidency of the then College of New Jersey in 1868. His stature as a leading philosophical realist in the Scottish tradition—not to mention a Scottish accent—assured that he would be taken seriously within the American academic establishment. Besides, his Free Church sympathies, evident ever since his siding with Chalmers during the Disruption of 1843, meant that Presbyterian Princeton—with a staunchly Calvinist clerical presence on the faculty and intimate connections with the neighboring seminary then dominated by Charles Hodge—was specially congenial to his academic and theological tastes.[20] Indeed, he had received, but declined, an energetic approach from the Free Church College in Glasgow to assume the chair of apologetics in 1856 and also testified that Chalmers (followed by Hugh Miller and Baron Bunsen) was the greatest intellectual force he had ever encountered.[21]

McCosh's assumption of the presidency, however, occurred right on the cusp of the college's perceived need to retrieve its position of national academic leadership through broadening its outlook even while retaining its theological heritage. McCosh embraced this challenge with vigor and insisted that Princeton "would be a Christian university, in a traditional sense."[22] In his efforts to achieve this aim he accorded a central role to moral philosophy, undergirded by religious conviction, within the college curriculum in opposition to what he saw as a faddish elective system that did not pay sufficient attention to the limits within which student freedom needed to be exercised. His debate with Charles Eliot of Harvard in 1885 revealed his abhorrence of a curricular system where music, French plays, and novels could oust mathematics, logic, ethics, political economy, and the sciences; it likewise displayed his horror over the possibility that a student could "gain a Harvard education without being taught anything of either morality or religion."[23] And these two elements were intimately connected, for McCosh would not let Eliot forget his own admission that "nobody knows how to teach morality effectively without religion."[24]

In his own efforts to preserve the ideals of Christian higher learning, McCosh had to grapple with two issues of momentous intellectual concern—Darwinism and biblical criticism. Suffice at this point to note that his espousal of a Lamarckian reading of evolution history, suitably fortified by a robust providentialism, permitted the Princeton circle to navigate its way through the Darwinian storms.[25] With a long-standing belief that science and Scripture were compatible, Princeton concordism faced a more serious challenge over biblical criticism and emerged, with McCosh's wholehearted support, in recondite opposition to higher critical views. McCosh himself, moreover, played a key role in the Presbyterian controversies over the historicism that permeated the work of the Old Testament scholar Charles Briggs and, towards the end of his life, he pronounced with solid, if urbane, conservatism on the matter.[26]

The significance of McCosh "holding the line at Princeton," to use Marsden's words, was evidently of considerable dimensions. And while it is true to say, as Marsden does, that McCosh came "from Scotland to the Princeton presidency,"[27] this is only indirectly the case. For McCosh had spent a decade and a half, immediately prior to his transatlantic move, as professor of logic and metaphysics at Queen's College in Belfast, having been appointed to that post in 1852. From that point in time until his departure for New Jersey in 1868, McCosh was engaged in a range of educational (and indeed other) pursuits that were crucial to the molding of the McCosh curriculum in the New World.

The story of higher education in Ireland is inextricably bound up with religious history given the central importance of the need for clerical education. Prior to 1793, and since its foundation in 1591, the University of Dublin—Trinity College—had been closed to all but Anglicans. Thus during the early nineteenth century, it was Catholic and Presbyterian dissatisfaction with educational provision at the university level that largely lay behind moves for the widening of higher education.[28] So far as the Presbyterian community was concerned, the general certificate that was issued by the Academical Institution, which came into being in Belfast in 1810, was recognized by the Synod of Ulster and the Secession Synod as equivalent to a degree.[29] The effect was that soon the majority of ministers for the Presbyterian Church, who had previously studied at the University of Glasgow where moderatism had begun to prevail, were now being trained in Belfast. Under these new arrangements, however, matters did not fare much better for those with conservative inclinations, and the prevalent Arianism at the Academical Institution fostered an ever-growing evangelical party in the General Assembly intent on severing links and providing theological education elsewhere. In due course a new college was erected and opened in December 1853 under the control of the Presbyterian Church's General Assembly, just one year after McCosh moved across the Irish Sea to Belfast.

In the meantime, a new university—the Queen's University in Ireland—had come into being as a response to problems of higher education for the laity. The new body incorporated three new non-denominational colleges—in Cork, Galway, and Belfast—where students were free of religious tests. The scheme came to fruition in 1850 and while these colleges were condemned by Pope Pius IX "as intrinsically dangerous to the faith and morals of Catholics," the Belfast college flourished, in contrast with the other two, not least because from the start the new Presbyterian College (the General Assembly's College) fully cooperated with the local Queen's College.[30]

Given the issue of providing mixed or nonsectarian education at Queen's, it is not surprising that curricular questions were to the fore in the early days of the institution.[31] In general, the range of subjects to be taken for an arts degree went beyond that required in many other universities at the time as the colleges sought to supplement the traditional curriculum based on classics and philosophy with elements of modern literature and science. But the issue of religious and moral instruction had to be faced, and the university instituted a detailed scheme to monitor student behavior, which involved a variety of penalties for such offenses as habitual failure to attend a place of divine worship approved by parents and regular neglect of the religious instruction provided in licensed boardinghouses. These measures, no doubt, were intended to compensate for the absence of theology from the curriculum, an understandable arrangement given the nondenominational character of the system and one which led the Presbyterian Church to proceed with the establishment of its own college. The outcome of a sequence of prolonged machinations that surfaced on the floor of the General Assembly was that Presbyterian students could receive their literary education at Queen's College and their theological training in the church's own institution. The fact that Henry Cooke—relentless harrier after heresy, crusader in the cause of political conservatism, and anti-Catholic partisan—was appointed dean of the Assembly's College ensured that the fears of the orthodox Presbyterians were in good measure assuaged.[32] The Catholics, however, decisively condemned the whole system and determined to found a university of their own—a scheme which came to fruition in the foundation of the Catholic University of Ireland under the rectorship of John Henry Newman in 1854.[33]

This was the environment into which James McCosh's educational career was launched when, in 1852, he was appointed professor of logic and metaphysics at Queen's College, Belfast. McCosh's predecessor in the post was Robert Blakey, the author of the four-volume *History of the Philosophy of Mind* (1848) and numerous other philosophical works, not to mention several publications on angling and shooting.[34] If nothing else, the enthusiastic endorsement of Blakey's work by the French philosopher Victor Cousin, himself the author of *La Philosophie Écossaise*, attests to the influence of Scottish Common Sense philosophy at Queen's College, Belfast, right from its earliest days. Blakey's commitment to philosophy, however, seems to have been greater than his commitment to the university, and persistent absence from his post led to his formal dismissal in October 1851.[35] Within a month the position had been filled by James McCosh, minister of the Free Church, Brechin, and author of the influential *The Method of Divine Government, Philosophical and Moral*, which had appeared in 1850. Lord Clarendon, the lord lieutenant of Ireland, was extraordinarily impressed by the book's efforts to reconcile traditional Christian theism and modern science, and it was largely on this account that McCosh was able to secure the Belfast chair.

Despite Clarendon's enthusiasm and the eulogies appearing in some portions of the press, the appointment was not received with universal approbation. Some expressed disappointment that the position had not gone to a local scholar. Others suspected that religious sentiment, and therefore political incentive, had obtruded. Indeed the fact that it was William Gibson, a professor at the Assembly's College, who had put Clarendon in possession of McCosh's treatise, not to mention the encouragement that Gibson personally gave to McCosh, lends support to these suppositions.[36]

Whatever the precipitating circumstances, there is no doubt that the Belfast years were McCosh's most fertile. Here he worked out his distinctive rendition of the Scottish tradition as he sought a via media between sensationalist empiricism and transcendentalism. During the 1860s, in such works as *Intuitions of the Mind* (1860), *The Supernatural in Relations to the Natural* (1862), and *An Examination of Mr. J. S. Mill's Philosophy* (1866), he displayed his distaste of both French materialism and Kantian idealism as equally metaphysically sinister. This perspective, cultivated in anticipation of its religious implications, emphasized the intimate corresponding connections between mind and nature. Standing, as Hoeveler puts it, "at the juncture of the Scottish philosophy and nineteenth-century evangelicalism," McCosh integrated these elements into a powerful, if rapidly dating, "Protestant scholasticism."[37] Throughout, he protested vigorously against the collapsing of mind and matter, a stance no doubt influential on B. B. Warfield, who later quipped, "What is mind? No matter! What is matter? Never Mind!"[38]

Given McCosh's personal intellectual pedigree—he had come under the profound influence of the moderate Sir William Hamilton in philosophy and the evangelical Thomas Chalmers in divinity during his student days—coupled with the highly developed taste for philosophy that characterized Scotland's universities in the era of what Davie has called "the democratic intellect,"[39] it is not surprising that McCosh's Belfast inaugural address was a vigorous call for the institution of inductive philosophy along the lines of the Scottish curriculum. Here, to the intervening cheers of an enthusiastic audience, McCosh laid out the groundwork of his subsequent intellectual mission at Queen's in a lecture, "On the Method in which Metaphysics Should Be Prosecuted," steering his own course between the Scylla of contemporary materialism and the Charybdis of mere intuitionism. French sensationalism and German romanticism—his twin bêtes noires—were thus the subjects against which he railed, as he turned for inspiration to his Scottish philosophical roots. Only by the rigorous prosecution of inductive method had science made progress; for he believed that "Bacon, like Moses, led us forth at last, / The barren wilderness he passed." It must be the same for metaphysics: "the precise nature of the intuitive principles of the human mind must be discovered by induction." The underlying reason was not hard to discern:

> The same God who gave to the planets their laws gave to the human mind its laws. The laws of the planets operate spontaneously—the laws of the human mind do also operate spontaneously; and, in order to discover either the one or the other, there must be a course of accurate and painstaking induction.[40]

Reid, Brown, Hamilton, Cousin, Butler, and Chalmers had all in varying ways demonstrated the benefits of following such a course, of promulgating "moral Newtonianism," as it has been called.[41] This thoroughly empirical turn, moreover, was intimately bound up with McCosh's moral perspective. Writing in his monumental 1875 History of Scottish Philosophy, a work which, incidentally, performed the strategic historiographic role of imposing coherence on the idea of a "Scottish School," he underscored the moral dimensions of inductive inquiry into the nature of the human constitution:

> At a time when the Scottish metaphysicians were discoursing so beautifully of moral virtue, there was a population springing up around their very colleges in Edinburgh and Glasgow, sunk in vice and degradation. . . . But the institutions which aim at lessening the sin and misery of the outcast and degraded—such as missions, ragged schools and reformatories— have proceeded from very different influences, and a philosophy embracing the facts they contemplate must dive deeper into human nature and probe its actual condition more faithfully than the academic moralists of Scotland ever ventured to do.[42]

Not surprisingly, McCosh wanted to assure his Belfast hearers that the reason he had "come to this place [was] not to earn an honorable livelihood, not to hold a place of honor, but in order to establish in the minds of the youth of this district . . . certain great intellectual principles, which will abide with them through life, and guide them in all their future inquiries." For it was precisely at this critical point in their lives that "character is formed."[43] The thoroughly ethical import of the whole undertaking was plain.

By turning in like manner to the methods of natural science, Protestant moral philosophers in America, of whom McCosh would become a leader, sought to milk metaphysical meaning out of mundane science, transcendental truths out of the mere material. Whatever the value of this strategy in keeping lines of communication open between science and moral philosophy, it ran the risk of a pan-mechanization that could even engulf human nature and social polity. Yet the constitutional strictures of the Republic were forcing advocates of moral philosophy to seek for ways of preserving a Christian public order without any coercive appeal to orthodox Christianity. The main route they could find was to say that the scientific study of the human constitution inevitably would display the very universal moral sense adumbrated in Christian theism.[44] For McCosh, it was simply a presupposition that the harmonious fit between moral laws and physical laws could only be accounted for by a God who had "so ordered his physical government, that it is made in various ways to support his moral government."[45] So he had declared in 1850—in the very book that assured his appointment to Queen's.

To the extent that McCosh later became a key figure in the emergence of the New Psychology in the United States, there is plainly supporting evidence for Graham Richards's contention that, instead of locating its ancestry solely in German experimental psychology and British evolutionary thought, there were strongly moral concerns at the headwaters of the new movement as articulated in the work of figures like James Mark Baldwin, William James, and G. Stanley Hall.[46] The issue of how to ground moral authority had certainly been an enduring problem since the foundations of the Republic; and transatlantic philosophy, in the shape of the Scottish tradition, held pride of place in the attempt to address it. In the latter part of the nineteenth century, the Christian philosophizing by the likes of Noah Porter and James McCosh—at Yale and Princeton respectively—turns out to have been instrumental in bringing to birth the New Psychology, a project which, according to Richards, was "a translation into more secular terms of the same ethical concerns which pervaded mental and moral philosophy." For these figures, he maintains, were "positively supportive of men who are considered as canonical 'founding fathers' of the New Psychology."[47] Thus even as they issued hostile commentary on the tradition of moral philosophy,[48] advocates of the newest psychology actually drew sustenance from the discipline's disowned parent. If indeed this is so, and the historiography which dismissed the relatively short life of American moral philosophy (it lasted for a little less than a century) as outrageously outré and intellectually moribund is misconceived, the foundations of the pastoral concern for students which Richards sees as crucially emblematic of the moral project undergirding the New Psychology were, in McCosh's case, laid during his years in Belfast. His own recollections of student life in Glasgow where, due to lack of pastoral care, many "contracted vicious habits . . . and fell into intemperance, or dissoluteness, or gambling, and came speedily to ruin," prompted him to take an active interest in the lives of the Belfast students, frequently inviting them to his home.[49] Not inappropriately, these later reflections were delivered in Belfast when he returned to participate in the 1884 conference of Reformed Churches just a few months before his debate with Eliot in New York.

Given McCosh's fundamentally *moral* conception of higher education, together with his desire for the democratization of intellectual life, it is understandable that during his Belfast years he would do all within his power to extend the scope of educational provision. Within a year or so of his arrival he had embarked on a lengthy and indefatigable campaign to foster the development of a national system of intermediate education, which would both enable children with academic talent to secure upward social mobility and at the same time provide a feeder system for the Queen's colleges.[50] A reconnaissance trip through continental Europe in 1858 afforded him the opportunity of surveying educational provision there, and the experience he accumulated was to become a crucial consideration in his later candidacy for the Princeton presidency. Indeed Sloane ventured to suggest that the "scientific study of educational systems," which McCosh pursued during his Belfast years, was "the most important of [his] avocations."[51] Also shortly after his arrival in Belfast, he became aware that there was an underrepresentation of the commercial and merchant classes within the student body and, with a number of colleagues, determined to rectify the situation. Accordingly, on being elected to the College Council, he availed himself of the opportunity to voice his feelings on the matter.[52] Later in 1857, when appearing before the Queen's College Commission, appointed to report on progress within the colleges of the university, he further pressed his concerns. The consequence was that, in due course, approval was secured for the institution of an appropriate course of teaching which ran, with only limited success, until 1874. Predictably curricular issues rapidly surfaced, and equally predictably McCosh took a dim view of the suggestion that the course should be heavily weighted towards science, modern languages, and political economy at the expense of logic and metaphysics. Academic specialization, even for day release students in commerce, was uncongenial to him; and the debates here foreshadowed what would soon come. What he wanted, as Hoeveler nicely puts it, was for mammon to "lie down with the muse."[53]

McCosh's subsequent expression of grave concern over the inroads into classical university culture that an unbounded elective system would make in American higher education thus had its origin in early disputes about curricular reform at Queen's College. Proposed changes in the ordinance prompted him to pen a letter to the university's secretary in which he complained about what he saw as a curtailment in the scope of the mental sciences in a system which permitted students to ignore metaphysics altogether. Compared with the Scottish system this was altogether deplorable, especially when subjects less fitted to "discipline the mind"—such as French, Italian, and modern history—could be substituted for metaphysics, political economy, and jurisprudence.[54] After all, moral philosophy had held pride of place in the Scottish curriculum for generations and was regarded as crucial no less to theology than to politics, economics, and social thought. Besides, the moral consequences of specialization were grave. Had not "the exclusive study of the material sciences had a materialistic tendency" in France—where the trend became so pernicious that it had prompted none other than Cousin to head up "a movement which

. . . ended in the higher institutions of France giving an important place to the study of the human mind".[55] The later debate with Eliot in New York, it seems, was merely a distant echo of culture wars already fought—and lost—in Ireland a quarter of a century earlier. For McCosh's opponent, Professor William Nesbitt, currently at Queen's College, Galway, and subsequently Belfast, did not hesitate to point out that "History and Metaphysics are the two subjects in our curriculum, the teaching of which is regarded with suspicion by the various religious communities into which the country is divided."[56] Princeton, McCosh was determined, would not make the same mistake. For it was these experiences in Belfast, it would seem, that prompted McCosh during his inaugural speech at Princeton to warn of the dangers of too much specialization. "Let the student first be taken, as it were, to an eminence, whence he may behold the whole country . . . and then be encouraged to dive down into some special place, seen and selected from the height, that he may linger in it, and explore it minutely and thoroughly."[57] The curricular philosophy that McCosh articulated at Princeton was evidently a compound product of Scottish philosophical principle and Ulster educational practice.[58]

EVANGELICAL: DEFENDING REVIVAL AND REVELATION

Within a couple of years of arriving in New Jersey, McCosh found himself reporting to the trustees of the college, for the year 1870, that "by far the most important occurrence that has taken place in our College . . . is a blessed revival of religion among the students."[59] Such sentiments, of course, were thoroughly in keeping with McCosh's evangelical sympathies, for revivalism was a favored mode of personal and communal transformation among evangelicals. McCosh, moreover, saw to it that the student body was well supplied with visiting preachers who would fan any pious sparks into revival flame. The result was that 1876 witnessed the most remarkable of the virtually routine revival seasons that Princeton had undergone over a number of generations. Having discerned among the students a growing spiritual momentum indicated by prayer meetings, strenuous personal evangelism, and earnest seeking after salvation, McCosh invited D. L. Moody and Ira D. Sankey to the campus to conduct services in the Second Presbyterian Church, and McCosh himself presided over a large communion service during their visit.[60]

American revivalism came in a wide variety of styles, assuming differing dispositions and deploying different techniques. And while it may be too strong to suggest that the mode of revival at Princeton that McCosh championed was rather more likely to be of the bowdlerized—or at least sedate—variety, certainly compared with what Hatch calls the "inflammatory practice" of earlier figures like Charles Finney who "gave Princeton theologians every reason to cringe,"[61] there is no doubt that he possessed the rhetorical and intellectual resources to finesse the more vulgar rantings of revivalist excess and eccentricity. These skills, I suggest, had been finely honed nearly twenty years earlier in Belfast as he encountered the religious awakening that swept through Ulster in 1859.

Since the early part of that year, and with even greater intensity since April, the north of Ireland had found itself overtaken by a tide of religious revival—a spiritual awakening accompanied in part by "convulsions, swoons, visions, and other extraordinary effects that seemed to spread through the province of Ulster like an epidemic."[62] "Monster meetings" in Belfast and Armagh presented the public face of a movement, which transformed personal life, spawned prayer groups, and fostered family devotions. As we have already noted, however, this awakening was not exactly produced by spontaneous spiritual combustion. News of American revivals in 1857–58 had induced the General Assembly of the Presbyterian Church in Ireland to dispatch representatives to inquire into the spiritual conditions of the former colonies. And these reports from afar, widely discussed at presbyteries and church meetings, transformed an endemic yearning for the retrieval of the earlier Sixmilewater renewal of 1625 into "active revival prayer meetings."[63] And yet the work of professional revivalists is conspicuous only by its absence, for the movement spread through the zealous activities of humble laymen, particularly those who recalled with deep conviction their own personal transformation. Indeed, according to the Presbyterian historian W. T. Latimer, this was the moment when for "the first time in the history of Ulster Presbyterianism laymen became as prominent as preachers."[64]

While in general revivalism was not part of the heritage of Scottish Presbyterianism, compared with Methodism for example, the Reformed support for the new enthusiasm that was expressed by Edgar and Gibson on the basis of their American experience doubtless carried much weight. Gibson, for example, the Assembly's College professor of moral philosophy, published in 1860 *The Year of Grace*—the standard history of, and theological apologia for, the Ulster revival. Here Gibson charted the local origins of the movement, cataloged its historical geography, presented a county-by-county inventory of its effects, and called upon the theological support of Princeton's Charles Hodge and Archibald Alexander in defense of its physical manifestations. All led him inexorably to the conclusion that the movement's "origin and progress unequivocally attest it as divine."[65] Not everyone saw it quite this way. Rev. Isaac Nelson, for instance, penned a virulent deprecation in a lengthy review of *The Year of Grace* candidly entitled *The Year of Delusion*. Deploring what he saw as the complete absence of reason, Nelson castigated those revival supporters who despised Enlightenment rationality and urged—in terms reminiscent of the Scottish philosophy—that any genuine "work of the Omnipotent Spirit . . . is done according to the operation of the natural laws of the mind." His conclusions were unmistakable: "we think that the so-called Revival of 1859 has been disgraceful to Christianity, a corruption of Gospel truth, and the means of filling the Presbyterian Church with vice and immorality under the sanction of religion."[66]

In turn, despite the savage censure issued by Nelson and no doubt due to the influence of John Edgar and William Gibson, J. Addison Alexander at Princeton reflected favorably on Ulster's "great awakening" as he gratefully observed that the revival seemed to have originated in the Presbyterian Church and was "still instrumentally promoted chiefly by the labors of its ministers and members." To Alexander, it was, all in all, a "wonderful event."[67] Ulster newspaper reports of Edgar's warm reception by American Presbyterian bodies as he relayed news of the Ulster re-

vival confirmed the close fraternal, if transatlantic, relations between these evangelical Calvinists.[68] As for denominational consequences, the revival's impact on Irish Presbyterianism was far from
negligible. In a short time, according to Robert Allen, it had the
effect of "more than doubling the size of some of the classes" in
the new Assembly's College.[69]

This, then, was the environment into which James McCosh
launched his own diagnosis of the revival and in particular of its
physiological manifestations. Towards the end of September 1859,
the Evangelical Alliance convened in Belfast. As one of its two sec-
retaries (the other being none other than William Gibson) approached the rostrum, he was greeted by a derisive chorus of hiss-
ing and booing from at least some of the assembled company. Rev.
William M'Ilwaine's reputation had preceded him. An evangelical
Anglican who had been present at the inaugural meeting of the
Alliance in 1846, a regular contributor to its annual proceedings, a
member of the executive council since 1857,[70] and a local anti-
Catholic controversialist of some notoriety,[71] M'Ilwaine had, however, blotted his copybook in the eyes of the evangelicals gathered
in Belfast, over the most pressing issue of current concern—the
Ulster revival.

William M'Ilwaine, the rector of St. George's Church in Belfast,
had welcomed the spiritual exercises that the revival had induced.
But he expressed his opposition to their physiological "excesses"
so vehemently that thereafter some evangelicals cast him as an enemy of God. As he rehearsed his queries, voices from the assembled company felt the need to murmur "Tut, Tut," to vociferously
inform him "You're wrong," to ask him "Are you converted your-
self?" and finally to declare "You are not of the Church of God!"[72]
Subsequently, in both popular print and medical treatise alike,
M'Ilwaine conducted his campaign against "fanaticism of the
wildest type," a fanaticism, moreover, which was both class- and
gender-biased towards "the ignorant, uneducated, hard-worked,
and easily impressed class, and, in the proportion of nineteen out
of every twenty, young and excitable females."[73] No doubt it was
because this assessment had appeared some weeks earlier in September as a follow-up to sermons that M'Ilwaine had delivered on
the subject in July (and which he subsequently pursued in the Jour-

nal of Mental Science) that he was the object of the Alliance's vilification.[74] But more: M'Ilwaine's Episcopalian convictions disposed him to query the laity-led character of a movement which removed it from the sphere of clerical management. Appeals for financial support by earnest female converts only confirmed his judgments, and those who duly made monetary contributions were condemned as rendering "a whole class of persons [unfit] for their lawful worldly occupations."[75]

There were, however, other voices to be heard that very day at the Evangelical Alliance. Perhaps it was because of greater rhetorical subtlety. Perhaps it was on account of the sympathetic tone of his apologia. Perhaps it was a consequence of a more democratic ecclesiology favoring lay participation and tidily in keeping with the democratizing thrust of his educational philosophy. Whatever the reason, James McCosh found himself acclaimed as the Evangelical Alliance's intellectual champion of revival. Indeed he did note that the revival was one of the "two great topics—public topics—which are at present engaging the thoughts of the people of Ireland." (The other, predictably, was the opposition of "the Romish hierarchy" to the arrangement of the Queen's colleges.)[76] The fact is, however, he too had certain reservations over what he termed the Ulster revival's "physiological accidents." But his strategy on that same September day in his paper to the Alliance was to relieve the revival movement of the burden of prejudice that its accompanying bodily manifestations had fostered in the minds of unsympathetic critics. To him these physical displays were mere "accidents," explicable as purely natural reactions to extreme emotional experience and largely attributable to Irish ethnic temperament. Cerebral associationism and psychological proclivity were thus co-contributors to the revival's visual drama. But—and this is crucial—McCosh cast his diagnosis in the language of defense by insisting that the "deep mental feeling" that induced somatic convulsions was itself "a work of God."[77] Speaking in advance of M'Ilwaine, and evidently unaware of any growing sense of dissent, McCosh was delighted to reflect that at the Alliance's meeting "there was not a gentleman who spoke but declared that he believed this to be the work of God."[78] His address was well received; by late October one Belfast bookshop had sold some 8,000 copies of the pamphlet. So, despite their shared reservations, M'Il-waine found himself cast as the villain of the piece, while McCosh emerged as the revival's apologist. On revival questions, McCosh had learned in Belfast how to use words wisely and how to avoid the acrid polemics of those inclined to demonize or valorize either the cultured despisers of spiritual renewal or the feverish advocates of revivalist enthusiasm.

The evangelical convictions that McCosh displayed in his endorsement of revival were fully matched by his defense of revelation against the onslaughts of modern critical methods. We have already noted his critique of Briggs's historicism—issued towards the end of his life—which gave succor to those of conservative theological conviction. But it was, again, in Belfast that he had first encountered the force of the new biblical criticism. No sooner had he given his pronouncements on the Ulster revival than copies of *Essays and Reviews* began to appear on the bookshelves in 1860. Authored by seven Church of England ministers, this collection caused a storm in the English-speaking theological world on account of its open deployment of critical methods—the self-same methods used in the interrogation of ancient texts—and its insistence on the need to take seriously poetic, legendary, parabolic, even mythic dimensions of the biblical documents.[79] The unifying assumption of the authors was simply that the Bible should be interpreted just like any other book. Such too was the thrust of John William Colenso's treatise on the Pentateuch, which came out two years later and propounded his belief that the Old Testament narratives should not be read as history but as the medium for conveying spiritual truths. Predictably evangelicals took a dim view of these maneuvers.

McCosh's 1862 volume on *The Supernatural in Relation to the Natural* afforded him occasion to express his alarm at these most recent machinations. Focusing especially on Baden Powell's chapter on miracles, McCosh provided a characteristically philosophical reading, locating the malaise in the influence of German skepticism. McCosh's strategy was to provide a theological account of natural law that could circumvent the mechanistic materialism that he believed afflicted Powell's scientific thinking. Yet these metaphysical concerns did not go to the heart of McCosh's disquiet over *Essays and Reviews.* What bothered him most of all was the crisis of intellectual and social authority that the undermining of biblical inspiration might induce. Put directly, sensuality and godlessness would ensue.[80] McCosh's conservative diagnosis placed him firmly alongside figures like Henry Cooke and J. G. Murphy, who pronounced no less vigorously on these matters.[81] Nor did McCosh restrict his expression of concern to this manifestation of German philosophical disease. When Ernest Renan produced in 1863 his controversial *Vie de Jesus*—a further contribution to a growing tradition of work querying the account of the life of Jesus in the synoptic Gospels along the lines already promulgated by David Friedrich Strauss—McCosh delivered two lectures on the subject to the Belfast branch of the Y.M.C.A. Under the title "The Life of our Lord, a Reality and not a Romance," McCosh castigated Renan's speculative endeavors, which, he said, ought not to be dignified with the term "history," but were rather a mere "romance." To McCosh the entire undertaking was based on thoroughly gratuitous naturalistic assumptions and left him no option but to "hiss it off the stage of history."[82]

EVOLUTIONIST: FORGING A SCIENTIFIC CREDO

Given the conservatism that McCosh displayed on matters of biblical criticism, not to mention his support of evangelical revivalism, his stance on the question of evolution—for which he is now probably best remembered—may seem somewhat odd. For McCosh came to acquire the reputation of being the foremost Victorian reconciler of evolutionary theory and Protestant theology. The details of his modus vivendi have been scrutinized by numerous commentators, and it suffices to simply record his adoption of a providentialist reading of evolutionary history in a Lamarckian mode.[83] Thus, speaking at the 1873 New York meeting of the Evangelical Alliance, McCosh told his hearers that, instead of denouncing the theory of evolution, "Religious philosophers might be more profitably employed in showing . . . the religious aspects of the doctrine of development; and some would be grateful to any who would help them to keep their new faith in science."[84] While some deployed the strictures of Baconian induction to resist Darwin's proposals, McCosh's empiricist inclinations encouraged him to treat with seriousness the data Darwin had accumulated—data which convinced him of the *fact* of evolutionary change, even while steadfastly resisting the naturalistic mold in which Darwinian *theory* was cast. McCosh was eventually to espouse such an all-embracing providential evolutionism that he came to locate the events of the *Heilsgeschichte* in the Christian era in the wider context of the progressive development of the great chain of life. The advent of the human species and the coming of the Holy Spirit at Pentecost were to be understood as inaugurating new stages of human existence. As he put it in 1890:

> In all past ages there have been new powers added. Life seized the mineral mass, and formed the plant; sensation imparted to the plant made the animal; instinct has preserved the life and elevated it; intelligence has turned the animal into man; morality has raised the intelligence to love and law. The work of the Spirit is not an anomaly. It is one of a series; the last and the highest. It is the grandest of all powers.[85]

In the light of these intimations it is hardly surprising that Ernst Benz sensed reverberations between McCosh's evolutionary eschatology and Teilhard's "Omega Point."[86] McCosh's enthusiasm for the Duke of Argyll's *The Reign of Law*, moreover, reveals just how far he was prepared to go in locating divine design within the intrinsic operations of natural law.[87] In all this, as we shall see in our next chapter, McCosh diverged markedly from the stance adopted by Belfast Presbyterians in the 1870s and 1880s, by which time he was firmly established in New Jersey.

Although McCosh's major pronouncements on the Darwinian intervention occurred after he had left Ulster, there is good reason to suggest that the foundations of his subsequent endorsement were laid during his years at Queen's. Even before leaving Scotland, his first book already showed the seeds of the accommodationism that characterized his later scientific perspective. For he had already come to realize that Paley's version of natural theology—a version which received a body blow from Darwin's natural selection mechanism—was not the only rendition of teleology. A homological alternative, stressing the ways in which divine wisdom was manifest in the *general* operations of laws rather than in *specific* organic adaptations, provided a valuable means of discerning the providential governance of the world order.[88] This version of the design argument was rather better placed to enable its advocates to adjust to an alternative, evolutionary account of adaptation.

But it was his experience of working on their co-authored *Typical Forms and Special Ends in Creation* with George Dickie (the Queen's College professor of natural history and a fellow Scotsman who had come to Belfast from Aberdeen) that further persuaded McCosh of the potential of this alternative reading of teleology. Traditionally this collaborative volume has been regarded as representing both the high watermark *and* the last gasp of scientific natural theology before the Darwinian onslaught and thus as shortly to be outmoded. But the book was very largely patterned on the morphological system of Richard Owen, who had worked with the conviction that anatomical structures were organized according to transcendental plans and that corresponding parallels (homologous relations, as they were called) between animal structures were readily detectable.[89] The value of such "idealist" reasoning to those with natural theological sympathies is plain,[90] and it enabled a number of clergymen-scientists in the years prior to the publication of Darwin's *Origin of Species* to adjust to the evolutionary speculations emanating from Paris materialists.[91]

What the precise division of labor was in *Typical Forms and Special Ends in Creation* is not known. But since George Dickie's research interests lay in botany and zoology—he presented numerous papers at the Royal Society and was the author of several botanic guidebooks—it seems likely that the detailed empirical data within the book were his. What is absolutely clear, however, is that he exhibited a profound fascination with morphology, and the mark of Owenite thinking is indelibly stamped on the joint volume. Besides, McCosh had earlier familiarized himself with Owen's output by authoring a lengthy review of his monograph *On the Archetype and Homologies of the Vertebrate Skeleton* (1848).[92] Moreover, he had in 1851 already ventured some theoretical speculations on botanical matters and was delighted that Dickie found these to be of value.[93] The result of their collaboration was an architectonic portrait of a creation designed to display a cosmic aesthetic not unlike that elucidated by the amateur Scottish geologist and journalist Hugh Miller. Certainly the authors perceived their joint work as in keeping with the tradition of Paleyite natural theology, but their espousal of Owen's morphology displayed a wider teleology, which in due course would facilitate the construction of an evolutionary natural theology. Thus while they insisted that "the recent discoveries in regard to the homology of parts can never set aside the old doctrine of the teleology of parts," they were equally sure that British natural theology needed to be supplemented by continental-inspired transcendental morphology. Continental writers like Oken had highlighted themes which must no longer "be overlooked in a natural theology suited to the middle of the nineteenth century."[94]

If these suspicions are well founded they make much sense of the stance that McCosh adopted in his first major systematic foray into evolutionary questions after he moved to the New World. In *Christianity and Positivism*, the published version of his 1871 lectures at New York's Union Theological Seminary, he deployed those very ideas developed in Belfast in accommodating to the latest evolutionary theses when he affirmed that

> There is proof of Plan in the Organic Unity and Growth of
> the World. As there is evidence of purpose, not only in every
> organ of the plant, but in the whole plant . . . so there are
> proofs of design, not merely in the individual plant and indi-
> vidual animal, but in the whole structure of the Cosmos . . .
> The persistence of force may be one of the elements conspir-
> ing to this end, the law of Natural Selection may be another.[95]

McCosh's adoption of evolution, then, was never of precisely Darwin's own variety. It was always a providential-teleological reading of evolutionary history that McCosh promulgated. But what facilitated even this degree of accommodation to the empirical component of the Darwinian theory was his capacity to conceive of divine design in terms other than that of Paley's perfect adaptationism. As we will shortly see, a few years later, when seeking to fill the chair of biology at Princeton, McCosh sought to perpetuate this same perspective by resorting to the services of a young Ulster

Presbyterian clergyman, George Macloskie, whose thinking will feature prominently in our next chapter.

James McCosh's Belfast years, it turns out, were infinitely more than a lacuna between his time in Scotland and America. To the contrary, his educational preoccupations, his revivalist inclinations, his stance on the new biblical criticism, and his evolutionary leanings were all materially marked by his experience at Queen's College. The democratizing impulse that energized his views of higher education and predisposed him towards religious revival had been hammered out in the crucible of mid-nineteenth-century Ulster society. It may not be too much to suggest that it also inclined him towards an account of organic history that favored progressive development from below, as it were. When cast in moral terms, the survival of the fittest, according to Boyd Hilton, "suited the progressive developmentalism of incarnational thought better than the rigors of competitive capitalism."[96] With such convictions McCosh found himself opposed by those like M'Ilwaine who, more concerned with clerical control, found both revivalism and Darwinism entirely uncongenial. But more, it was in the environment of Ulster's religious polarization that McCosh learned how to use words wisely, how to combine theological conservatism with social tolerance, and how to hone his rhetoric in such a way that censure was palatable and enthusiasm judicious. Such idiomatic skills and intellectual flexibility were precisely what enabled him to transform the local College of New Jersey into the international Princeton University.

Two Science and Scripture

Transatlantic Transactions

During the final decades of the nineteenth century, Presbyterians in Belfast and Princeton discovered a novel item on their theological agendas. The new theory of evolution promulgated by Charles Darwin and his doughty disciples Thomas Henry Huxley and John Tyndall had to be confronted. Numerous studies of theological reaction to Darwinism are now available and, in general, these have done much to dispel the old conflict interpretation of the relations between science and religion.[1] Indeed there is now evidence to suggest that where conflict was stirred up, as often as not, it was promulgated less by reactionary clergymen than by the Darwinians, as the advocates of scientific naturalism might be collectively identified, who were at pains to advance the position of science in late Victorian culture. Having said this, there is an increasing body of opinion affirming that general models of how science and religion have interacted in the past are doomed to failure since they do not take with sufficient seriousness the particular circumstances and contingent conditions in which debates were domiciled.

Here we wish to examine in some detail how Ulster-American Presbyterianism—as expressed in the citadels of Princeton and Belfast—met the perceived threat of the Darwinian moment. It might be expected that communities with an identical theology, a common curriculum, and shared ecclesiastical icons would respond in similar ways to such intellectual challenges. The common heritage that these Presbyterian cultures espoused, it turns out however, did not guarantee a common transatlantic response to the new biology. Accordingly we explore here the reception of Darwinism in the American and Ulster Calvinist heartlands, focusing particularly on one or two key players in the drama whose connections between Princeton and Belfast were both deep and lasting. In both cases local circumstances were at least as significant as shared theological commitments in conditioning how the new science was encountered. Through pursuing these particular responses something of the subtle nature of transatlantic Presbyterian cultural connections may be glimpsed.

ROBERT WATTS: CONTROVERSIALIST

Robert Watts missed his train connection from Dublin to Belfast on Saturday, 28 March 1863.[2] He had just arrived by boat from the United States of America and had traveled that same day from Cork. Watts's wife had already returned from the New World in 1861 for health reasons, and he had been forced to resign his pastorate of the Westminster Presbyterian Church in Philadelphia in order to rejoin her. Prior to taking up that charge he had studied at Princeton Seminary in New Jersey under such Reformed luminaries as Charles Hodge, J. Addison Alexander, and W. H. Green. The Princeton experience was truly formative for Watts and was to dominate his outlook for the rest of his life. Old Princeton was an ever-present force, and he battled long and hard to reproduce its spirit and ethos on the other side of the Atlantic.

It was missing that train, however, that secured his reentry into Irish Presbyterian life. For having failed to make his connections, Watts found himself preaching from the pulpit of Dublin's Lower Gloucester Street Presbyterian Church on that Sunday evening. What had happened was that James Edgar, the minister of the church, had suddenly died on the very day Watts stepped off the boat, and Watts was prevailed upon to occupy the pulpit in the dire circumstances. In due course he was unanimously invited to take up the ministry of Lower Gloucester Street as Edgar's successor later that year. But it was to be a brief pastorate. For within three years, in 1866, on the death of Dr. John Edgar, Watts was appointed to the chair of theology at the General Assembly's College in Belfast—a position he eagerly embraced, not least because it afforded him unlimited opportunity to promulgate the theology of Old Princeton at the very heart of Irish Presbyterian intellectual life. Therefore it is no surprise to find the historian of the Presbyterian College, Robert Allen, commenting that "One cannot think of Robert Watts without thinking of Charles Hodge."[3]

During his tenure of the Assembly's chair, Watts further cultivated his reputation as a controversialist. Even before returning to this native Ireland he had published a critical commentary on Barnes's treatise on the atonement for the July 1859 issue of *The Princeton Review*. And this was only to be the start of a long campaign on behalf of conservative Calvinism against what he took to be a variety of foes of the faith.[4] From his Belfast chair, he issued vigorous repudiations of Arminianism, Darwinism, German rationalism, Roman Catholicism, and Robertson Smith's biblical criticism.[5] But perhaps his dominating passion was the issue of biblical authority, and he sought to provide a rigorous, and indeed rigid, defense of verbal inspiration in the face of various revisionist proposals, particularly in his Carey lectures for 1884.[6] Throughout, he received the approval of evangelical Calvinist stalwarts like Charles Haddon Spurgeon, who found him to be both sound and scriptural. Others were less laudatory. Marcus Dods, doubtless appalled by the truculence of Watts's language, quipped that he was "one of those unhappily constituted men who cannot write unless they are angry."[7] Watts's literary energies and general theological predilections are not the subject of our immediate concern, however; instead, we choose to focus on his role in the Darwinian controversies in late Victorian Belfast in the context of the Princeton connection, which he had labored long and hard to tend. Thereby some of the broader cultural ramifications of Ulster-American Presbyterianism may be highlighted.

THE TYNDALL EPISODE

The *Northern Whig* enthusiastically announced the coming of the "Parliament of Science"—the British Association for the Advancement of Science (B.A.)—to Belfast in its pages on Wednesday, 19 August 1874. The meeting would, the editor was sure, provide pleasant entertainment, a temporary respite from "spinning and weaving, and Orange riots, and ecclesiastical squabbles," and perhaps a little drama arising from "the hot discussions" predicted for "the biological section," between advocates of human evolution and those "intellectual people—not to speak of religious people at all—who believe there is a gulf between man and gorilla."[8] With Thomas Henry Huxley (Darwin's bulldog), J. D. Hooker, and John Tyndall all speechifying, it promised to be quite an event.[9] For if the new scientific priesthood, which they represented, planned to launch an attack on the old clerical guardians of Scripture and social status, there could scarcely have been a better venue than Calvinist Belfast. Tyndall's pugnacious performance did not fall short of expectations. In an Ulster Hall garnished with accompanying orchestra, he delivered—with nothing short of evangelical fervor—a missionary call to "wrest from theology the entire domain of cosmological theory." His conclusion was that all "religious theories, schemes and systems which embrace notions of cosmogony . . . must . . . submit to the control of science, and relinquish all thought of controlling it."[10] The gauntlet had been thrown down.

Robert Watts was quick to pick it up. The very next Sunday he issued a virulent attack at Fisherwick Church in downtown Belfast. Watts had good reason for spitting blood, moreover, having had a paper which he submitted to the organizers of the biology section of the B.A. flatly turned down, even though it was a plea for "peace and co-operation between science and religion".[11] Evidently the B.A. wasn't interested in conciliation. And the rebuff doubtless stung. But any chagrin that this expulsion may have fostered was nothing to the anger that Tyndall's address aroused in him. The commendation of Epicurus was especially galling; that name had "become a synonym for sensualist," and Watts balked at the moral implications of adopting Epicurean values. To him it was a system that had "wrought the ruin of the communities and individuals who have acted out its principles in the past; and if the people of Belfast substitute it for the holy religion of the Son of God, and practice its degrading dogmas, the moral destiny of the metropolis of Ulster may easily be forecast."[12]

Of all the applause Watts received for his Tyndall offensive, none pleased him so much as the enthusiastic endorsement of Charles Hodge. On reading the address, Hodge wrote to him saying it "will do you great credit, and the cause of truth great good.

Tyndall and Huxley have done nothing but openly avowing what it was plain they really held. The German scientists of the same school, who pride themselves in their atheism, do not hesitate to include their English co-laborers in the same category with themselves. They ascribe their reticence to fear of the religious public in England. It seems they have at last got courage to speak out. . . . The evil . . . for the time being is tremendous." Since Watts regarded Hodge as "the author of the greatest work on systematic theology which has ever issued from the pen of man," he was clearly flattered by the letter, and so he had it read to the Belfast Presbytery, printed in *The Witness*, and reproduced in the pamphlet version of his sermon.[13]

Tyndall's speech cast a long shadow over Ulster Presbyterianism for more than a generation. Plans were hastily laid for a course of evening lectures to be given at Rosemary Street Church during the winter months on the relationship between science and Christianity.[14] During that 1874–75 winter of discontent, eight Presbyterian theologians and one scientist joined together to stem, from Rosemary Street pulpit, any materialist tide that Tyndall's rhetoric might trigger. Just as the villagers of medieval Europe and colonial New England annually beat the bounds—marked out the village boundaries—so the Presbyterian hierarchy needed to reestablish its theological borders. But the ripples did not stop even there.

Just over a year earlier, the Catholic serial *The Irish Ecclesiastical Record* had presented an evaluation of Darwinism in which its correspondent castigated the "Moloch of natural selection" for its "ruthless extermination of . . . unsuccessful competitors," its lack of evidence for transitional forms, its failure to account for gaps in the fossil record, and its distasteful moral implications.[15] As for the latest clash in Belfast, the Catholic archbishops and bishops of Ireland issued a pastoral letter in November 1874 in which they repudiated the "blasphemy upon this Catholic nation" that had recently been uttered by the "professors of Materialism . . . under the name of Science." This certainly was no new warfare, they reflected; but the Catholic hierarchy perceived that this most recent incarnation of materialism unveiled more clearly than ever before "the moral and social doctrines that lurked in the gloomy recesses of [science's] speculative theories." Quite simply it meant that moral responsibility had been erased, that virtue and vice had become but "expressions of the same mechanical force." Such was the brutalizing materialism that now confronted the Irish people.[16]

Notwithstanding the congruence between these evaluations and those of the redoubtable Watts, the sectarian traditions in Irish religion ensured that opposition to a common threat would do nothing to bring Protestant and Catholic together. In a subsequent reprint of his pamphlet "Atomism: Dr. Tyndall's Atomic Theory of the Universe Examined and Refuted," Watts thus incorporated in an appendix "strictures on the recent Manifesto of the Roman Catholic Hierarchy of Ireland in reference to the sphere of Science." It was "painful," he noted, "to observe the position taken by the Roman Catholic hierarchy of Ireland in their answer to Professors Tyndall and Huxley."[17] This required not a little rhetorical finesse and Watts's reasoning was far from clear as he sought—with little conviction—to distance himself from their proposals. What it boiled down to was an attempt to say that his objections to Tyndall's machinations were reasonable; theirs were not. But the detail is not important. What is significant is that the furor surrounding the Tyndall event became yet another occasion for Ulster nonconformity to uncover its sense of siege. By seeking to cast secularization and Catholicism as subversive allies against the inductive truths of science and the revealed truths of Scripture, Watts found it possible to conflate as a single object of opprobrium the old enemy, popery, and the new enemy, evolution. To Watts these were indeed the enemies of God, of Ulster Presbyterians . . . and of Ulster itself.

The strongly political character of Watts's reading is not difficult to discern. Writing to Charles's son, A. A. Hodge, in 1881 for example, he observed: "Communism is at present rampant in Ireland. The landlords are greatly to blame for their tyranny, but the present movement of the Land League, headed by Parnell, is essentially communistic. He and his co-conspirators are now on trial, but with six Roman Catholics on the jury there is not much likelihood of a conviction."[18] And later in an 1890 letter to the Princeton theologian B. B. Warfield, halfway between Gladstone's two Home Rule Bills, in which he castigated both the Free Church and the United

Presbyterians in Scotland, he added: "Both these churches are so bent on Disestablishment that they are quite willing to sustain Mr. Gladstone's Irish policy & deliver their Protestant brethren into the hands of the Church of Rome, to be ruled by her through a band of unmitigated villains."[19]

As for evolution, Watts maintained his antagonistic attitude for the rest of his life. At the 1884 pan-Presbyterian meeting in Belfast, even while George Matheson and Henry Calderwood (Scottish Presbyterians) were endorsing an evolutionary viewpoint, Watts told the company that evolution was a "mere hypothesis" with "not one single particle of evidence" to support it. Again in 1887 he wrote: "Despite the efforts of evolutionists, the laws which protect and perpetuate specific distinctions remain unrepealed, and Science joins its testimony to that of Revelation in condemnation of the degrading hypothesis that man is the offspring of a brute."[20] Here we witness a much narrower biblicist rejection of evolution than was ever evident at Princeton.

Not surprisingly Watts utterly repudiated the efforts of the Scottish evangelical publicist Henry Drummond to evolutionize theology. To him, Drummond's project was just a mess—theologically and scientifically. To be sure, his aim of removing "the alleged antagonism" between science and religion was a worthy objective. But the Drummond strategy ultimately was "not an Irenicum between science and religion or between the laws of the empires of matter and of spirit" at all. Rather it only displayed the expansionist character of natural law. Watts found the whole project so bizarre that, as he worked up to his conclusion, he felt "inclined to apologize for attempting a formal refutation of a theory which, if it means anything intelligible, involves the denial of all that the Scriptures teach, and all that Christian experience reveals."[21]

Drummond, of course, was not the only Scottish writer to fall under the whiplash of Watts's tongue. The professors of biblical criticism did not escape with fewer scars. By now Watts had grown entirely disillusioned with the Edinburgh New College network and cultivated links with Princeton with greater vigor than ever.[22] Writing in 1889 to Warfield, for instance, he began: "It would seem as if Princeton is going to absorb Belfast. Here I am asked to introduce to you, I think, the fifth student, within the past few weeks. Well, over this I do not grieve but rather rejoice. I am glad that our young men are setting their faces towards your venerable and orthodox institution instead of turning their backs upon orthodoxy and seeking counsel at the feet of men who are trampling the verities of Revelation under foot."[23] And in introducing yet another student to the Princeton campus he wrote to Warfield in 1893: "I am greatly pleased to find that our young men have turned their eyes to Princeton instead of Edinburgh, and I owe you my warmest thanks for the great kindness you have shown them."[24] He had already reminded Warfield that he had been writing a series of articles on the changing attitudes towards inspiration in the Free Church, reporting at the same time on the current heresy hunting of A. B. Bruce and Marcus Dods. Predictably, Watts took a dim view of these teachers. "How has the fine gold of the disruption become dim!" he lamented. "The men of '43 would have made short work of these cases."[25] Later that same year, having sent Warfield two days earlier a copy of his new book *The New Apologetic, or the Down-Grade in Criticism, Theology, and Science,*[26] he concluded yet another letter with the comment: "I dread the influence of the Scotch Theological Halls, as you may learn from my book."[27]

And yet for all this there is evidence to suggest that the sturdy Ulsterman was beginning to have suspicions that even Princeton was failing to hold a firm anti-evolution line. Take, for instance, his reply to Warfield in 1894 thanking him for sending a copy of William Brenton Greene's inaugural lecture.[28] Watts felt constrained to comment:

> I admired Dr. Greene's Inaugural, but I am sorry that he passed such high eulogium upon Mr. Herbert Spencer. My revered father, Professor Wallace, author of an immortal work, entitled "Representative Responsibility," had, for Spencer, supreme contempt as a professed philosopher. Immediately after the meeting of the British Association in Belfast, in 1874, I reviewed Spencer's Biological Hypothesis, & proved that he was neither a philosopher, nor a scientist. Someone sent him a paper containing only one half of my review, &, assuming that what the paper gave was the whole of my ad-

dress, he took occasion in an issue of his book, then passing through the Press, to charge me with misrepresentation. I called his attention to the mistake of his correspondent, but he had not the courtesy to withdraw the charge. Dr. McCosh's successor in the Queen's College here, trots out Spencer to our young men in their undergraduate course, and one of my duties, in my class work, is to pump out of them Mill & Spencer.[29]

Clearly even after twenty years his recollection of the Tyndall event had not faded, and Watts neither would, nor could, release his grip on that bitter memory. Watts's suspicion that Princeton was beginning to drift away from his own persistently dogged confessionalism was not entirely without foundation. Indeed, other Princeton champions had already reacted far more enthusiastically to evangelical apologists for evolution. Thus while, as we have seen, Watts vilified Henry Drummond's efforts, A. A. Hodge found *Natural Law in the Spiritual World* to be an "interesting and original work" and its author's theology "essentially, sometimes profoundly, orthodox." His conclusion was that the "book is unquestionably written in the interest of orthodox and spiritual Christianity. It is original, suggestive, and must prove instructive. The author has undoubtedly assisted in opening a vein of important truth."[30]

Evolution was not the only issue on which a transatlantic rift was beginning to appear. When his earlier, bitter critique of Robertson Smith appeared in 1882, entitled *The Newer Criticism and the Analogy of the Faith*, it was reviewed by one of Watts's luminaries, none other than W. H. Green, doyen of Princeton Old Testament scholars.[31] Green graciously began with some soporific commendations on the high esteem in which the work was held, necessitating a reprint within a few weeks of publication. But while he approved of the Reformed confessionalism that was Watts's chief mode of critique, he was evidently unimpressed with the work as a scholarly treatise. He found that Watts's line of argument failed to "furnish a complete answer to the hypothesis" and did not even constitute any serious grappling with critical methods. Besides, he conceded that Watts did "not sufficiently take account of the progressive nature of divine revelation." Again and again Green felt constrained to highlight a precarious line of reasoning here, an inconclusive argument there, and weak evidence elsewhere. Watts might certainly have been a doughty confessional publicist and rhetorician, but there is more than a hint in Green's reflections that sublime rhetoric was no substitute for serious research.[32]

THE MACLOSKIE-MCCOSH COALITION

Even while Robert Watts was injecting anti-Darwinian rhetoric into Ulster Calvinism, others were exporting pro-evolution sentiments to the intellectual hub of American Presbyterianism. In 1875 Rev. George Macloskie crossed the Atlantic to take up the new chair of natural history at the College of New Jersey. He was delighted by the appointment, though reportedly not a little surprised to receive the invitation from his old Belfast professor, James McCosh, with whom he had also fought in support of Gladstone's disestablishment policies.[33] He is said to have mused that he only accepted the position because "he wanted to see America for a few years and thought he might learn enough natural history on the way over to keep ahead of the boys."[34] Whatever Macloskie's supposed feelings on the matter, however, his appointment took place at a crucial moment in the history of the New Jersey college.

The early 1870s were stormy years among Presbyterian intellectuals concerned with keeping abreast of the latest scientific theories. As we have just seen, Charles Hodge informed the readers of *What Is Darwinism?* in 1874 that the theory was nothing less than atheism—the very same year that John Tyndall preached his gospel of scientific naturalism in Belfast. In the United States the solid opposition to Darwin from Louis Agassiz, James Dana, and Arnold Guyot remained firm. But by the middle of the decade there were abundant signs that the newer generation of scientific professionals was finding Darwin's theory empirically and conceptually rewarding. To be sure there was a host of competing suggestions as to what the mechanisms of evolutionary change might actually be, but there was less and less doubt that evolution occurred.

It was into this intellectual ferment that McCosh launched his proposal in 1871 to establish a chair of natural history in the newly created John C. Green School of Science at Princeton. It was a crucial position, not least because it would indicate to the scholarly world the stance that Presbyterian Princeton was adopting on the new biology. Filling the post proved far from easy, and the symbolism of the difficulty has not escaped commentators. As Bradley Gundlach puts it: "McCosh's inability to find a suitable candidate went down in the annals of American education as a prime illustration of clerical obstruction of scientific progress, on the assumption that the ministerial faction on [the] board of trustees, led by Charles Hodge, blocked McCosh's every move to bring a working evolutionist to Princeton."[35] In fact the story was far from that simple, as Gundlach shows. For one thing McCosh strenuously sought a few years later in 1878 to engage the talents of the Canadian John William Dawson, a noted anti-Darwinian geologist, and engineered a hitherto unprecedented invitation from both the seminary and the college in the endeavor to secure his services. Though McCosh was himself a convinced evolutionist, when it came to the well-being of his beloved Princeton he much preferred to appoint a pious anti-Darwinian than an unbelieving evolutionist.

Either way, it certainly was the case that McCosh had difficulty filling the new position. Edward Drinker Cope, a Quaker and a Lamarckian paleontologist, had been suggested, but McCosh soon broke off negotiations with him. Similarly Theodore Gill and Charles Frederick Hartt failed to secure the position despite recommendations. And so McCosh turned to George Macloskie, probably because his old pupil's brand of evolution was thoroughly domiciled within a Presbyterian theology. It lacked the extremes of materialism and idealism that other candidates seemed in danger of espousing and retained a robust confidence in the explanatory power of teleology. Gundlach comments: "It seems likely that it was Macloskie's reliable, Presbyterian devoutness that the more intransigent trustees had missed in the other candidates."[36]

Clearly what McCosh wanted was a colleague who could engage the apologetics of antimaterialism, even while retaining a belief in the fact of evolutionary change; and he was prepared to sacrifice the professionalizing aims he had for the college, even if only as an interim measure, to preserve theological integrity. Macloskie's appointment may indeed have been a stopgap measure, but that the Irishman possessed the ideological qualities that McCosh wanted attests to the continuing significance of the Belfast-Princeton cultural axis.

Although Macloskie affected surprise at McCosh's invitation, he had long entertained hopes of a transatlantic academic career. Certainly he had the paper credentials for a scholarly life. For his student work in natural history at Queen's College in Belfast he received a gold medal, having studied with such scientific luminaries as George Dickie, Thomas Andrews, and Sir Wyville Thomson. Subsequently he undertook theological training and was ordained to the ministry of the Presbyterian Church in Ireland, serving in the parish of Ballygoney between 1861 and 1873. During his time there he pursued legal studies as an external student at the University of London, from which he also received a gold medal for academic excellence. An honorary D.Sc. from Queen's and an LL.D. from London further attest to his scholarly accomplishments. Macloskie, evidently, was nothing if not polymathic. Indeed he sported a letter, dated 14 March 1865, from the then vice president of Queen's, Thomas Andrews, lauding the young man's linguistic competencies to qualify him for a chair of Greek and Latin, and a similar 1868 recommendation about his scientific accomplishments from George Dickie, his former Queen's professor currently holding the chair of botany at Aberdeen.[37] Moreover, Macloskie himself had written to his old teacher McCosh expressing interest in making a career for himself in the New World and received from McCosh the following reply written on 29 August 1871:

> I am truly glad to hear from you. I had heard of your honors in a general way but not specifically and I am pleased to find that you remember me and give me the details of yourself. I have been considering how all these things may tend to your usefulness in Ireland or elsewhere. There would be fine fields of usefulness for you in America but the difficulty would be to get you a stranger introduced to them. I really do not know whether you are a popular preacher (I have never heard one way or other) whether you mean to devote yourself to the work of the ministry the noblest in which you can

be engaged or whether as having gifts you are seeking an academic position. In all these walks there are wide fields here. The difficulty is to get you known. I give no advice. The responsibility must be with you. But I will be glad to hear from you as to your views and intuitions.[38]

Macloskie, then, was not far from McCosh's mind during those difficult days when he was casting around for a suitable candidate for the chair in natural history in his new Green Science School. By that point in time, moreover, Macloskie had already made some tangential observations on the Darwinian theory in his consideration of "The Natural History of Man" in 1862 (just one year after his ordination). Here, while expressing some hesitancy about the universal claims of the Darwinian system, Macloskie paused to affirm that the principle of natural selection could account for human racial differentiation. Indeed he insisted that he had "already employed this principle, to explain the diversity that exists in the different tribes of mankind, whilst the specific unity is still preserved."[39] Certainly the deductive character of the Darwinian theory was, at this stage, bothersome to Macloskie, though in years to come he would—as we shall see—defend the necessity of scientific speculation. But this early stance already displayed some of the very qualities that McCosh would espouse, namely, openness to evolution's empirical findings and resistance to its materializing inclinations. Later in Princeton he penned the following concluding words to his notes on the protozoa—observations which encapsulated McCosh's own sentiments perfectly:

> The study of Natural History forces on the mind the conviction that there is knowledge and wisdom and a controlling mind behind these things. No mind is so strong in its naturalism as to get over this conviction and recent discoveries are proving more than ever that whatever share secondary causes and accidents have had in making things what they are, behind and above all there is some intelligent one who is directing them all according to the counsels of His own will.[40]

The explicit teleology expressed here was characteristic of evolutionary thinking in the McCosh-Macloskie mode. "Christian evolutionists," he wrote in 1882, "(and there are many such) hold that God made every species, out of inorganic matter by changing it into protoplasm in an orderly way, first into movers, then into amoebae, and so on."[41]

George Macloskie was certainly not a scientist of the first rank. Prior to leaving Ireland he had published on the silicified wood of Lough Neagh[42] and later was the author of a textbook on *Elementary Botany* (1883). In addition, he prepared the botanical sections of the three-volume *Reports of the Princeton Expedition to Patagonia* and wrote on the housefly for the *American Naturalist*. He regarded his discovery of the poison-fang and poison-glands of the mosquito as his most important scientific contribution. Besides this he provided a transcription of "John Brainerd's Journal," a record of the missionary's work among the native peoples of the New Jersey region.[43] He was also a keen participant in the Scotch-Irish Society of America and an enthusiastic advocate of Esperanto. But he reflected that during his years at Princeton his "most useful work [was] the discussion of the hot questions of science and the Bible." His position on these questions, he reminisced, "consisted largely in my hearty belief in both; not in all or many of the unverified deductions that some people draw from the Bible and other people draw from science; but that both, in the main, are all right if we can wisely interpret what they say."[44]

Macloskie maintained this perspective throughout the remainder of his life at Princeton. In the early years of the twentieth century, in unpublished notes on the drift of modern science, he still sought to keep the worlds of scientific specialism and Christian conviction in conceptual tandem. Thus on the one hand he endeavored to maintain the freedom of scientific investigation from theological incursion by arguing that Christians were "sometimes retarded by prejudices derived from [their] theological training." If an Assyriologist, he urged, "entered on his investigations with the determination beforehand to find them either for or against the Old Testament," such assumptions would undermine the authenticity of the findings. On the other hand, however, he was only too aware of the materialist tendencies in science induced by increasing specialization: it was "excessive specialism," he reckoned, that had progressively blinded the scientific community to the realms of the nonmaterial. Mechanical or physico-chemical conceptions that had "replace[d] the older supernaturalism" were all right in their place; but the extension of the methods of the naturalist beyond their appropriate domain rendered "students color-blind to the higher things of life." To Macloskie, then, biblicist science was as pernicious as its skeptical counterpart. So he not surprisingly sided with Asa Gray—over against Charles Hodge—when he commented: "We have no sympathy with those who maintain that scientific theories of evolution are necessarily atheistic." Indeed by now he was even prepared to accept the possibility that the human "soul as well as the body" might have been derived from animal forebears, "or even from inanimate matter."[45]

For Macloskie, all of this was in keeping with his Protestant heritage, and he looked askance at the expulsion of the president of a French geological society, on account of his evolutionary convictions, through the efforts of the Jesuits.[46] Such sentiments could well be expected of an Ulster Protestant, of course. He thus kept a scrapbook of clippings for 1873–74 on Vatican Decrees and Civil Allegiance[47] and in a notebook on "The Scotch-Irish, Their Services in Education" recorded statistics displaying considerably higher rates of criminality and comparably lower rates of literacy among Catholics compared with Presbyterians.[48] And yet, for all that, he was fully aware that all was not well among the Presbyterians on the science question. Not only had he lived through the scenes surrounding Tyndall's Belfast address which we have already scrutinized,[49] but his papers contain the detailed record of the action taken in 1890 by the presbytery of Charleston, South Carolina, against James Woodrow, leading to his dismissal over the issue of evolution.[50]

If McCosh's dominating concern at Princeton was to preserve the college's Presbyterian heritage by fighting materialism and promoting a Christian university,[51] even while domesticating evolutionary biology, Macloskie certainly fitted the bill. In the years that followed his appointment Macloskie took on something of the mantle of keeping the Presbyterian community in touch with scientific thought through his numerous publications in church-related serials. In the late 1880s and 1890s he drew the attention of his fellow Presbyterians to a range of matters of pressing scientific and theological import: the role of speculation in science, accommodationist strategies, and theistic evolution.[52] In 1887, for instance, he defended not just the legitimacy but the necessity of speculative theorizing in science—a not insignificant twist of argument given the typical Presbyterian nervousness about theory emanating from a deep attachment to the Scottish philosophy. Here he subverted standard Baconian induction and went so far as to suggest that "Hypotheses that conflict with recognized principles of science, of philosophy, or of theology are all legitimate subjects of examination."[53] Not that this implied any unorthodoxy on his part. In an 1889 piece for the *Presbyterian Review*, for example, he made it abundantly clear that he was convinced that "in the actual intent of the Scripture, we shall find no mistakes." What he did insist was that accepting the doctrine of the plenary inspiration of Scripture did not imply, much less necessitate, any biblicist science: the laws of nature simply could not be deduced from incidental scriptural references to physical phenomena. "We are not at liberty," he remarked, "to erect our science upon the Scripture, and then to turn round and prove the Scripture by our science."[54] Scriptural geology had thus proven to be a dead end, and Macloskie railed against the strained efforts of the concordists to "geologize" Genesis. What such schemes ignored was the old Calvinist doctrine of Scripture's "accommodating itself" to conventional human talk.[55] To recognize this principle would enable Christians to approach Darwin's theory with poise and patience. Instead of castigating evolution, it would be wiser to "refrain from committing ourselves to or against it, till the way be clear; and above all to resolutely decline to place the authority of the Bible in either scale of an uncertainty."[56] To follow the creationist tactics of Louis Agassiz—"not a theologian and scarcely a Christian"[57]— would be nothing but folly.

Crucial to Macloskie's own domestication of Darwinian declarations was his conviction that he had resolved—to his own satisfaction—the issue of teleology, and he repeatedly spelled out his resolution to his Presbyterian readers. Such a stance enabled him to maintain intimate connections between the light of Scripture and the light of reason. In the first issue of B. B. Warfield's new *Presbyterian and Reformed Review*, Macloskie thus cut his way through the border terrain between rationalism and "unintelligent Scripturalism" in order to leave space for the testimony of nature.[58] Neither did materialism nor Hutchinsonianism—the latter named for the seventeenth-century English clergyman who sought to erect a biblical science entirely on scriptural statements—hold any attraction for him.[59] A better candidate was Princeton's own W. H. Green (to whose work Macloskie persistently reverted[60]) who had found the resources to tame higher criticism in precisely the same way that a believing scientist could bend Darwinism to Christian purposes. Accordingly he argued the case for a chastened form of theistic evolution in 1898—an essay replete with testimonial gobbets, from figures like Fiske, Temple, Gray, and McCosh, affirming an evolutionary teleology. Indeed, for at least a decade, he had been greedily fastening on Huxley's admission that while Darwin's theory "does abolish the coarser forms of Teleology, it reconciles Teleology and Morphology. The teleological and the mechanical views of nature are not mutually exclusive."[61] Now he protested vigorously that evolution committed no theological impropriety. "The Christian evolutionist," he urged, "is able to believe in the miraculous birth, the theanthropic personality of Jesus Christ, in His miracles, in His resurrection after death and in His ascension to glory."[62] Macloskie held vehemently to these sentiments even while acceding to the real possibility of human evolution. To him it was entirely conceivable that the human physical form was the result of a naturalistic evolutionary process even if the "spiritual nature" was the consequence of special divine intervention. "As a member of the animal kingdom," he later suggested, "man was created by God, probably in the same naturalistic fashion as the beasts that perish; but unlike them, he has endowments which point to a higher, namely a supernaturalistic, order of creation."[63] Macloskie was convinced that the monogenetic implications of the Darwinian theory had actually done much to confirm the biblical narrative.[64]

All of this was entirely in keeping with McCosh's vision. In 1903, for example, Macloskie looked back with enthusiasm and appreciation to McCosh's early efforts to Christianize evolution; McCosh's system, he mused, while once the subject of sharp criticism was now being "universally accepted" as an explanation "for the creation of new species."[65] Not surprisingly he reflected that McCosh's efforts had done much to "prevent a disastrous war between science and faith."[66]

Macloskie, of course, did not confine his reconciling efforts to the pages of learned journals. He delivered many addresses on such topics, for example, in the college chapel. In 1892, for instance, he opened a notebook entitled "Preliminary Talks on Science and Faith."[67] The topics taken up for exposition that year included "The Iconoclasm of Science," "Creation," "Evolution: The Right Attitude," "Creation of Man," "Paradise and Eve," "Antidiluvian Times: Popular Errors," "Preadamites," and "The Deluge." In these he reiterated the self-same arguments he was putting into print. Concerning the early chapters of Genesis, for example, he told his hearers that "If Darwin himself or a poet like Milton, thoroughly versed in Darwinian thought, had been called upon to present the evolutionary theory in a popular form to the contemporaries of Moses they could not have described it in a more striking manner. Any improvement upon the Mosaic account which could be suggested are mere trifles and matters of detail."

Even if he had to temporarily sacrifice the professionalizing vision McCosh had for science in his beloved Princeton, in the appointment of Rev. George Macloskie he found in his former Belfast student the perfect candidate to marry the old theology and the new science.

THE HISTORICAL GEOGRAPHY OF A
CULTURAL CONNECTION

While the cultural and theological links between Belfast and Princeton remained both deep and lasting throughout the Victorian period, there is evidence to suggest that, on the issue of science and Christianity, the trajectories substantially diverged. Evidently, shared theological sentiments did not guarantee a monochrome response to the latest intellectual challenges facing Calvinist communities. It turns out, in fact, that local circumstances were crucial to the ways in which the new science was encountered, to the rhetorical strategies available to interlocutors, and to the degrees of freedom permitted within the very theological spaces that publicists had done so much to reproduce. The bellicose speechifying of Tyndall in Belfast set limits on the extent of possible rapprochement with the scientific enterprise; his materialist rendition of the atomic philosophy and its evolutionary implications made it extraordinarily difficult for Robert Watts, as spokesman for Calvinist conservatism, to negotiate the sorts of modus vivendi with Darwinian biology that James McCosh, George Macloskie, and B. B. Warfield could effect in the New World. The different cultural geographies of Princeton and Belfast, together with their variant political topographies, thus had a crucial role to play in their diverging assessments of evolution theory. To be sure, in both spaces pro- and anti-evolutionary sentiments found expression in the post-Darwinian era; but the dominant voices by the last decade of the nineteenth century in the two places were calling on the same theology to support different evaluations of evolution. Here, then, we find exposed a historical geography of evangelical responses to Darwin for too long subsumed under the simple rhetoric of either conflict or concession. The contingency of this-worldly circumstances are, if the story told here is to be believed, crucial to understanding the historical connections between science and Christianity in general, and Ulster and American Presbyterianism in particular.

Three   Contending for the Faith

Presbyterians Face up to Modernity in America and Ireland

Willa Cather once observed that "the world broke in two in 1922 or thereabouts."[1] The historian Robert T. Handy, focusing more specifically on religious institutions, sees the break coming in 1935, when the Protestant era in America ended.[2] These observations lend point to a thought about the cultural history of the 1920s and 1930s and, in the context of this inquiry, about transatlantic Presbyterianism. If one does not take 1922 or 1935 too literally, we can nevertheless see the usefulness of such a notion about the substantial breaking of fellowship in the 1920s in the Presbyterian Church in the United States of America (PCUSA) and the Presbyterian Church in Ireland (PCI). Even allowing for local variations on the theme, one sees important connections and convergences. The issues were similar and the results the same.

The PCUSA and PCI were forced to confront from, say, 1875 onwards what Paul Carter has called "the spiritual crisis of the Gilded Age."[3] At stake were issues which, taken together, meant the degree to which the churches would face up to modernity. These issues were methodological, theological, and ecclesiastical: methodological in that theologians in both countries wrestled with the meaning of the scientific study of religion in the years following the publications of Darwin; theological in that the basis for authority in the church and in the Christian life—the Bible—was subjected to a critical analysis which, for some, threatened the very nature of the Christian faith; ecclesiastical in that Presbyterians had to decide the degree to which toleration of differing views would or could be allowed within the fellowship of the church. In respect to these issues, both the PCUSA and the PCI "broke in two." The party in the churches that favored openness to the scientific methods, revised views on the Bible, and on broad membership was victorious in the controversies of the 1920s. They gained control of the church institutions and especially of the theological schools at Princeton and Belfast. The party that favored rejection of, or was ambivalent about, the new science, that held traditional views of Scripture, and that favored a narrower membership was defeated in the controversies. A portion of the latter party withdrew from the larger churches, established new denominations and, in the American case, a new theological school.

The background of these controversies was the so-called "fundamentalist-modernist" controversy, a set of events at once much larger than the two Presbyterian churches, and of which the Presbyterian churches themselves were not fully representative. Fundamentalists were later to be characterized broadly by a radical separatism that few Presbyterians shared. Fundamentalists also came to assert a literalist biblicism that the more confessionally-minded Presbyterians found confining. Furthermore, few Presbyterians found resonance with the fundamentalists' novel theology of premillennialism and its pessimistic assumptions about society and culture. On the other hand, most Presbyterians in the victorious party were not really full-blown modernists. While opposing the more bizarre aspects of fundamentalism (e.g., dispensationalism), they were moderates on the questions of science, Scripture, and tolerance. Very few leaders, in either America or Ireland, favored the naturalistic, relativistic religion of the true modernists. While the Presbyterian churches in America and in Ireland were not perfect representatives of the fundamentalist-modernist controversy, they are arguably the most interesting because they took theology very seriously and provided articulate spokesmen for similar controversies in other less theologically inclined denominations.

Historians of Presbyterianism and of fundamentalism in Ulster and in America are not unaware of the connection and convergences between the PCUSA and the PCI. In the standard work on Presbyterianism in Ireland, Finlay Holmes acknowledges that the climate of antagonism and controversy in Ireland was heightened by an injection of American-style fundamentalism.[4] On the American side, George Marsden's various works on Presbyterianism and fundamentalism are without peer.[5] Marsden observes that, while

fundamentalism is an American phenomenon, the one place outside the United States that may have nurtured a home-grown fundamentalist movement is Northern Ireland.[6] Other historians, such
as Steve Bruce on the Ulster side, and Lefferts Loetscher and
Bradley Longfield on the American side, also acknowledge the connections and convergences.[7] But, to date, no work has attempted
to portray the Presbyterian version of the fundamentalist-modernist controversy on a transatlantic canvas. This chapter attempts to
do that by building upon the work of the scholars noted above and
by utilizing some hitherto little-used sources.

We hope to explore the explanatory power of both institutional
and ideological analysis. While there were two Presbyterian parties
on the main issues, there was always a third party too, a kind of
silent majority that cared more about preserving the denomination than about the proximate causes of conflict. This large group
in the middle, whom William Weston and others call "loyalists,"
is the group that putative liberals or conservatives had to cultivate
if one of the latter was to be victorious. In the United States, the
liberals were soundly defeated in the first skirmishes in the 1890s.
After that the liberals seem to have learned that their task was to
try to convince the loyalists to broaden the theological consensus
in the PCUSA. The conservatives, having won fairly easily in the
1890s, seemed to think that they would be victorious in future disputes if they only held the line. They were wrong. Their inability
to convince the loyalists of their constitutional exclusivity was fatal to their cause.[8] However, institutional analysis leads us only so
far. By the end of this chapter we hope to have established the
ideological and epistemological differences between the two main
factions, and why one party was able to carry the loyalists in Ireland and America with them.

The controversies of the 1920s did not come to churches, either
in Ireland or America, whose histories were testimonies to unbro-
ken fellowship and ecclesiastical harmony. To the contrary, both
the PCUSA and the PCI had broken apart and rejoined, split and
reunited in the mid-eighteenth century and in the mid-nineteenth
century. It is the latter division and reunion that interests us most
in the present context. While the divisions may have occurred because of several proximate issues, the two-party division in both

the United States and in Ireland turns on the relative appreciation for (or against) the revivals that swept across the ocean in the mid-nineteenth century. In this "North Atlantic culture" it was inappropriate to ask on which side of the ocean the revivals began. There was plenty of traffic to and fro, as J. Edwin Orr and Richard Carwardine have demonstrated.[9] As much as immigrants ignored national boundaries in the great migrations of the nineteenth century, so did religious revivals which began on one side of the ocean and soon found reflection on the other. Whether or not the great revival of 1857–59 began in Wales then went to America or vice versa is difficult to determine. What is definitely known is that a committee of Irish Presbyterians headed by William Gibson, later to be moderator of the General Assembly of the Presbyterian Church in Ireland, was sent by the General Assembly of 1858 to America to observe and report on the revival there. His reports from Philadelphia provided an important stimulus to the great 1859 revival in Ulster, which began in county Antrim in March of that year.

We need not try to tell the story of the revival here, other than to observe the two schools of interpretation that followed the revival's conclusion. William Gibson, who welcomed the method and results of the revival, wrote a still-useful account of it called *The Year of Grace*.[10] Rev. Isaac Nelson, writing from the viewpoint that deplored the lay participation of the revival, its ignorance of Reformed confessions, and its "enthusiastic" concomitants, called his pamphlet *The Year of Delusion*.[11] Whether or not the revival of 1859 was, in fact, a work of grace or delusion or some of both cannot be answered here. Yet one observes that the perception of the revival created a fault line in the memory of Irish Presbyterians that emerged again in the controversies of the 1920s.[12] The moderate/modernist victors in the twenties were, at best, ambivalent about the revival and about its echo in 1922 under W. P. Nicholson.[13] The conservative/fundamentalist losers in the twenties held high the memory of 1859, even as they deplored their church's moving away from what was said to be the history of true Presbyterianism.

In some ways this fault line mirrors the experience of American Presbyterians who found themselves dividing into two affinity groups in respect to the "new measures" of the revival in America, especially as it focused on the career of Charles G. Finney. Yet it would be wrong to divide Presbyterianism, on either side of the ocean, into two factions on the revival that ineluctably led to division in the fundamentalist-modernist controversy in the 1920s. Even if we were to make such a division, it would be unclear as to which side advocated views that led to what. While avoiding a simple causal connection for American Presbyterians, one historian observes that those who accept new measures in one place and time, as opposed to traditional doctrines and confessions, are likely to welcome new measures in an altered time and place.[14] So in America, theological seminaries founded in the spirit of the revival, the so-called "New School" (most notably Union), were also the seminaries that first welcomed aspects of theological liberalism. Correspondingly, the seminaries that were uneasy about the revival, the so-called "Old School" (most notably Princeton), were opponents of liberalism when it arrived from Europe later in the century.

In Ulster, which had just one theological school, the pro- and anti-revival parties were both present on the faculty and on the board. In that case, the reverse of what we found in America seemed to be true in Ireland. Pro-revival people tended toward the conservative end of the spectrum in the twenties while the anti-revival people, emphasizing rationality and science, tended toward the liberal end of the spectrum.[15] In another view, the seceding element in American Presbyterianism represents a continuity into the twenties and thirties of the basic tension within Presbyterianism about revivalism; thus both factions on revivalism are present in both factions in the later division.[16] No such systematic study has been done on the Irish side of the ocean, but one suspects it may also have been as true there as it was in America. In any case, since most Presbyterians, clergy and laity alike, remained in the PCUSA and the PCI after the controversies and divisions of the 1920s, it would seem statistically unlikely that the small seceding group was composed of all the members of either the pro- or anti-revival factions.

Differing perceptions about the revivals created fault lines in Presbyterianism, thus making later breaks in the church unsurprising. But those perceptions were not so much causes as precur-

sors of the great uproars of the early twentieth century that cul-
minated into the bitter divisions of the 1920s. In the PCUSA and
in the PCI, there were relatively few out-and-out modernists, in
any classic definition of that term. Also, there were relatively few
out-and-out fundamentalists in the PCUSA or in the PCI. Most
clergy and laity attending solemn assemblies were typically moderates who loved their church enough to allow some tolerance as
to differing views. The existence of this broadly loyalist middle in
both the PCUSA and the PCI would have great consequences for
the ultimate determination of the controversies of the 1920s in
both churches. What Loetscher wrote for the American Presbyterians could equally be said for their Irish co-religionists: In the
first third of the twentieth century "there was a pragmatic conception of the church"

> which, in the interests of avoiding divisions that would in-
> jure the church's work, has substituted broad church inclu-
> sion of opposing theological views for theological answers to
> them. To adapt Santayana's figure, the Church's theology has
> been living in a modest colonial house, more and more over-
> shadowed by the skyscraper of the church's active work.[17]

Despite the irenic nature of the loyalist, inclusive party, many
conservatives in both the PCUSA and the PCI nevertheless articulated an exclusive attitude in asking if there were, or were not,
some essential points which must be held by Presbyterian clergy.
In the United States, the General Assembly of the PCUSA declared
in its meeting of 1910, and reaffirmed in 1916 and 1923, that there
were five points "essential and necessary" to maintaining the doctrinal standards of the church. The five essential doctrines were:
1) the Holy Spirit so inspired the writers of Scripture "as to keep
them from error"; 2) "our Lord Jesus Christ was born of the Vir-
gin Mary"; 3) Christ offered up himself as "a sacrifice to satisfy
divine justice"; 4) "he arose from the dead, with the same body
in which he suffered"; 5) Christ "showed his power and love by
working mighty miracles." As Loetscher points out, this rendering
of orthodoxy became the fundamentalist-conservative faction's
rallying cry. There can be little doubt of its fundamentalist origins

because these points (while leaving premillennialism out) resemble very closely the main points of orthodoxy as articulated by the Niagara Bible Conference of 1895.[18]

While the Irish Presbyterian Church never went on record as its American counterpart did as to the essential points of Calvinistic Christianity, the conservatives in the PCI could rest assured that sound doctrine (to them) was being taught in Belfast. The professor of systematic theology at Belfast from 1866 to 1895 was Robert Watts, a Princeton graduate and close disciple of Charles Hodge, his teacher at Princeton. Watts taught Hodge's *Systematic Theology* for thirty years in the church's college in Belfast and was himself such a stout defender of infallibility and inerrancy that his work was quoted by the Princetonian Benjamin B. Warfield in the latter's *Revelation and Inspiration* (1927).[19]

The death of Robert Watts in 1895 marked the end of a theological era for the Presbyterian Church in Ireland and for the Presbyterian College in Belfast. As one recent commentator suggests, "teaching continued to be conservative but Watts's successors were more prepared to listen to those from whom they differed, than he, or his contemporaries had proved to be. The younger men saw some insights of value where the older men saw none."[20] The older tradition of valuing the confessions and orthodox belief was continued by Matthew Leitch, who was president from 1902 to 1922. The newer direction of thinking, especially in biblical theology, was led by Thomas Walker, appointed to the chair of Old Testament in 1888. The historian of the college has written of Walker's "unequivocal acceptance of the results of modern criticism."[21] Another professor, Thomas Hamill, while according high value to the Westminster Confession of Faith, nevertheless insisted that it was "the product of its age, but the Holy Spirit, abiding ever in the church, guides her in adapting the presentation of her theology to changing circumstances."[22] Whether or not to adapt to the new methods, especially in biblical criticism, was the question that rocked the college at Belfast in the early years of this century. With Walker setting the biblical lectures on the course of modern criticism, the college's president, Matthew Leitch, tried to point the college in another direction. In an 1902 article "Modern Criticism and the Preaching of the Old Testament," President Leitch wrote the following:

> So far all evangelical churches have refused to adopt these new critical theories. And the reason is not far to seek. In biology one of the first laws of life is the law of self-conservation. Every living organ sets itself against anything in its environment that tends to destroy itself and its kind. It is this instinct of self-conservation that leads Christian teachers and Christian churches to oppose theories about the Bible which they feel would be destructive of or injurious to the Christian life. A criticism of the Bible which was really the product of the intellectual and spiritual life of the Church itself, and was in sympathetic contact with the spiritual work and aims of the Church, would be welcomed by every earnest preacher as a helper in his work. But the criticism of this analytical school is not a growth that has developed out of the Church's life, but a parasite that has fastened on it. It originated in English deism and grew up in German rationalism and philosophic naturalism, and in all its transformations it carries with it a taint of the soil in which it grew, and is always noxious to the faith and life of the Church.[23]

We do not have a direct written reply from Thomas Walker, though it cannot have pleased him or have failed to cause wonder among Presbyterian students and clergy alike to had have the college's president assert that the very methods being taught in the biblical department were a parasite on the life of the church and noxious to its faith.

The question of what was essential to belief, and to what standards intending clergy should be required to adhere, was to come up repeatedly in the first two decades of the twentieth century in both the American and Irish Presbyterian Churches. While controversy was already swirling around the theological schools at Princeton and Belfast, and soon would return to them, it was not in the first instance theological education that brought matters to a head. It was the mission field, or perhaps the perceptions at home of what was going on in the mission field, that caused the matter to arise as to minimum essentials and the degree to which the church could tolerate diversity of theological opinion. In both churches the controversy centered on China.

In America the first shot was fired not by a Presbyterian but by an Episcopalian, William H. Griffith Thomas, in an address to the Presbyterian Social Union of Philadelphia on 24 January 1921. He asserted that many missionaries in China, including Presbyterians, were much affected by modernism, saying that the same question obtained in China as at home, i.e., "the trustworthiness and divine authority of the Word of God." For Rev. Griffith Thomas the main difficulty in China was the attempt "to find and to show points of agreement between Christianity and Oriental religions by graduates of liberal theological seminaries."[24] The Presbyterian Board of Foreign Missions was disturbed by the allegations and asked that Dr. Griffith Thomas name the Presbyterian missionaries in China who had compromised the faith, but the critic would not comply with the board's request. It seems clear that conservative critics were not so much attacking the missionaries as the whole policy of inclusive and exclusive definitions of what was "essential" to Presbyterian Christian belief. The defender of the Board of Foreign Missions, Dr. Robert E. Speer, was its secretary as well as a well-known evangelical and a contributing writer to The Fundamentals. Yet Speer was also a churchman who believed in a more inclusive definition of churchmanship than many other evangelicals in the PCUSA. Speer's determined and patient leadership of the Board of Foreign Missions was a vital factor in resolving the question in a more inclusivist direction. The General Assemblies of 1921, 1922, and 1924 received many overtures from presbyteries questioning the orthodoxy of Presbyterian missionaries in China, and each time the Board of Foreign Missions was able to satisfy the General Assembly on the soundness of its missionaries.

The missionary controversy did not surface again for many years, and, perhaps to anticipate prematurely a later part of the story, it might be said here for the sake of completeness that in 1930 the matter of missionaries would come up once again, and this time actually cause a split in Presbyterianism. In 1930 a book was issued by an independent group, though the PCUSA was a member of the interdenominational body that sponsored the research. The book, Re-Thinking Missions: A Layman's Inquiry after One Hun-

dred Years, was based on a survey of the state of mission work in Asia. The chairman of the committee issuing the book was Professor William Hocking, of Harvard's philosophy department. The ideas presented in *Re-Thinking Missions* were surely modernist, by anyone's definition, and presented a dilemma for Dr. Speer at PCUSA's Board of Foreign Missions. Despite the good standing that Speer enjoyed among conservatives (he had been a contributing author to *The Fundamentals*) and his personal opposition to *Re-Thinking Missions*, conservatives saw a great danger signal in his apparent waffling. Two years passed before the board was able to offer substantial criticism of the report, and even then the board's strategy seemed awkward and defensive, both to conservative criticisms of the report and to liberal praise of it.[25] But the mere existence of *Re-Thinking Missions* and the continuing, but unsubstantiated, reports that the Board of Foreign Missions was covering up the existence of modernists in the mission field were enough for Dr. J. Gresham Machen, of Princeton Seminary, to launch a renewed campaign against the work of the board. Machen proposed that his presbytery overture the General Assembly on the board's lack of orthodoxy, which he cast in terms of the "five points." Not only was Machen's proposal rejected at presbytery level, but the same body sent an overture to the next General Assembly commending the word of the Board of Foreign Missions. In 1933 an evangelical group, committed not only to the "five points" but also to the defense of the entire Westminster Confession, formed an Independent Board for Presbyterian Foreign Missions, with Dr. Machen at its head. In respect of Machen's continued participation on the Independent Board, the Presbytery of New Brunswick suspended Dr. Machen from his ministry in the Presbyterian Church.[26]

In Ireland, there was a similar story. Rev. James Hunter, a clergyman in the Knock congregation in Belfast, had for some time been concerned about possible modernist tendencies in the Presbyterian Church in Ireland.[27] In 1915, Hunter tried unsuccessfully to initiate charges against Rev. F. W. S. O'Neill, a missionary in China. Back in Britain, O'Neill had given a series of lectures at the major universities on Chinese religions. He described himself as teaching "a reasonable Biblical theology." His self-confessed difficulty in teaching and preaching in China was linguistic: he could not readily translate into Chinese the western-based metaphysical assumptions embedded in, say, the Westminster Standards. He found translation of the narratives of the Bible into the Chinese language and thought patterns quite easy, but what he found difficult were the abstract formulations in the epistles. In his own words, O'Neill's theological approach to China was as follows:

> The message of the West to the East is given in the words which sum up the Gospel, God was in Christ. The Father of Jesus is God, and there is no other God. Whatever trait of personality belonged in the days of His flesh to the Son has always belonged to the character of the Father. Conversely, action of any kind impossible to Jesus can never be possible to God. Only by living with Jesus and working in His companionship under the guidance of His Spirit from day to day can we find the Father and be changed into His likeness. It is at the Cross that the very heart of God's uttermost love is revealed. Because Christ bore our sins in His own body on the tree, we have come to know the awful truth that as long as sin remains unrepentant anywhere, the greatest sufferer for the sin is not the erring child, but his Father. And with our eyes wide open to the desperate condition of the world without and to the treachery of our fickle hearts within, we who belong to Christ are to believe in the coming triumph of His Kingdom: we dare to believe that the Kingdom of Love is a social ideal, which can be put into operation now.[28]

O'Neill was never tried by mission board, presbytery, or assembly and was later acknowledged by the General Assembly for his work by being made moderator in 1936. Although James Hunter was unsuccessful in this case, it would not be the last that the PCI was to hear of him. The field of battle would soon move back to the theological schools.

In 1924, thirteen students of the Presbyterian College (the General Assembly's College) in Belfast wrote a letter to the College Committee of the General Assembly, asking that body to inform them of exactly what obligation was imposed upon a clergyman in signing the formula of subscription. James Hunter was closely involved with this request, as he was a member of the College

Committee of the 1924 General Assembly. Further, he was to be a member of the special committee appointed by the General Assembly to determine if changes in the questions and formulas of subscription should be made.

Even as the special committee began its work, James Hunter, under the auspices of the newly formed Presbyterian Bible Standards League, addressed large and enthusiastic audiences across Ulster on the question of modernism in the church and especially in the Presbyterian College. In the spring of 1926 he circulated leaflets describing the college as "a seed-bed of rationalism." These were unorthodox methods of attack, especially in view of the existence of the special committee. The Presbytery of Belfast censured James Hunter for using unconstitutional means of attacking the college, since he had constitutional means at hand to advance his grievances. He appealed this censure to the General Assembly of 1926 and was rejected by a vote of 499 to 115.[29]

James Hunter, despite his lack of success in the case of Rev. O'Neill and his censure in respect to the Bible Standards League, was not ready to give up. In late 1926 he began what was to be his last effort to save the Presbyterian Church in Ireland from what, in his view, was a fatal accommodation to modernism. At the December 1926 meeting of the Presbytery of Belfast, Rev. Hunter introduced a motion to bring charges of heresy against Professor J. Ernest Davey of the Presbyterian College, Belfast. Early in 1927 the Presbytery fixed the date of February 15 to begin the trial which took fourteen sessions, concluding on 29 March 1927. Though less spectacular than the Scopes Trial in America (July 1925) and surely conducted with more decorum, the trial of J. E. Davey was as important for the resolution of the long-building controversy in Ulster as the more celebrated event in Tennessee was for America. With historical hindsight, we can now see that this trial was the turning point in the struggle for the soul and mind of the Presbyterian Church in Ireland.

J. Ernest Davey was a "child" of Irish Presbyterianism in all affective senses of the word. He was the son of Dr. Charles Davey, who was for many years the pastor of St. Enoch's Church, one of the more influential and celebrated Presbyterian congregations in Belfast.[30] Moreover, Davey was later described by Professor J. M.

Barkley, a prominent scholar, as "the most brilliant and versatile scholar Irish Presbyterianism had produced"[31] up to that time. Thus, for James Hunter to accuse J. E. Davey was to bring accusation to the very heart of Irish Presbyterianism.

Davey was the youngest person ever to be appointed to a chair at the Presbyterian College. He taught church history from 1917 to 1922, when he was appointed to the chair of biblical criticism (later known as the chair of New Testament language, literature and theology). He moved to the Old Testament chair for a few years in the early 1930s but in 1934 returned to New Testament teaching and writing. He was later to be principal of the college, moderator of the General Assembly (1953) and, in general, one of the most influential people in Irish Presbyterianism in the twentieth century. He died in 1960, at seventy years of age.[32]

We will, below, note carefully the charges brought against J. E. Davey in 1927. However, by way of introducing the subject, we should try to see it the way that Professor Davey himself saw it. Two years after his trial, in a sermon delivered in Belfast, he set forth the idea that had, and would, guide his life, i.e., the task of seeking the rapprochement of the historic Christian faith and the requirements of modern scholarship. In this regard it is vital to note that Davey did not see this task as mere compromise between the two, much less allowing modern thought to set the agenda. In 1929 he quoted from a former principal of the college: "There is no more difficult position today, nor one which evokes less sympathy, than that of the minister who has to stand between the world of modern knowledge on the one hand, and the world of traditional religion on the other, and mediate between them."[33] Davey saw his role as one of mediator, and even his critics acknowledged that through all the difficulties that attacks on him brought, his responses were characterized by an unfailing grace.

The essence of the charges brought against Davey turned on a related question: could, or ought, Christianity and higher criticism find common points of mediation? Davey's opponents never doubted his sincerity or honesty. But, the question remains, was he trying to do what cannot be done? If rapprochement means bringing into cordial relations formerly opposed persons or views, the critics insist, is it not giving away the historic faith to treat cordially that which strikes at the faith's very heart? While exonerated in his trial, Professor Davey himself suggested that 1927 would not be the last time for asking such questions.[34]

It was Davey's book, published in 1923, that was to be scrutinized in his trial. *The Changing Vesture of the Faith* was, as its title suggests, Davey's attempt to see the historic Christian faith in a new light—not an attempt to undermine the faith. First delivered in lecture form in 1921, the published version—because of the heresy trial—was much read and discussed in Ireland. In essence, what Davey did in *Changing Vesture* was to apply a method akin to what Karl Mannheim would call the sociology of knowledge. Davey's intent was to discuss "the origins and development of Christian forms of belief, institution and observance"[35] and especially the sociopsychological states and motives which underlie them. For Davey, the value of forms consists in their ability to conserve and nurture the life that had created them. But when forms outlive their useful life, they become destructive rather than sustaining. The judgment on the church throughout its history, then, is the inability to know when forms of thought and belief are no longer relevant to, and sustaining of, life. As Davey wrote, "Life must always, for a healthy Christianity, dominate forms, but it cannot dispense with them; and it must seek to create or recreate them continually after the pattern shown to it in the mount."[36]

Protestant hearers or readers of Davey's thoughts cannot help but have granted his general point. Protestantism rests on the prior acceptance of the method Davey employs, i.e., that at the time of the Reformation, the forms of thought and belief were confined by outdated, even "dead," practices that inhibited the true Christian life. The question, however, to divide Davey from his critics was this: did the forms developed at the time of the Reformation enhance or entrap Christian life in the twentieth century?

The five charges brought by Rev. James Hunter and others in late 1926 and on which Davey was tried in 1927 can be divided into two parts, doctrinal and biblical. The four doctrinal points (imputation, the origin of sin, the nature of Jesus, and the character of the Trinity) can be laid to one side until and unless the most important one is resolved. For both sides of the controversy, the most essential question reduced to this: what kind of book is the Bible? Specifically, the third heresy charge alleged that "Professor Davey taught what is contrary to the Word of God and the Westminster Confession of Faith regarding the inspiration, infallibility and Divine authority of the Holy Scriptures." Unless that charge was resolved, arguments about the other charges were of little more than scholastic interest.[37]

On 23 March 1927 J. Ernest Davey spoke at length to the court in defense of his views on the Scriptures. He immediately went to the vital issue of what was really on trial. He said, "I am fortunately not on my trial, let me say at once, regarding the theology of the Princeton theologians of this or last century, but as regards the Scriptures and the standards of our Church, which have been greatly misinterpreted and misconceived in popular thinking."[38] In the Westminster Confession, Davey pointed out, it says in the section on Scripture that "God gave man a revelation of Himself, and *afterwards* this was committed to writing, thus making Scripture most necessary to men. That is, we start with the admission that the Bible is not the revelation itself but the *record* of a revelation, a revelation given to Old Testament saints and consummated in Christ and the life of the Christian Church. The true revelation of God is Jesus Christ and all that leads up to Him and flows from Him. He is the living Word of God, and our Scriptures are the written Word of God as preserving and recording that revelation."[39] The Westminster Confession, Davey continued, insisted that the Bible be "a rule of faith and life," which is defined in the following words: "The whole counsel of God, concerning all things necessary for His own glory, man's salvation, faith and life, is either expressly set down in Scripture or by good and necessary consequence may be deduced from Scripture." And given the Protestant belief of the priesthood of all believers, the meaning of the Bible is not so obscure as to be read only by an educated person. To the contrary, Davey said, "even the unlearned may attain to a sufficient understanding of it. Indeed, our Presbyterian doctrine is a doctrine of the sufficiency of Scripture, not of its inerrancy."[40]

While Davey was correct to observe that he, not the "Princeton theology" of the Hodges and Warfield, was on trial in 1927; those in the court and in the interested public surely knew the connection between the charges against Davey and Princetonian views on the Scriptures. One of the main evidences brought against Davey was the testimony, and vitally, the notebook, of a student, William J. Grier. Converted by W. P. Nicholson in 1922 in Belfast, Grier had been a student at Princeton and had come back to Belfast for his final year (1925–26) of theological training prior to ordination in the Presbyterian Church in Ireland. The notebook of Grier's classroom work under Davey became an extremely contentious part of the trial, especially as to whether it was complete and unchanged from the time of the note-taking to its presentation in evidence by James Hunter and others.[41] Moreover, "the recent book" by J. Gresham Machen, presumably *Christianity and Liberalism*, was mentioned in Davey's trial by one of the accusers, Rev. Samuel Hanna, as a book that should be read by all.[42]

The question was, according to Davey, whether or not the Westminster Standards allowed for later scholars to employ historical and literary methods for the critical study of the Bible. For Davey, his affirmation of the *Confession's* assertion of Biblical infallibility ("all things necessary . . . ") and his acceptance of Divine inspiration in no way precluded historical and literary analysis. But, aware as he was that his trial was formally about his work in the context of the historic Westminster divines, Davey also knew that part of the charges against him turned on his work in relation to the contemporary Princeton divines. In short, there were two matters at issue in the trial: was Davey's work acceptable to the historic Reformed formulations and to the reformulations of Reformed thought by such luminaries as Belfast never produced, Benjamin B. Warfield, Charles Hodge, and A. A. Hodge?

Davey carefully pointed out where he differed with the Princeton scholars, especially in what—he believed—was their error in moving from infallibility to inerrancy ("inerrant" original texts are no longer extant; and, why would God inspire an inerrant text, then leave it to chance in the fallible hands of translators and scribes?). Even so, Davey thought himself in broad agreement with the Princeton scholars, especially on the question of the human side of biblical origins. In Davey's testimony on 23 March 1927 he quoted favorably from A. A. Hodge. It is important enough to quote at length here (and to note that the parentheses in the quotation are Davey's, added as commentary, not Hodge's): The writers, Hodge says,

> wrote from human impulses, on special occasions, with definite design. Each views his subject from an individual standpoint. They gather their material from all sources (the documentary theory of the books)—personal experience and observation, ancient documents and contemporary testimony. They arrange their material with reference to their special purpose, and draw inferences from principles and facts according to the more or less logical habits of their own minds. The limitations of their personal knowledge and general mental condition, and the defects of their habits of thought and style, are as obvious in their writings as any other personal characteristics. They use the language and idiom proper to their nation and class. They adopt the *usus loquendi* of terms current among their people, without committing themselves to the philosophical ideas in which the usage originated. Their mental habits and methods were those of the nation and generation. They were for the most part Orientals, and so their writings abound with metaphor and symbol; and although always reliable in statement so far as required for their purpose (one of the points in question—their purpose in God's providence) they never aimed at the definiteness of enumeration, of chronological or circumstantial narration, which characterizes the statistics of modern Western nations. Like all purely literary men of every age they describe the order and fact of nature according to their appearances (an echo of Charles Hodge), and not as related to their abstract law or cause. Some of these facts have, by many careless thinkers, been supposed to be inconsistent with the asserted fact of Divine guidance (note the word). But it is evident, upon reflection, that if God is to reveal Himself at all, it must be under all the limits of human modes of thought and speech. And if He inspires human agents to communicate His revelations in writing, He must use them in a manner consistent with their nature as rational and spontaneous agents.[43]

This concession to contextualizing the origins of the Bible, and an openness to the concerns of modern scholarship, was what Davey wanted. In sum, if Davey's work was acceptable under the Westminster Standards and if it was in some substantial agreement with the reformulations of Reformed ideology as from Princeton, there was little doubt in the minds of the vast majority of the Presbytery of Belfast that it was also acceptable to be taught at the Presbyterian College, Belfast. On the charge of biblical heresy the Presbytery exonerated Davey by a vote of 65 to 11. James Hunter and his colleagues appealed the result to the General Assembly of the Presbyterian Church in Ireland. On 10 June 1927 the General Assembly dismissed the appeal by a vote of 707 to 82. Part of the motion to dismiss read as follows:

> The General Assembly, in finding Professor Davey not guilty of the charge brought against him takes the opportunity to declare afresh its own loyalty to the Standards of the Church as described in the Rule of Faith (Chap. II of the Code), and reaffirms the duty incumbent upon all Professors in its Colleges (while not refusing light from any quarter) to maintain in all their teaching conformity with the said Standards, and to build up in the faith those whose duty it will be in the coming days rightly to divide the Word of Truth.[44]

The important parenthesis, "while not refusing light from any quarter," reaffirmed the historic Presbyterian attitude of not binding consciences but also affirmed that modern scholarship would be valued in the training of clergy. Not long after, James Hunter and the as-yet-unordained student from Princeton and Belfast, William J. Grier, withdrew from the Presbyterian Church in Ireland and were prominent among the founders of the Irish Evangelical Church, later the Evangelical Presbyterian Church. Grier later became editor of the small church's magazine, The Irish Evangelical, and in 1945 published his version of the events of 1927. In that booklet he asserted that "The Irish Presbyterian Church has given herself over to Modernism," and that it was the duty of Christians to separate themselves from fundamental error.[45] The notion, on the other hand, that the vast majority of the PCI did not see the events of 1927 as a struggle between truth and error but of toleration of differences within a more inclusive church, in which several views were loyally accepted, was unappealing to James Hunter and William Grier.

In the United States the battle for control of the soul of the Presbyterian Church did not have the lightning rod of a heresy trial to focus on Princeton Seminary. Yet, events were moving ineluctably toward a broad church, or inclusivist, conclusion that was the functional equivalent of the resolution in Ireland. In outline, the General Assembly of 1925 appointed a Special Commission with a brief "to study the present spiritual condition of our church and the causes making for unrest, and report to the next General Assembly, to the end that the purity, peace, unity and progress of the church may be assured."[46] This special theological commission of fifteen members issued a report that was adopted in 1927. The General Assembly of 1926 appointed another special commission to investigate the questions surrounding theological education at Princeton. Its report was accepted by the General Assembly of 1929. The two reports (1927 and 1929) taken together were to commit the Presbyterian Church in the U.S. to inclusivist churchmanship. Not surprisingly, some conservatives withdrew in 1929 to form a new theological seminary and later a new denomination. The relationship of the two special commissions, and their reports, is worthy of further specification, which can, for present purposes, be summarized from the work of Loetscher, Longfield, and Weston.[47]

The moderate-liberal group of the PCUSA was, at first, alarmed by the decision of the 1925 General Assembly to appoint the Special Commission. Mindful of the General Assembly's 1910 statement on "the five points" and its reaffirming of them twice later, the moderate-liberal group was afraid that the commission's report might, once again, reaffirm "the five points," thus causing great difficulty for people of a theologically inclusivist persuasion. The commission made a preliminary report in 1926 and its final report in 1927. Already in 1926, it was clear which way the commission would tend. Without naming J. Gresham Machen's *Christianity and Liberalism* directly, the commission took dead aim at it and categorically repudiated Machen's views as articulated in his book that there were two distinct religions coexisting within the Presbyterian Church. Moreover, another part of the commission's report noted carefully the history of Presbyterianism in America, observing that there was never a time when one set of views characterized the whole church, but that the center of gravity in the church was a mediating one. Further, the report put forth, in constitutional language, an argument that meant the end of the campaign by the conservative-fundamentalist group for the Assembly to define orthodoxy. For doctrines to be essential and necessary they now had to emerge from the Westminster Standards and had to quote the article as it appeared in the original. Thus, in a stroke, the statements of the General Assemblies of 1910, 1916, and 1923 were rejected. Well can one conclude that "the work of this Special Commission of 1925 was therefore a turning point in the theological history of the church since the reunion of 1869."[48]

The final battle in the inclusivist-exclusivist controversy was to turn on decisions taken by the General Assembly in respect to theological education at Princeton Seminary. Although by the 1920s Princeton was one of many accredited Presbyterian theological schools, it was, by virtue of its history as the first and most prestigious of the seminaries, the most important institution of the PCUSA. As historian John Mulder has noted, the struggle for the soul of Princeton was much more important than one theological school. Rather it was "a virtual war over the theological identity and future of American Presbyterianism."[49] The essential question at Princeton during the 1920s was similar to that which had torn the fabric in Belfast: to what degree, if at all, would the seminary allow the teaching of modern scholarship? Under the leadership of Benjamin B. Warfield, arguably the most learned theologian in America during the half-century of 1875–1925, Princeton had led the forces that wished to hold the line against the incursions of modern scholarship.

With the retirement of Francis L. Patton as Princeton's president in 1913, and the appointment of J. Ross Stevenson, structural changes began between denomination and seminary that would have great consequences for the issue of modern biblical criticism. Patton began and Stevenson pursued a course of leadership at Princeton intended to bring the seminary into closer touch with the life of the Presbyterian Church. The historic, theologically rigorous tradition of the seminary was, by the early 1920s, being ably led by Professor J. Gresham Machen, who consciously sought to continue the theological position developed by the Hodges and Warfield. Even liberal critics of Machen could admit, as late as 1924, that his views were shared by a majority of the faculty. But the minority group on the faculty, while surely conservatives, were people of a moderate and irenic spirit as compared to Machen. Significantly, this minority group had all served pastorates in the church, while the majority had little, if any, experience of ministry in the church. This may, at least partly, explain the differences in tone as the two groups on the Princeton faculty articulated their positions on the key issues of modern scholarship, biblical criticism, and membership.

In 1926 (when across the ocean James Hunter was preparing charges against Professor J. E. Davey) the redoubtable J. Gresham Machen became the focal point of controversy at Princeton. In May 1926 Machen was elected to the chair of apologetics and ethics. But, in view of the deep divisions among the directors and trustees of the seminary, reflecting faculty division, several directors and trustees requested the General Assembly of 1926 to investigate conditions at the seminary "alleged by these Directors and Trustees and by others to be subversive of Christian fellowship and to be jeopardizing the usefulness of the Seminary."[50] A committee of inquiry was duly appointed by the General Assembly, but, the question arose, should the appointment of J. Gresham Machen be approved? In what must have been a stunning moment at the General Assembly meeting, President J. Ross Stevenson arose and spoke to the issue of Machen's appointment. Casting his argument in the rhetoric of broad church ideology, he stated that he wanted Princeton Seminary to "represent the whole Presbyterian Church and not any particular faction of it." Stevenson further observed that certain men "on the platform," presumably the leaders of the General Assembly, "could not be invited to the Princeton Theological Seminary because of the line of demarcation drawn by those who believe the time has come to make the differences clear."[51] It seemed apparent to all that the appointment of Machen would be the lightning rod. The General Assembly appointed a special committee to investigate the situation of Princeton and postponed the appointment of Machen until the committee reported.

In the autumn of 1926 the so-called Committee of Five visited Princeton Seminary. The controversy, long building, could not have come to more pointed and bitter clarity. The majority of the faculty repudiated Stevenson's speech of the prior General Assembly on the point of wanting the seminary to represent the "whole church." They believed that vigorous action was needed to save the seminary and the PCUSA from modernism. For his part, President Stevenson replied in kind, asking whether or not it was in the interest of the Presbyterian Church to have Princeton "swing off to the extreme right wing so as to become an interdenominational Seminary for Bible School-premillennial-secession fundamentalism?"[52] The Committee of Five could not, nor did it believe itself empowered to, immediately resolve the situation at Princeton. In its report to the General Assembly of 1927, it recommended the creation of a new committee to bring forward recommendations to reorganize the structure of Princeton under one board so as to make it more responsive to the needs of the church and to end the divisive spirit. Importantly, Machen's election was again deferred.

The reconstituted committee of inquiry into affairs at Princeton—now called the Committee of Eleven—reported to the General Assembly of 1928 and recommended a plan for reorganizing the structure of Princeton. They recommended a single Board of Trustees to replace the (more faculty-oriented) Board of Directors and the (more church-oriented) Board of Trustees, with composition to be drawn, in thirds, from the two current boards and from General Assembly appointments. This plan, it was said, would more clearly fix responsibilities as to who spoke for what and whom in the seminary and the church. Most observers of both persuasions in the church understood the importance of the plan, i.e., it would surely make Princeton a more inclusive seminary. For the majority of the existing faculty the issue was whether or not orthodoxy and toleration were compatible. For the majority in the church and in the General Assembly, the issue was whether or not one viewpoint among many should be allowed to typify, even control, Princeton. The report was not acted on in 1928 because the mediating majority in the General Assembly requested a year's truce of discussion about Princeton and asked that a vote be deferred for one year, hoping that cooler heads might prevail.

In 1929 the General Assembly adopted the reorganization plan. Many noted conservatives opposed the plan, but, when it was adopted, they learned to live with it. The fact that conservative leaders like Clarence Macartney and William Courtland Robinson could see their way clear to remain in fellowship with other Presbyterians after 1929 was good indication that most conservatives still believed that they had a significant and valued role to play in the PCUSA. A minority of the conservatives, those of a more polemical temperament, later seceded from the PCUSA. With J. Gresham Machen the clear leader, the movement was centered in the always-conservative Philadelphia area. The Presbyterian Church of America (PCA), later the Orthodox Presbyterian Church, Westminster Theological Seminary, and the Independent Board of Presbyterian Foreign Missions became the institutional creations of those conservatives who believed they could no longer work within the larger Presbyterian Church. As Loetscher points out, for the seceding conservatives, the creation of their new institutions was the last phase of a struggle "characterized by the earnestness of despair." Marsden agrees: "The formation of the PCA marked the last entrenchment in a war that had been all but lost." [53]

The notion of a lost cause to which one still might be faithful resonates deeply in American history, especially for white southerners. The idea—and ideals—of the Confederacy was, to many southerners, the "everlasting South," despite (possibly because of) the lost cause of the Civil War. Bradley Longfield's important work brings this insight to bear upon the Presbyterian controversies. He reminds us that Machen was a southerner by heritage and conviction, a person who "brought to the Presbyterian conflict a profound respect for a particularly southern solution to disagreement: secession." Longfield further notes well that Machen, in thinking and feeling that secession was an acceptable and honorable tradition, separated himself from conservative allies in the North. This was especially true for Machen's close friend and ally, Clarence Macartney, equally conservative, but influenced by the culturally dominant tradition of northern evangelicalism. Macartney elected to stay within the larger church because he believed his opportunity to influence both the church and society would be greater there.[54]

A view contrary to the one offered here has been ably argued by D. G. Hart's recent biographical study of Machen. Hart makes the valuable point of distinguishing between Protestant liberals and cultural modernists. On the one hand, such ideas as the relativity of religious truth and the adaptation of religion to science were clearly part of the modernist project. On the other hand, most liberals in the mainstream churches wanted merely to make adjustments in traditional Christianity so that the gospel might be relevant to the present age, which would preserve Protestantism's historic and privileged role as moral guardian of America. For Machen, as Hart presents his views, it was worse to be a Protestant liberal than a cultural modernist because the latter had clearly moved beyond authentic Christianity, whereas the former was trying to adapt Christianity to modern culture. This was dangerous, according to Machen, because in hoping to maintain the church's role as cultural guardian "they had confused influence with faithfulness."[55]

Part of Hart's argument is persuasive, that liberals in the churches in the 1920s rarely were full-blown modernists. Rather they were progressive people adjusting religious belief and practice and seeking to have (in good Presbyterian fashion) religion set the tone for American life.[56] But, in his approving discussion of Machen's classic and controversial *Christianity and Liberalism* (1923), Hart shows decided sympathy for Machen's allegations that liberals are not merely misguided Christians but purveyors of another religion, thus inviting these false speakers to leave the church. *Christianity and Liberalism* was popular because it was controversial. Without the scholarly nuance that characterized Machen's other work, this book went for the jugular, as Machen himself said, "to present the issue as sharply and clearly as possible."[57] Late in 1923 Machen recycled a few of his ideas into a sermon ("The Present Issue in the Churches") at the First Presbyterian Church of Princeton. Hart calls Machen's language "feisty,"[58] but surely it was more than that: "The plain fact is, disguised though it may be by the use of traditional language, that two mutually exclusive religions are contending for the control of the church today."[59] Machen's language is clearly provocative, and it cannot be squared, though Hart tries, with the irenic spirit shown by Machen in the evolution controversy. Machen refused to go to Dayton, Tennessee, to testify at the Scopes trial. Moreover, he would try to construct "a mediating position between modernists and fundamentalists that reconciled the seemingly backward ideas of traditional Protestantism with the findings of modern science."[60]

Which is the real Machen, the one who saw no common ground between two different religions, or the one who refused to grandstand about a volatile issue and tried to find common ground between liberal-modernists and traditional-conservatives? Hart has made an important contribution to the discussion by showing that Machen was fundamentalism's lone modern scholar; but he seems to allow Machen to have it both ways, in militantly insisting on the doctrinally pure church and in accepting the need for common ground in other strategic areas. To be sure, biblical fidelity was of prime importance to Machen, thus making all other issues side issues. Perhaps we are asking too much of Machen to have been consistently militant on all volatile issues. As Hart suggests, it was possibly merely a tactical matter to avoid evolution. Yet given our concerns here with science, and especially the evolution controversies, we recall that other conservative Presbyterian leaders, such as William Jennings Bryan, saw evolution as precisely focusing the questions of biblical truth. We are not persuaded that the puzzle about the ideas and motives of Machen and his fellow seceders has been fully solved yet.

In the two cases under review here, concerning the Presbyterian Church in the United States of America and the Presbyterian Church in Ireland, we have seen remarkable connections and convergences as the two churches confronted modernity in the 1920s. In both cases the majority elected to pursue a course of ecclesiastical inclusiveness, even if it meant having fellowship on mission boards, in pulpits, and, vitally, at theological schools with those who deviated from what was said to be summed up in historic Calvinism's "five points." But was the formulation of "five points" as true to the historic nature of Calvinism in its Presbyterian form as its advocates insisted? Loetscher suggests that the "truest theological character of the PCUSA was rediscovered in the 1920s, in that moderate, mediating ecclesiology triumphed over strict and polemical attitudes."[61] However, as we shall see below, the issue cannot be so neatly resolved.

In Ireland, Robert Allen, the historian of the Presbyterian College, Belfast, asks why so few people supported James Hunter at the General Assembly of 1927 and why so few followed him out of the PCI to form the Irish Evangelical Church. If James Hunter in Belfast, and the same might be said for J. Gresham Machen in Princeton, stood as a pillar for truth against heresy in the church, why did he, or they, receive so little support? In the Irish church, Allen suggests there is "a congenital dislike of logical extremes, and it is this which saves it from stark dogmatism." The true face of Irish Presbyterianism emerged, it is suggested, when it decided to include and to broaden, not to exclude and to narrow.[62] Moreover, in the standard history of Irish Presbyterianism, Finlay Holmes implies that the conservatives and seceders had little cause to worry in any case. To the allegation that the PCI apostasized in the 1920s, Holmes insists that "The Irish Presbyterian Church had not apostasized, there was no departure from essential orthodoxy on the part of theological professors, ministers or church members."[63] Austin Fulton goes even further in support of this tendency of thought, i.e., that the difficulty in the fundamentalist-modernist controversy was created not by those who brought in new ideas but by those who fearfully resisted them. To this end, Fulton quotes favorably the final statement of J. Ernest Davey, in his defense before the General Assembly of 1927:

> Some of our Presbyterian Churches who have had this battle already over, would hardly even investigate them (i.e., the charges of heresy) seriously, but a section of our Church has been spoiling for a fight, and they have had no past heresy hunt to deter them since the distinctively modern study of religion and its forms began with the scientific revival of the last century. The issue before you is I believe, faith or fear— by which are we to be governed?[64]

Robert Allen agrees. What was particularly saddening to those who remained in the larger church while others departed was the apparent fear, indeed anger, on the part of the seceders. Would that they had been patient, argues Allen, with scholars investigating the historical and literary questions arising from the critical study of the Bible. Criticism, after all, is not necessarily heresy. In a vitally important insight, Allen writes, "In an age when new facts about the Bible are being discovered and investigated it may be difficult to sort the new knowledge into the mold that suited the old. The process of assimilating new elements of truth and co-ordinating them with the old requires time and care."[65]

In writing thus about "facts," Robert Allen is on to an important point, which he does not develop to its full significance. It is vitally important for our reinterpretation to insist that the neat dichotomy of dividing the conservative-fundamentalist faction (holding to "fears" and "outdated" ideas) from the moderate-modernist faction (holding to "facts" and "progressive" ideas) is not useful. Both factions believed it possessed facts, and that those facts accorded with true science. Modernists were not more "thoughtful" and the fundamentalists were not more "fearful." While there is an important intellectual difference between the two factions, it is not the one often assumed and articulated, either by apologists at the time or by later historians.[66]

George Marsden's *Fundamentalism and American Culture* (1980) and his many essays, some of which were collected in *Understanding Fundamentalism and Evangelicalism* (1991), have opened up a new line of inquiry on decoding the acrimonious controversy that went on in Presbyterianism in the 1920s. Marsden's arguments about American Presbyterianism are of importance in our attempt to understand Irish Presbyterianism and to connect the transatlantic world that broke in two in the 1920s. In summary form, the point is this: the two sides to the fundamentalist-modernist controversy approached the questions at hand with two differing sets of presuppositions: in a phrase, the difference is between common sense realism and interpretation (in the "higher criticism" sense of the term). At the very marrow of the discussion is the nature of history.

For most twentieth-century historians, there is little regard for "absolutes" most of which have dissolved in respect of historical subjectivity. For J. Gresham Machen, and for James Hunter and William Grier, the starting point for "facts" about God was the

Bible. For J. Ernest Davey and for the newer Princeton men, facts emerged from the Bible through interpretive structures. Neither view is more scientific or fact-oriented than the other, but the two views are radically different as to presuppositions. Facts, according to most twentieth-century historians, not only do not speak for themselves but may not even exist except in the human memory of them. On the other hand, as Machen wrote in *What Is Faith?* (1925), "the facts of the Christian religion remain facts no matter whether we cherish them or not: they are facts for God: they are facts for angels and for demons; they are facts now, and they will remain facts beyond the end of time."[67] For someone like J. E. Davey to assert that one can discover new facts through the modern, critical study of the Bible is almost to speak in a different language from Machen, and surely from different presuppositions. The first statement that Machen made to the incoming students at Westminster Seminary in its inaugural year, 1929, was to question the whole idea of interpretation.[68]

Machen's ideology was in the tradition of so-called Scottish Common Sense philosophy, developed by Thomas Reid (1710–1796) and taken abroad wherever Scottish Presbyterians went. It formed the method in which most intellectuals, and surely most Presbyterians, in the North Atlantic culture thought. Reid taught, and most Presbyterians before approximately 1875 seemed to agree, that the human mind can know the real world as a direct object of our thought. On the other hand, Lockeans interposed "ideas" between humans and the real world. When Machen tried to articulate some of these concerns at the 1929 General Assembly of the PCUSA (in the context of the Princeton reorganization debate), some hearers were incredulous.[69] What seems to have been at stake, though few of the antagonists would have put it thus, was whether or not in the twentieth century theological inquiry would be based on the historic notion of common sense or on critical interpretation. Historian Lefferts Loetscher sees the significance of this: "The debate thus often presented the spectacle of apparent contradictions in statements of facts, which were actually agreements as to facts, but disagreements as to their theological significance."[70]

Machen in America and Hunter in Ireland seemed to have been driven to their unpopular and unsuccessful campaigns not by theologies necessarily different from that of their opponents but by differing presuppositions about the way any person can know truth. The advent of modern biblical criticism marked, for the conservatives, a different way of knowing, and thus they regarded it as fundamentally corrosive to Christian belief. The person—then or now—working within the presuppositional categories of common sense would regard most acts of interpretation as fatal to what he or she would call "Biblical Christianity." The person—then or now—working within the presuppositional categories of modern historical interpretation would regard the "fact" orientation of common sense realism to be at least charmingly antique or possibly intellectually dishonest. With paradigms shifting so seismically it is little wonder that, given the other fault lines, the world of transatlantic Presbyterianism "broke in two in 1922 or thereabouts."

Four Keeping the Covenant

Militant Protestantism and the State in Ulster and America

The last third of the twentieth century has offered many surprises, most notably the disintegration of the Soviet Union and the fall of the Berlin Wall. Even as pieces of the wall formerly dividing East and West Berlin were being sold as tourist curios, authorities in Belfast were shoring up and extending the wall—the "peace line"—that divides the warring communities there. Those communities are known by different names: on one side it is Catholic, nationalist, and republican; on the other it is Protestant, unionist, and loyalist. While the names in each set are not exactly interchangeable, there is an affinity between them that the respective participants understand and act upon. The state of Northern Ireland, created as a stop-gap measure by Britain following the establishment of responsible government for most of Ireland under a Dublin-based parliament, existed for a half-century (1922–1972) with its own parliament at Stormont. In 1972, because of Stormont's apparent inability to govern the province, the British government in London intervened, prorogued the provincial parliament, and asserted direct rule from Westminster. If Stormont failed, it did so because it lacked that ingredient essential for all successful governments, a sociopolitical consensus.[1] The historian does not take a position on the unionist desire to see Northern Ireland work or on the republican desire to see it fail. One merely notes that the events from at least 1969 onwards have illustrated the bitterly contested nature of the state's legitimacy.

A commonplace expression when referring to Northern Ireland has it that "the inevitable never happens while the unexpected always does." By "inevitable" it is meant that Ireland as a whole is "natural" for the nation state. John Donne to the contrary notwithstanding, an island can be a thing unto itself, and in the view of many outside observers, it must be "inevitable" that the peoples inhabiting an island realize their essential commonality and, in the end, form a nation. By "unexpected," in the expression noted above, something has always emerged to prevent the seeming inevitability that all people on the Irish island will accept that their collective future depends on no one but themselves alone (e.g., the name of the republican, nationalist, and Catholic political movement, Sinn Fein, or "ourselves alone"). The loyalist, unionist, and Protestant faction, of course, is the group that supplies the objections which, taken together, prevent the supposed inevitability from happening. They are therefore put on the defensive when asked to explain themselves to an incredulous world opinion when it observes the two factions engaging in a horrific civil war in the north of Ireland, historically known as the province of Ulster.

The loyalist, unionist, and Protestant group is a numerical majority in the state of Northern Ireland, and they have repeatedly exercised their constitutional rights in voting to remain a part of the United Kingdom. They believe that they already have a nation to which they belong, and to live in an all-Ireland republic would be an unacceptable change of nationality. As to why they abhor so deeply living with their fellow islanders, the loyalists note that they would become a minority in a state at least guided (some would say dominated) by a church whose ideas and values they cannot accept.

Until now in this chapter we have carefully referred to the two factions using political, attitudinal, and religious terms. While one would not wish merely, or simplistically, to reduce the subtle interconnection between the three terms, it is necessary to single out the religious component for explicit analysis because many of the participants themselves (especially Protestants) see it that way. It is, as noted above, the bedrock objection of Ulster Protestants to an all-Irish nation state that Ireland is a "confessional state," informed by a church they disdain. Even as much as one sees the multidimensionality of the so-called "troubles," the religious dimension has—in the view offered here—been relatively discounted in scholarship over the past twenty-five years. The remainder of this chapter has two objectives: to restore the balance in the discourse about the troubles in respect to religion; and to look again at the 1920s to examine the founding of the state of Northern Ireland and the role of evangelical, revivalist Protestantism in cementing a broad consensus among all social classes which would result in the unique solidarity that continues to say "no" to the putative inevitability of an "Irish" nation. As elsewhere in this book, we will look to the United States for comparative possibilities in linking Protestant evangelicalism and political conservatism.

The difficulty of interpreting Northern Ireland does not obtain because scholars have too little information with which to work. To the contrary, the province of Ulster has been one of the most studied parts of the world over the past twenty-five years (one thinks of T. S. Eliot in wondering about the wisdom that eludes us in gaining information). While new discoveries of fresh data are always welcome, the question that concerns us here is: what frames of reference do we employ in our studies, i.e., how do we interpret Northern Ireland?[2] And, since we are asking about the connection between revivalist Protestantism and the state in Northern Ireland, we need to inquire into the intersection of religion, society, and politics in a state that has not functioned well.

Most serious writers, in trying to decode the subtexts that cause disfunction in Ulster, have suggested that religion has had little more than a superficial role. While acknowledging that the participants in civil strife refer to themselves by religious names, nearly all historians and social scientists have insisted that the realities of conflict lie elsewhere. Duncan Morrow, a political sociologist in Ulster, argues that the answer to why academics cannot see religion's importance lies in the social construction of knowledge among British academics. As Morrow reminds us, the British academy is decidedly secular, therefore assuming a world in which religion either has disappeared or exists only among socially marginal peoples. "At its worst religion is equivalent to obscurantism and superstition. In this context religion, particularly in its organized form, is a strange and difficult territory, easier to dismiss than to explore. The obsessive religiosity of the Irish is at best embarrassing and at worst dangerous."[3]

If social scientists believe religion to be epiphenomenal in Ulster, it may well turn not on the intrinsic merits of the case but on their own failure of imagination about the persistence of religion in the modern world. Scholars whose presuppositions insist that the institutional forms and cultural effects of religion cannot be significant social phenomena often, therefore, accuse of "false consciousness" those participants in Ulster whose self-description insists that religion is vital in shaping their worldview and in guiding their actions. Having used the term "false consciousness" we must say a word about the contribution of Marxist scholars, especially those in sociology and political science.

In the mid-to-late 1960s, Marxist interpretations of all sorts were gaining a wide hearing in all areas of social analysis, no less so in interpreting the civil strife that began again in Ulster in 1969. James Connolly (1870–1916), of the revolutionary generation, had restated in Irish terms the basics of Marx's and Engels's ideology, i.e., that national independence and democratic socialism had to proceed hand in hand in Ireland. Indeed, even noting the knotty problem of Ulster Protestants, Connolly held the position still held by many nationalists, that when Ireland was united the true class interests of Ulster workers would become clear to them, and they would, either out of conviction or necessity, align themselves with their class allies throughout Ireland. Of the many Marxist works to appear since 1968, Liam De Paor's *Divided Ulster* is one of the most often discussed.[4] He uses the colonial argument, both because it is dear to the heart of Marxist orthodoxy, and because, prior to 1921, it was probably a correct description of relations between Britain and Ireland. Further, by 1970, the time of De Paor's writing, to make the colonial argument stick in a postcolonial era was to seal the doom of British control in Ulster. Yet the argument's greatest weakness is that were the British government to withdraw its troops from Northern Ireland, it would not mean "Brits out," because a majority of the population in Ulster would nevertheless regard themselves as British. To summarize, the colonial argument—appropriate as it may have been for all of Ireland prior to 1921—does not apply to contemporary northeast Ireland because the absence of the putative colonial power would not change the ethnocultural realities in the area.

Michael Farrell's otherwise interesting, well-researched, and well-written work of 1976, *Northern Ireland: The Orange State,*[5] is equally defective in its reasoning from a Marxist viewpoint. He founds his argument on the classic Marxist staple of the manipulation of the Ulster Protestant working class. While he, and other writers, are onto a valuable theme in articulating the economic and social differences between working-class and bourgeois Protestants, the argument breaks down if pressed to the conclusion that the Protestant proletariat would assert Irish consciousness if liberated from the double duplicity of Protestant identity and bourgeois manipulation. Even fellow Marxists Paul Bew, Peter Gibbon, and Henry Patterson[6] allow for an objective reality in Protestant consciousness. Further, as to the question of the essential Marxist assumption that Ireland must be united and independent to be socialist, Gibbon and Patterson, in their own specialized studies, revised the Marxist model of interpretation even further, to allow for an objective reality in Protestant resistance to a unified, socialist Ireland.[7] Well does John Whyte remark that "during the 1970s, then, the unity of the Marxist school of thought on Northern Ireland disappeared,"[8] and with it, one might add, much of its interpretive power (though toward the end of this chapter, we will return approvingly to that staple product of Marxist analysis, i.e., cultural alienation). Economic and class conflict is undeniably present in all nations and no less so in Ulster. But as an explanation of the current conflict such emphases take too little account of culture, in the broadest sense of that term.

Richard Jenkins, an anthropologist, goes the farthest in terms of a social scientific mea culpa. He asks if social scientific analytical models of reality are intrinsically more accurate than folk models (taking into account religion and culture) of the same reality. In short, are historical and/or contemporary actors in society guilty of false consciousness if they insist that cultural concerns are of vital interest to them? Or, Jenkins asks, does the social scientist, like mother, know best? Jenkins, correctly in my view, insists that social actors' self-understanding should be accorded respect, and that social scientists are not necessarily better placed to make sense of a conflict situation than the immediate participants themselves.[9]

If the conflict in Northern Ireland is not fully or solely about class and economic conflict, and if we should take the self-description of the participants seriously, then why should we not use the political names they give themselves and ask, concurrently, if the conflict is not really best understood in political terms? There are various meanings of "nationalist" and "unionist." These are political terms, revealing a political historical consciousness and political objectives. Simply put, a nationalist is one who wants an Ireland united and independent from Britain. A unionist is one who wants to maintain the British link between Northern Ireland and the United Kingdom. In both views, it is agreed that the main conflict is between Britain and Ireland, with nationalists traditionally blaming Britain for Ireland's troubles and with unionists traditionally blaming Ireland for Britain's Ulster troubles. In the discussion to follow we will distinguish between traditional and revisionist nationalist and unionist definitions of the political problem of Northern Ireland. This helps us to see how far understanding has come in a relatively short while.

The traditional nationalist interpretation of the Northern Ireland problem turns on two notions: that the island of Ireland forms a natural national unit for whatever people reside thereon, and that the problem of an Ireland divided against its natural self is to be laid to the door of Britain. This view is best articulated by Frank Gallagher in *The Indivisible Island*,[10] in which he argues that Irish people, of any political stripe, never really wanted partition. He maintains that Northern Ireland was never viable in either political or economic terms and that British subsidies alone keep the province going. This viewpoint is also articulated in the Irish Constitution, in which that new nation asserted its right "to the unity and integrity of the national territory." These assertions, let it be noted, took no notice of the existence of, or the feelings of, the people who formed the majority in the six counties of northeast Ireland. However, the viewpoint of traditional nationalists has been challenged by people who are also undeniably nationalist, i.e., desiring a united Ireland, but who see the division not between Ireland and Britain but rather between the peoples of Ireland themselves.[11] Since the onset of the troubles again in 1969, the revisionist historiography accelerated, most notably in the writings of such southern Irish political luminaries as Garret Fitzgerald and Conor Cruise O'Brien. Taken together, their works conclusively shift the focus for division in Ireland from British machination to Ulster Protestant reluctance.[12] By allowing for an objective reality for another people residing on the Irish island, the bedrock of traditional nationalist interpretation was eroded.

The traditional unionist interpretation of the Northern Ireland problem also turns on two notions: that there are two distinct peoples in Ireland, and that the problem resides in the refusal of nationalists to accord to the Protestants a political right of self-determination that the former claim for themselves. This view was best articulated in M. W. Heslinga's *The Irish Border As a Cultural Divide*,[13] which is the direct counterpart to Frank Gallagher's work, noted above. For Heslinga, and for most unionists, the real nation, and natural unit, is the British Isles, with the real affinities being east and west and the differences being north and south. In this view, Ireland has no historical or sociopsychological basis to claim that the island should be one state. Such views sustained unionist ideology for a long time, in which people in Ulster would chant slogans about a "Protestant parliament for a Protestant people." Yet reality began to overtake such unionist perspectives when the troubles broke out anew in the late 1960s, most notably in the writings of the academic historian A. T. Q. Stewart, who wrote trenchantly that

> most people, if asked to define the chief symptoms of the Northern Ireland troubles, would say it is that the two communities cannot live together. The very essence of the Ulster question, however, is that they *do* live together, and have done for centuries. They share the same homeland and, like it or not, the two diametrically opposed political wills must coexist on the same narrow ground.[14]

Writers who portray unionist ideology, whether or not descriptively or normatively, began, by the late 1970s, to admit that in Ulster there resided a minority community that had rights and legitimate aspirations. Thus the tendency of revisionist unionist writing was to converge, paradoxically, with that of revisionist nationalists, i.e., that all could now admit the legitimate existence of Protestant and Catholic institutions and ideology.

The seemingly unassailable point that there are two communities in Northern Ireland and that the conflict is between them—not Britain and Ireland—is an astonishingly new interpretation. But it quickly became the consensus interpretation. Despite their longevity, traditional nationalist and unionist interpretations—i.e., blaming Britain or Ireland—are now quaintly passé. Writers articulating the internal-conflict interpretation may still and nevertheless be unionists or nationalists, but they are focusing, at long last, on the two communities themselves. Having said that, however, there is one last point to be considered in this context. In view of the concerns of this chapter—to what extent is religion at the heart of things in Ulster—we need to ask if politics is the main concern. In one of the best books on contemporary Ulster, Stewart's *The Narrow Ground*, we read the following:

> The fact is, however, that the quarrel is not about theology as such and remains, in its modern form, stubbornly a constitutional problem, though religion is the shibboleth of the contending parties. Essentially the conflict in Ulster is not different from other conflicts in the modern world: it is about political power and who should wield it.[15]

Having seen that social class and economic conflict are necessary but not sufficient causes for the troubles, we need to answer Stewart's point about politics. Is the conflict about politics, like other modern conflicts, and is religion merely "the shibboleth of the contending parties"? We have previously agreed that social scientists do not necessarily know better than participants themselves, so we should look at what they say. In answer to Stewart's concern we should grant immediately that, of course, the conflict in Ulster is "about political power and who should wield it." But, such a statement does not answer the significant question about the meaning of politics, i.e., wielding political power to do what?

Herein is a significant interpretive difficulty. The Catholic-nationalist group sees the conflict mostly in political terms. Their politics are about requiring the state to meet the legitimate needs and aspirations of the minority community in Ulster, whether or not within an all-Ireland context or in a United Kingdom context. The Protestant-unionist group is not of so single a mind,[16] and they attend church less frequently than Catholics, thus making categorical judgments about them problematic. Yet, while there are some Protestants who view the conflict in political terms, many, if not most, see the conflict in religious terms. For them religion is vastly more than shibboleth and vital to their worldview and to the actions that spring therefrom.

At this point the critical reader will want to ask: can one really and seriously say that religion, as commonly defined, is at the heart of the troubles, at least for Protestants? This invites the subsequent question: what do we mean by religion as commonly defined? Religion, one supposes, for most people, is either a matter of private psychological comfort or of institutional allegiance, involving adherence to doctrines or theological positions. But, is this enough of a definition of religion?

John Hickey's work helps us here in talking about explicit religious beliefs and their social importance. What Hickey contributes to the discussion is the insight that social scientists and historians express a disinclination to believe that there is a "concept of commitment, or the ensuing fact that people are capable of ordering their actions on the basis of commitment."[17] Commitment to religious belief—apart from social origins and effects—is not the stock in trade of academic analysis. Hickey sees the historic roots of the Reformation as still operative in Northern Ireland.

> The forces that are provoking that "problem" find part of
> their roots in the religious tradition that has influenced
> Europe and America at least since the sixteenth century. The
> peculiarity about Northern Ireland is that the conflict which
> took place in the remainder of Europe and in the United
> States some centuries ago is taking place in this province now.
> The other societies have found some means of dealing with
> that problem and producing a "modus vivendi" for the
> conflicting groups. Northern Ireland has not.[18]

Hickey details the pattern of perceptions among Protestants—especially of the Reformed, Calvinist Protestants of Ulster—about the Roman Catholic Church. While these assumptions about worldviews may be said to describe more of the pre–Vatican II Catholic Church and are therefore outdated, they nevertheless represent the deeply held views of many, if not most, Ulster Protestants. The argument proceeds as follows: The mission of the Catholic Church may be to convert the world but, within that, a central purpose is to protect the *depositum fidei*. This means that the organizational structure of the church must remain separate from the state. So, while the church may claim to intervene in activities that are the moral functions of the state, it cannot accept the reverse; that, political leaders be allowed to intervene in the affairs of the church. Thus, the Roman Catholic Church could never become an established church, like the Church of England, because secular political leaders, whether a hereditary monarchy or an elected parliament, could never be accorded directive and controlling power over the church. To Protestants, this is all wrong. They see religion as functioning to bring Christians together to form a "holy city," a city created by the voluntary association of like-minded persons who find the warrant for their authority not in the church but in the Bible. As Hickey concludes: The religious divide in Northern Ireland is not based purely on the symbolic membership of a group with different political ideologies but is rooted in different interpretations of the Christian faith, which, in turn, help to form attitudes as to what society and its institutions should be about.[19] Historians David Hempton and Myrtle Hill agree: "Any attempt to unravel the complexities of the Irish Protestant psychology must take as its starting point the overriding sense of moral responsibility with which evangelicals were imbued, and which blurred the distinctions between religious and political activities. For evangelical contempt for the Roman Catholic Church emanated not only from its doctrinal 'heresies' but from their social and political consequences."[20]

It is in this context that one can begin to understand the desire of Ulster Protestants to maintain the state of Northern Ireland, because it is, for them, their last line of defense in a logical argument that began with a different Christian worldview. For Protestants, the theological notion of covenant is both deeply ingrained in their religious thinking and is easily transferable to social contract thinking. Like their Calvinist co-religionists in South Africa, the Protestants of Ulster are fond of writing covenants that combine religion and politics in nationalistic context.[21] Indeed, on the fiftieth anniversary of the founding of the Northern Irish state, some 334,000 men and women signed their names to the Ulster Covenant. It stressed that the forces trying to undermine the government of Northern Ireland were "subversive of our civil and religious freedom . . . " thus requiring them to "hereby pledge ourselves in solemn covenant throughout this our time of threatened calamity to stand by one another in defending our cherished position of citizenship in the United Kingdom."[22]

John Whyte, the best overall recent interpreter of the Northern Irish scene does not like Hickey's viewpoints and calls them "extreme."[23] But what is "extreme" in them seems to be that Hickey takes religion very seriously. Whyte wonders why religion can cause strife in Ireland whereas the terms "Protestant" and "Catholic" in other countries "mark a purely religious difference."[24] Whyte seems to have misunderstood what it means to say "purely religious." Religion is never sealed off from its social context; in fact, the very sort of Protestants we are studying here—mainly Presbyterians—found their religious ideology in conjoining religion and culture, and they eschew attempts to make religion solely a private matter. The viewpoint argued here is that it is unimaginative, even sterile, to try to distinguish between the discreet domains of religion and politics. As aptly stated by the anthropologist Richard Jenkins, "Religion often concerns itself with issues that are apparently political, and politics may equally be self-consciously religious."[25] This is the case in Ulster, where Protestant politics and Protestant religion are not only interconnected but spring from a single worldview.

Frank Wright, a political scientist, helps the discussion at this point with his subtle and nuanced analysis of Protestant ideology. While he does not discuss the ideology's origins, he notes its affects and effects by laying down a gauntlet to conventional social science in writing that, in Northern Ireland, "Ideology tends to structure experience rather than the other way around."[26] This ideology is, importantly, an autonomous one, in that it lives in a self-fulfilling world of its own, relatively untouched by empirical reality. So, when Catholics are openly hostile, Protestants say that their real face is showing; when Catholics are cooperative and ecumenical, Protestants wonder what ulterior purpose the Catholics are trying duplicitously to pursue. At the bottom of this attitude is a foundational belief about the nature of Protestantism and of Catholicism. In sum, it is a version of the Whig theory of history, that God (or, as Jefferson said, "Nature's god") wants the right to triumph in the end. In this view of things, the right means the continual expansion of liberty and the conquest of tyranny. The internal mechanism of this progressive development is religion, with Protestantism always on the side of liberty and Catholicism on the side of tyranny.

Protestantism in Ulster, however, is not a monolithic social force. A useful distinction, if not pressed too far, between Protestants has been offered by Owen Dudley Edwards. For Edwards, there are at least two types of Protestants, the "confident" who tend to ignore Catholics and the "fearful" who are hyperconscious of the Catholic presence in their midst.[27]

The Rev. Dr. Ian R. K. Paisley is the most faithful representation of this fearful ideology in contemporary Northern Ireland. He was born in county Tyrone in 1926 and raised in the staunchly unionist town of Ballymena in county Antrim. After some Bible school training he was ordained in 1946 in an independent church. His career is another example of the transatlantic connection. Paisley's honorary doctorate was given by Bob Jones University, in South Carolina, known as the most militantly fundamentalist university in America. In 1951, Paisley founded the first congregation of the Free Presbyterian Church, a small denomination of which he has been the sole moderator. While the denomination itself is quite small, the sociopolitical ramifications of "Paisleyism" are Ulsterwide. It will do no good to try to dismiss Paisley, as some scholars have, by calling him a "fanatic," his rallies "stunts," and his rhetoric "ranting hyperbole," "neanderthal," "laughingly recondite," and even "antediluvian."[28] Far better to see Paisley as many Protestant people in Northern Ireland see him, as a legitimate political leader with religiously informed views that many Ulster people share but would not state so boldly in public.[29]

In one of his own publications Paisley put forward, in 1966, the essence of Protestant religiopolitical ideology:

> Liberty is the very essence of Bible Protestantism. Tyranny is the very essence of Popery. Where Protestantism flourishes

Liberty flames. Where Popery reigns Tyranny rules. . . . As Liberty and Tyranny have no common meeting place, so Protestantism and Popery cannot be reconciled. Popery is tyrannical in every sphere of life. . . . On the other hand Protestantism is the torch-bearer of Liberty. Protestantism, at a stroke, cuts down all the shackles of superstition and priestcraft. The soul is free to commune with its Maker. There is one mediator between God and man—the man Jesus Christ. . . . The Protestant's home is his castle. He brooks no interference from Pope, priest, pastor, preacher or prelate. . . . No one can control the Protestant's education or the books which he shall read. He is free born and trembles not at priestly threats or the Papal curse. . . . At the ballot box the Protestant exercises complete liberty. . . . In our province the battle lines between Papal Tyranny and Protestant Liberty are joined.[30]

Well does Frank Wright conclude that in Ulster religion and politics are inextricably bound, so that the continued crisis of political legitimacy is a "battle between two religious systems carried on in the fields of politics."[31] Despite the disinclination of some scholars to accept this point,[32] there has been ample qualitative and quantitative research to demonstrate that evangelical political ideology is formative (one does not say determinative) in Protestant thinking well beyond the merest numerical confines of the evangelical wing of Protestantism as such, as David Taylor and Martha Abele MacIver have shown.[33] Precisely because the state of Northern Ireland has endured the contesting of legitimacy since its founding, the social ramifications of evangelical ideology are shared by most Protestants (card-carrying evangelicals or not) because it affords them a secure sociopolitical identity in a confusing and conflictual situation. It should be emphasized, moreover, that religion's formative role is not merely functional, that is, derivative mainly from a desire for political cohesion. It is that, to be sure; but political ideas are generated by religious beliefs. In MacIver's sensitive and illumining inquiry into the beliefs of Protestant political elites, she notes the different views of the three political groupings among Protestants: Democratic Unionist (DMP), Official Unionist (OUP), and Alliance. The last was included for completeness, not because it is politically effective or much representative of Ulster Protestantism. The conclusion of her unique work indicates a strong symbolic convergence between conservative religious beliefs and conservative political views. The evangelical movement, in gospel halls and in Presbyterian, Anglican, and Methodist churches, has had a disproportionate share in shaping Unionist ideology and practice.

The evangelical movement is a multinational phenomenon that emerged in all Protestant denominations in the English-speaking world. From approximately 1740 onwards, this Anglo-American, pan-Protestant movement was to become both a revitalizing force within Protestantism and a major critic of "established" religion, whether socially or intellectually. Its signature was the desire to convert others to the Christian faith and therefore believed deeply in direct evangelism, both on an individual and communal basis. Since established church leaders often were either opposed or apathetic to evangelical zeal, evangelical leaders and laity alike prayed for what they called "revival," a communal turning of many people to the paths of righteousness.

Evangelicalism is a fairly broad movement that encompasses several types of churchmanship (from Anglican to Pentecostal) and varying perspectives on the relationship of Christianity to culture. At the far right of evangelicalism one finds fundamentalism, at once a part of the broader evangelical movement and its most severe critic. It is the fundamentalist faction within evangelicalism that gives the larger movement most of its bombastic firepower.

It is curious that this term—fundamentalist—has gained such wide usage in Ulster because it is of American origin. Specifically it refers to a set of religious doctrines and attitudes put forward early in this century in a series of pamphlets—The Fundamentals— by an organization called The World's Christian Fundamentalist Association, of Minneapolis, Minnesota. The movement that drew inspiration and cohesion from The Fundamentals was, and is, a militantly antimodern movement among evangelical Protestants. It draws its theoretical and theological foundations largely, though not exclusively, from Calvinism and its affect and élan from the Methodist and Baptist revivalist tradition, the hallmark of American Protestantism.[34]

George Marsden, in a groundbreaking article, compares American fundamentalism with its cousin, British evangelicalism. While the two share a tendency toward biblical literalism and a conversionist zeal, they differ markedly in one significant respect. British evangelicalism seems to understand the role of history in religio-cultural development, whereas American fundamentalists have a view of history that is distinctly antimodern.[35] Thus, the fundamentalist's religion is construed in terms of defending a heritage. This heritage often reflects the secular American self-definition of America being a unique place, exceptional in the world's history, in which Europeans might begin again.[36] If one can combine the notion of a religious covenant (the Calvinist God who purposes his inscrutable will) with a Whig theory of history about the constant expansion of liberty (and Methodist-Baptist free will), one has a very potent force indeed. This explicit conjunction of religious and political ideology is the essence of what Robert Bellah called "civil religion."[37] While fundamentalists in America are not the only upholders of civil religion, they are the most consistent of its contemporary defenders.

We cannot here fully rehearse, but can note, the historiographical sea change on fundamentalism and evangelicalism that has occurred over the past twenty years.[38] Prior to about 1970, religion was largely ignored by historians outside the confines of what was then called "historical theology" or "church history." When mainstream historians discussed religion at all (especially conservative Protestantism), they painted a picture of regressive protest to the developing consensus of American values.[39] Fundamentalism (and, to an extent, evangelicalism also) was often portrayed as anti-intellectual (though in reality it was much concerned with ideas), as rural and possibly southern (though in reality its ideas were generated in the urban North), and simplistic (though in reality a simple and straightforward idea that accorded with the Bible was thought to be "truth" to the fundamentalist believer).

Ernest R. Sandeen was the scholar who began the revision of fundamentalism. Rather than allowing religion, especially fundamentalism, to be defined as merely reactive to social change, Sandeen persuasively portrayed fundamentalism as a genuine religious movement. But as valuable as Sandeen's pioneer work was, he applied too narrow a scope to his work, insisting that fundamentalism be defined "partly, if not largely, as one aspect of the history of millenarianism."[40] He was challenged in this respect by George Marsden. The two exchanged views in a journal, and those comments would give shape to the historical debate for years to come.[41] Marsden's main concern was not to doubt fundamentalism's basic religious character but to correct Sandeen's having given too little of fundamentalism's social context, as well as the way in which the movement at once rejected and reflected American culture. Marsden's more fully rounded views, now widely accepted by historians and social scientists, see this religious movement as social, political, intellectual, and "American" phenomena.[42]

Sandeen's work was cut short by his untimely death, and scholars of religion are the worse for his inability to build on his seminal work. Yet in one of his last articles he was showing signs of incorporating cultural perspectives into his work. He was inquiring into an authentic conservative tradition in America that was religiously based. He noted the rapid advance of modernization and with it the secularization and alienation that ineluctably follow. In pointing people back to basics, "the process of rapid, technologically induced change seems destined to succeed where poets and historians have previously failed. By stripping every sector of American society to its bare essentials, to its irreducible commitments, this giant change machine is defining the American character."[43] Sandeen saw the epitome of the modern person as one able to adapt to all changes and to commit to nothing permanent, with values only functionally suited to adaptation. On the other hand he saw an authentically conservative American as a person with something to remember and to protect, i.e., both the central truths of the Christian faith and the American culture in which they had been so important for many years.

Returning our focus to Ulster, we need to ask if "real" fundamentalism can exist outside the United States. The leading historian of Irish Presbyterianism, R. F. G. Holmes, while noting the deep influence of American-style fundamentalism on Ulster's religious and political life, rightly observes that the research is not conclusive as to whether fundamentalism is native to Ulster or imported there.[44] George Marsden, while otherwise insisting that fundamentalism is an American phenomenon, drops a tantalizing footnote to the effect that the one possible exception to the rule might be Ulster.[45] Further, if it be true that the genius of American fundamentalism is its direct continuity with nineteenth-century revivalism, then Ulster could fit the definition because of the impact of revivalism in nineteenth-century Ulster. As Peter Brooke has shown, a coherent Presbyterian culture gave way, after the revival of 1859, to a less coherent but more inclusive Protestant and evangelical culture.[46] Moreover, Sandeen's suggestion about the role of modernization, with its alienating secularization, seems also to be true for the Protestants of Ulster. If modern change strips away other forms of sociocultural identity, it may drive people back to basics and cause them to reassert their identities based in memory; to remember again what, in another connection, Abraham Lincoln called "the mystic chords of union."

The idea of the covenant is important to discuss at this point. Above, on the way to another point, we observed the potency of conjoining the Calvinist idea of the covenant with the Whig theory of history. This is the essence of evangelical civil religion, that is, a belief that God has a special arrangement with a specific people, and that people's historic role is to stand for righteousness in society to enable the conquest of liberty and the defeat of tyranny. It is beyond dispute that such a belief lies at the heart of the American myth, that empowering story Americans deeply believe about themselves.[47] As Bernard Bailyn and Nathan Hatch have shown, religion and politics were so intertwined in the minds of the (especially New England) revolutionaries that the defense of political and religious liberty—the Whig theory—was one.[48]

In contemporary Ulster, Ian Paisley is the most important, and divisive, leader in both religion and politics. His ideas about politics and culture are accepted, even cherished, by Protestants in Northern Ireland well beyond the confines of the fundamentalist sects. He spoke for a majority of Ulster people in 1985, just after Margaret Thatcher and Garret Fitzgerald had concluded the Anglo-Irish Agreement. No better statement about the importance of the religiopolitical covenant can be imagined than Paisley's diatribe against Margaret Thatcher.

God has a people in this province. There are more born-again people in Ulster to the square mile than anywhere else in the world. This little province has had the peculiar preservation of divine Providence. You only have to read the history of Ulster to see that time after time when it seemed humanly impossible to extricate Ulster from seeming disaster, that God intervened. Why? God has a purpose for this province, and this plant of Protestantism sown here in the north-eastern part of this island. The enemy has tried to root it out, but it still grows today, and I believe, like a grain of mustard seed, its future is going to be mightier yet. God Who made her mighty will make her mightier yet in His Divine will.[49]

The critical reader of these words will want to ask how such a statement might represent Ulster Protestants in general, i.e., those outside of, or on the fringes of, fundamentalist evangelicalism. The recent insightful work of Donald H. Akenson helps us here. In a brilliantly conceived study of religiously based covenantal politics in South Africa, Israel, and Ulster, Akenson reminds us of the social importance of Scripture in certain cultures. The covenant that Yahweh made with Israel of old has been appropriated to the modern societies named who also claim that they are special in God's sight: one Jewish nation appropriating its own scripture, and two nations informed by Calvinist ideology and insisting that they are the modern fulfillment of the same scripture.

On 28 September 1912, virtually the entire adult male Protestant population of Ulster signed a document entitled "Ulster's Solemn League and Covenant." The political situation was at a knife edge. It appeared that the Home Rule Bill for Ireland would soon pass the House of Commons in London and become law. The General Assembly of the Presbyterian Church in Ireland passed a resolution outlining the general Protestant case for the Union and against political control from Dublin. In the autumn when Protestant leaders composed "The League and Covenant" they were aware of committing a possible treasonous act in appealing directly to the King over the heads of Parliament. They referred to the Home Rule Bill as a conspiracy, while declaring their loyalty to the Crown.[50] (See page 99 for a copy of "The League and Covenant.")

Ulster's

Solemn League and Covenant.

Being convinced in our consciences that Home Rule would be disastrous to the material well-being of Ulster as well as of the whole of Ireland, subversive of our civil and religious freedom, destructive of our citizenship and perilous to the unity of the Empire, we, whose names are underwritten, men of Ulster, loyal subjects of His Gracious Majesty King George V., humbly relying on the God whom our fathers in days of stress and trial confidently trusted, do hereby pledge ourselves in solemn Covenant throughout this our time of threatened calamity to stand by one another in defending for ourselves and our children our cherished position of equal citizenship in the United Kingdom and in using all means which may be found necessary to defeat the present conspiracy to set up a Home Rule Parliament in Ireland. ¶ And in the event of such a Parliament being forced upon us we further solemnly and mutually pledge ourselves to refuse to recognise its authority. ¶ In sure confidence that God will defend the right we hereto subscribe our names. ¶ And further, we individually declare that we have not already signed this Covenant.

The above was signed by me at _____
"Ulster Day," Saturday, 28th September, 1912.

God Save the King.

Well does Akenson conclude: "That this document, which is the nodal point around which all subsequent Ulster history revolves, was a distinctly Presbyterian artifact is yet another indication of the real (but frequently unrecognized) cultural hegemony that the Ulster-Scots held over the entire Protestant population of the north of Ireland."[51] Alvin Jackson makes a very valuable point in the same vein. He suggests that the events in Ulster prior to the First World War, and centering on 28 September 1912, "have served as a creation myth for Unionism in the twentieth century—as a kind of Orange Genesis."[52] Fundamentalism then in Ulster seems to conform to the typology of American fundamentalism, in both religious and political senses, i.e., by bringing the two together. But before we can say conclusively that Ulster fits the typology, we need to examine one more point, the sense of a cultural crisis.

American fundamentalism had been a long time germinating but came to full flower in the years following the First World War. As Marsden has shown, fundamentalists believed America to be at the brink of crisis.[53] They regarded attacks upon a number of views they cherished as threats to the moral warrant of Protestant cultural leadership. In politics, while Protestants never had total dominance, they exercised a hegemonic role that only rarely had been effectively challenged. With the political mobilization of the "new" immigrants from southern and eastern Europe under the leadership of the Catholic Irish, the "old" outsiders, the Democratic party was seen as a threat to the "natural" state of politics under Protestant control. Further, the realm of public morals was being threatened, at least as far as evangelical piety was concerned. Prohibiting alcohol and enforcing sabbath observance were highly charged symbolic issues for most Protestants. Right from the beginning of the evangelical hegemony a critical issue turned on who had the power to define the social meaning of drink.[54] Moreover, the education of children was slipping away from the intellectual control of Protestants. Post-Darwinian ideas, along with so-called progressive methods, seemed to threaten the learning of civic virtue, always the powerful, if hidden, agenda of the public schools.

In trying to understand the rise of fundamentalism one must place the question in appropriate historical context. By looking into context one does not try to reduce fundamentalism's essentially religious character. However, it is not enough to state that fundamentalists are extremely conservative Protestants; such folk have been around for a long time and have not come forth in this special and separate (and separatist) movement. It took a special moment of a heightened sense of crisis, even hysteria, for a special movement of religiously based militancy to arise. Militancy is crucial to their outlook. As Marsden observes, "Fundamentalists are not just religious conservatives, they are conservatives who are willing to take a stand and to fight."[55]

If the sense of a social crisis is necessary for a kind of fundamentalist militancy to arise among conservative Protestants, then Ulster seems to fit the pattern quite well. As other parts of this book demonstrate, Ulster Protestants faced perceived threats similar to their American co-religionists: they were accustomed to hegemonic leadership in Ulster society and resented the prospect of its loss; they worried about (what they called) the moral fiber of the society; theological liberalism in the churches and educational modernism in the schools were also viewed as singularly bad trends. The unique situation in Ulster, of course, was the proposed political changes within the United Kingdom that Home Rule would bring. They did not wish to become part of an Irish nation because they already had a nation toward which they felt deep loyalty. Moreover, in the great carnage of World War I, they had proven their loyalty to Britain in the thousands of Ulstermen who had given their lives in the killing fields of France on behalf of crown and country. For the Parliament of the United Kingdom to disown them after that sort of sacrifice was incredible to Ulster Protestants. The Home Rule Bill, whose implementation was postponed until after the war, seemed to many Ulster Protestants not only to be a conspiracy against them but a mean and spiteful one at that. Ulster people said "no" in the decisive winter of 1920–21, and many continue to say "no" to the time of this writing. It is often said that Ulster Protestants have a "siege" mentality, an allegation about which most Ulster men and women would be unembarrassed. They believe themselves to be committing everything they are and possess to a righteous cause. As David Miller has demonstrated, the intellectual origins of Ulster unionism in Scottish Presbyterian contract thinking cannot be ignored.[56]

Sociologist Steve Bruce has recently discussed what he calls the fallacies of "liberal" and "ecumenical" thinking in and about Ulster. Liberals, he suggests, generally believe that conflict is based on mutual misunderstanding and that conflict resolution would follow if groups would redefine their goals. Ecumenicals, on one hand, make a virtue out of accepting differences between religious groups. But ecumenicals also insist that such differences need not be threatening to any "tradition," and that both sides should try to learn from each other. Bruce points out, however, that the real constitutional aspirations of the two communities are deeply held and passionately believed in, and that liberal and ecumenical pronouncements seem—to ordinary people—to be out of touch with reality. The fact is that the equally legitimate aspirations of the two communities cannot be simultaneously fulfilled. At the same time there is a deep conviction on the Protestant side that their desires to remain British will, one day, be swept aside in some final negotiation between Dublin and London, thus deepening the Protestant sense of cultural anxiety.[57]

We have noted above the easy confluence of the notion of theological covenant and social contract thinking. Arthur Aughey's recent review of Ulster thought in the 1980s, following the Anglo-Irish Agreement, is excellent. Ulster unionism "is at one and the same time completely loyal and completely rebellious. It prostrates itself before the Union Jack and every sympathetic utterance of royal and politician alike and takes to the street with an almost anarchic fervor at the slightest hint of its absolute values being 'compromised'."[58] Thus the ambiguous nature of the state in Northern Ireland was, and is, the continued cause and sustenance of the sort of social crisis that brings conservative Protestants into a condition of wary militancy. In sum, fundamentalism may well be an American phenomenon, but it is not solely or uniquely so. For the reasons given above, we can suggest that the typology also fits Ulster quite well. Indeed, because of the peculiar circumstances in Northern Ireland—a province lacking consensus about its political legitimacy—militant fundamentalists have achieved a social and political role denied their comrades in America.

Five   Populist Ideology and Revivalism

W. P. Nicholson and the Forging of a Unionist Identity

In the review of literature in the previous chapter we noted the interpretive shift that has developed among scholars who try to explain the contested legitimacy in the Ulster state. Most notable is the shift from the colonial argument to the internal conflict argument. No longer is the Ulster question able to be laid at the doors of the United Kingdom and the Republic of Ireland; the conflict is between the two communities in Northern Ireland. But a concern that often arises when this viewpoint is presented turns on class analysis; in short, why do not working-class Protestant loyalists embrace their class allies in the Catholic, nationalist communities and work together for mutually beneficial social change in Ulster? There are two parts to the answer. On a practical level, many loyalists may believe themselves to be better-off in a British Ulster than in an Ulster under the dominion of Dublin, which may be the result if they make common cause with nationalist class allies. But perhaps more significantly, to many (if not most) loyalists, ideology is more important and satisfying than the supposed benefits that might follow from class solidarity. Yet the questions to this viewpoint persist: are not working-class Protestants being duped by the Protestant establishment to give up potential political and economic gains in exchange for the token of power given them by a distrustful establishment? This line of questioning does indeed have interpretive force, but it does not take into account the reality of the populist power enjoyed by working-class loyalists.

Paul Bew, Peter Gibbon, and Henry Patterson, the revisionist Marxist scholars noted in the previous chapter, have offered a very helpful suggestion. While working within a Marxist discourse, they nevertheless write trenchantly about the development of an independent, populist movement among working-class Protestants in the years following 1920.[1] In the years after World War I and the founding of the Soviet Union, political leaders in Britain and America were afraid of the spread of bolshevism, so they looked askance at trade union movements as potential nurturers of radicalism. In the special case of Ulster, radicalism and socialism were frequently linked to republicanism. There was, in fact, a real chance that Belfast workers would side with the British Labour Party, which would have weakened the solidarity of Unionism markedly. Edward Carson and others led the way among Protestants to develop a loyalist brand of Ulster trade unionism. They played on the fears and frustrations of unemployed ex-servicemen by giving the question of joblessness a sectarian twist; that while Ulstermen were away fighting for king and country, thousands of Catholic workers came to Belfast to take their jobs.

The several causes were soon to be rolled into one. So-called "vigilance committees" were set up at many of Belfast's largest employers, most notably the shipyards, to work with the Ulster Unionist Labour Association (UULA) to ensure the re-employment of Protestant workers loyal to the political union with Britain and opposed to socialism and its twin, republicanism. There were the inevitable clashes between armed Protestants and the security forces. In a bid to legitimate their authority, UULA leaders asked for the regularization of their own unofficial constabulary, created, they said, to protect Protestant areas. Despite some misgivings of the government and objections from the military, the special constabulary was given official status in November 1920. This marks a substantial shift in the Protestant community. As Bew, Gibbon, and Patterson write, "In its anxiety to re-establish a militant basis for resistance to republicanism which could operate independently of the British, the Unionist leadership had been obliged to concede a portion of bourgeois class power to the Orange section of the working class."[2] The state of Northern Ireland had not yet been created, but a very important force had been made—an independent paramilitary force of populist Protestant ethos, whose self-assertiveness would not be diminished once the state, as such, was created.[3] There were warnings that such a policy would run amok. The *Westminster Gazette* warned that the expedient of arming the rougher elements of the Protestant community would come back to haunt all concerned because "all the eager spirits who have driven nationalist workmen from the docks or have demonstrated their loyalty by looting Catholic shops will now be eligible."[4] The significance of giving semi-autonomous power to the populist element of militant Protestants cannot be overstated. The problem that has vexed establishment leadership since at least 1920 is how, at once, to benefit from the dirty work done by Protestant militants (in and out of official security roles) and to reign them in when politics or human decency demanded it. A recent study of a Unionist political leader, Edward Saunderson, demonstrates that the gentry leadership was often unable to control, or even understand, the sentiments of the Orange working class.[5]

The best single book on the impact of evangelical Protestantism in Northern Ireland is by David Hempton and Myrtle Hill.[6] In *Evangelical Protestantism in Ulster Society*, they cover the subject from 1740 (the plausible beginning of the evangelical movement) to 1890, when, the authors suggest, the Home Rule crisis brought together the various components of Protestant consciousness into an Ulster identity. One wishes the authors had extended the scope of their study to include the founding of the Northern Irish state, thus illumining the period under review. Nevertheless, some of their ideas have salience for the period after 1920, as the authors are correct to observe that the crisis of the 1880s became a more or less permanent crisis of legitimacy.

Our concern with the populist element in Ulster Protestant opposition to the British government in the Home Rule crisis is discussed by Hempton and Hill, who observe that rallies against Home Rule nearly always began with hymn-singing and prayer, thus giving a religious camber to political opposition. Moreover, the substantial presence of the Orange Order at the rallies "heightened the populist, militant atmosphere, and indicated the extent to which 'religious' values pervaded the wider culture."[7] Hempton and Hill go on to point out that the striking aspect of the Ulster Protestant world picture "is the extent to which it was a self-referentially coherent ideology, embracing past, present and future, as well as religion and politics."[8] One can scarcely overemphasize, it seems, the role of evangelical religion in stiffening the resolve of loyalist political opposition. At the same time we must make the realistic observation that this form of religion may not have been practiced by many Ulster people who nevertheless fought for, and embraced, its role in the shaping of culture.

This ideology gave Ulster Protestantism its radical edge, in which opposition to Catholicism and government alike was galvanized by populist self-righteousness. The rank and file of the Orange movement was virulently anti-Catholic after the 1880s, a sentiment encouraged by the gentry leadership. In fact, the main worry of the establishment was apathy by the rank and file; to avoid that, they tolerated all manner of Orange excesses, and in these excesses the ordinary folk of Ulster found their own voice. As Hempton and Hill observe, the mass rallies were addressed by men of property and standing. The elite on the platform "played oratorical games with their hearers, safe in the knowledge that any excesses of the mob would be directed not against them but against their shared religious enemy."[9] Thus, the function of evangelical Protestantism in Ulster, at least since the 1880s, was to be the cement that solidified an Ulster Protestant, loyalist identity. That cement has caused the boundary wall between the two communities to stand long after the Berlin Walls of this world have fallen elsewhere. Historian James Loughlin agrees. In a very valuable and subtle analysis of the Ulster ideology after 1886, he charts the creation of the myth that legitimated the new state. He shows how the overall and general attitudes of loyalty were successfully connected to the particular and everyday aspects of Ulster life. In this vision, populist religion was a vital part of what he calls "the integrating myth" and the desire for an all-class Protestant social solidarity.[10]

The populist nature of politics in Ulster was undergirded by populist religion. As demonstrated earlier in this book, it does no good to try to distinguish between Protestant religion and politics in Ulster because definitions of covenant and contract are perceived within the ideology of a culture which has accorded a Presbyterian-evangelical worldview with hegemonic leadership. Among the religiopolitical leadership, the populist element has been both a source of strength and of concern: strength because the leadership could count on grassroots agreement on essentials; concern because established leaders, in church and society, could not always control populist sentiments.

Revival meetings among Protestants are long-standing methods of renewal, and religious leaders are required to give at least tacit support to the evidences of grace supposedly going on outside the normal functioning of churches. However, as has been the case throughout church history, itinerant evangelists have been both bane and blessing to regular patterns of ecclesiastical authority. Revivals, often called "missions," were common in Northern Ireland. The view suggested here is as follows: revivals were very important in renewing conservative, evangelical Christianity in Ulster, but they were also structurally unstable. The special gifts (charisma) of evangelists were not always to the liking, or under the control, of established authority. If Bew, Gibbon, and Patterson are right in calling our attention to the populist element in politics, and since there is no meaningful distinction between Protestant religion and politics, we should look for the revivalist element that spoke to, and spoke for, the same (perhaps unruly) populist element of the Ulster population that allowed Ulster to say "no." But the "no" that Ulster said in populist terms was defiant of both a government in London that would conspire against them and of a middle-class leadership in Ulster that would use, but not always appreciate, them.

In the rest of this chapter, we will illustrate this point by examining the life and work of William Patteson Nicholson (1876–1959). Returning to his native Ulster in the 1920s, on secondment from the Bible Institute of Los Angeles where he was staff evangelist, W. P. Nicholson held a series of evangelistic missions throughout Ulster during the crucial years of 1921–26. We argue that Nicholson's unique work among working people, especially men, was of great importance in directing the loyalty of the Ulster's working classes toward Unionism. He was successful because he was able to speak from, and to, the populist ethos that makes Ulster Unionism so fascinating (as Aughey says, completely loyal and completely rebellious). If one wonders why the working people of Ulster, especially Belfast, are so boisterously loyalist in political terms, one must recall the comments of Paul Bew and his colleagues that common folks have been able to find their own voice within the practice of Unionist intransigence. By the same token the fundamentalist and revivalist group in Protestantism has had a considerable impact in restating timeless religious verities; doing so in their own way, and wary of the possible compromises of established authority in theological schools and denominational headquarters.

W. P. Nicholson was a man with great power to move others by his vivid and charismatic rhetoric. His missions in various parts of Ulster in the early 1920s were of great importance in helping to create a fundamentalist-evangelical populism that was, at once, solidly evangelical in religion and loyalist in politics. Scholars have not taken up the challenge of Nicholson, although there have been two popular, short studies on Nicholson by Murray and Long, and a short biographical sketch on Nicholson in a collection of his sermons edited by Ian Paisley.[11] The connection between Nicholson and Paisley is an important one. In Protestant Ulster, where heritage means a very great deal, people in the present who encourage Ulster to say "no" hold up the memory of Nicholson's Ulster career as being at the heart of the meaning of Northern Ireland. A story told by Paisley gives much insight into both the thinking of a current political leader of Ulster and the leading Irish evangelist of the twentieth century. When Paisley was ordained in 1946, Nicholson was in the congregation. Nicholson is reputed to have strode to the communion table and within the service he said, "I have one prayer for this young man, that God will give him a tongue like an old cow." He defined that as follows: "Young man, go into a butcher's shop and run your hand along a cow's tongue, it is sharp as a file." Then Nicholson prayed, "Please God, this man will have a tongue that will be as sharp as a file in the hearts of the enemies of the King."[12] It is remarkable that Nicholson did not mention the enemies of the state, of the church, or even of the gospel, but of the King. Now it is possible that Nicholson meant God the King and not King George V, but no more classic statement of loyalism could have launched the religious and political career of Paisley.

Nicholson was born near Bangor, in the eastern part of county Down. His parents, John Nicholson and Ellen Campbell, had seven children, four boys and three girls. His family moved to Belfast when he was quite young, and they lived in a comfortable area near Queen's College (later University). His first school was at the Fisherwick Presbyterian Church, and he later studied at the Model School, on the Falls Road section of West Belfast. A great influence in the young Nicholson's life was the church his family attended, the Albert Street Presbyterian Church, on the Falls Road. The minister was Henry Montgomery, "a powerful preacher, well known as an outspoken apologist for Reformed Christianity and for his determined advocacy of social justice."[13] Under Montgomery's ministry, the church founded the Shankhill Road Mission (also known as Albert Hall), which became a center for social welfare in the area. The latter work grew rapidly, and Montgomery resigned from the church to give full time to the Mission, where, some twenty-five years later, Nicholson would conduct one of his most important evangelistic missions.

Nicholson was uninterested in education, so after leaving school in 1892 at age sixteen he held various jobs, mostly at sea, but he also worked as a railroad construction worker in South Africa. He experienced a deeply felt conversion in 1899 at his mother's home in Bangor. Believing himself called to an active Christian ministry, Nicholson enrolled in the Bible Training Institute in Glasgow, Scotland. He was influenced by many people in Glasgow, but especially by three visiting lecturers, James Denney in New Testament, James Orr in Apologetics, and Alexander Whyte in Homiletics.[14] During his vacations, Nicholson came back to Belfast where he assisted Henry Montgomery at the Shankhill Road Mission. Montgomery had a great impact on the younger man. As S. E. Long writes, "Montgomery's militant evangelicalism was of a kind with the strong fundamentalist theology which Nicholson found so satisfying in his own thinking."[15] But Nicholson was also challenged by the sheer energy of his chief. Several times on the Shankhill Road, Montgomery would see a crowd, stand on a chair borrowed from a nearby home, and urge the hearers to repent. Sometimes he would ask Nicholson to get up and speak, saying to the younger man, "If you can't hold them, you haven't much of a message and you are not fit to preach."[16] Nicholson also learned from Montgomery a contempt for preachers who spoke of the faith in nuanced or muted tones, an attitude that would resurface years later when he was conducting a mission in Belfast just when the Bible Standards League was moving against Professor Davey in the theological college. In all, then, his work with Montgomery at the Shankhill Road Mission confirmed within the young Nicholson a conviction that he could, indeed must, work with people from the working class. He came to realize that he could speak with conviction and power in an idiom they could understand and appreciate.

Nicholson finished his studies in Glasgow in 1903 and began work as an evangelist with the Lanarkshire Christian Union. It was one of several countywide associations founded for evangelical follow-up in the aftermath of the revival that swept over Scotland under the ministry of Moody and Sankey in the 1870s. Nicholson worked in Scotland for four years, and he was reportedly very successful among men, often coal miners and steel workers. His unusual methods pleased his supporters, because he combined populist religion with populist style. At one meeting in Scotland he encouraged working men to chalk the pavements of the city with "Nicholson Mission" and an arrow pointing the way. Some took the advice too far and painted the letters and arrows in whitewash, for which they were charged and fined. One man could not pay the fine and was jailed. One can only imagine the populist glee with which Nicholson must have delighted the crowd at his meeting that night as he told them of the incident and then received a special offering to pay the fine.[17] At the end of his time in Scotland he married a local woman, Ellison Marshall.

Nicholson then began a three-year association with the American evangelistic team of J. Wilbur Chapman and Charles M. Alexander, mostly in Australia but also in the United States. In 1911 Nicholson took a temporary appointment back in Scotland. D. J. Findlay, pastor of the largest church in Scotland, St. George's Cross Tabernacle in Glasgow, went on a year's recuperative leave. The two experiences—on tour with Chapman and substituting for Findlay—confirmed for Nicholson the calling he was to pursue. By now a trained and experienced preacher, Nicholson decided that being a traveling evangelist was the life for him. He wrote in 1912: "I don't believe it is ever God's will to put a square peg in a round hole, or vice versa. He made me for an itinerant sort of life so I feel very much at home and enjoy the journeying here and there, doing God's work. To be a whole year in one place is a queer strain on my nature and the grace of God in me."[18]

There is no clear testimony from either Nicholson or his family as to why they moved to the United States in 1913, other than that it did not seem an unusual thing to do. According to Nicholson's daughter, Jessie, her father was never home for more than a week between his evangelistic journeys, lasting up to six weeks. The family, with the largely nonresident father, settled in Carlisle, Pennsylvania for about four years.[19] Nicholson's own account of those years was not about his family but about his work. He teamed up with a singer, Raymond Hemmings, an old friend who had worked with Nicholson on the Chapman and Alexander tour in Australia. Together they began to hold "tabernacle" meetings, by which they meant that a tent or rough structure would be built in a town, thus creating a neutral zone to which all denominations and traditions might feel free to attend.

In Pennsylvania, Nicholson became an ordained minister. There was, at that time, a large number of traveling evangelists, some of dubious qualification and integrity. Ordained on 15 April 1914, Nicholson was aware that he needed a more official standing than he had in order to do his work. He later wrote, "They knew now I was no 'wild-cat' irresponsible sort of evangelist. I came across some evangelists who, when asked what church they belonged to, would say, 'I belong to the Lord.' I always felt a wee bit suspicious about them."[20] Nicholson was indeed a credentialed minister in the Presbyterian Church in the United States of America, which allowed him to become more acceptable in the higher reaches of fundamentalist circles. Both because of his growing reputation and possibly because he was a Presbyterian clergyman, he soon found himself invited to preach at the Moody Church in Chicago and the Church of the Open Door in Los Angeles. In the summer of 1917 he visited, and preached at, the recently formed Bible In-stitute of Los Angeles. He impressed the people there enough for him to be offered a position as staff evangelist the following year.

The dean of the institute was Reuben A. Torrey (1856–1928), one of the architects of the fundamentalist movement in America. A

Yale graduate, Torrey held Congregational Church pastorates in Ohio and Minnesota before becoming superintendent of Moody's Chicago Training Institute (later Moody Bible Institute) in 1899. He soon proved himself to be a worthy successor to the heroic Moody because during the first decade of the century he preached to an estimated fifteen million people around the world. He came to the Bible Institute of Los Angeles in 1912 to serve as the Institute's first dean, and, after 1916, also served until 1924 as the pastor of the Church of the Open Door. Thus, for the august and Victorian patron of American fundamentalism, Torrey, publicly to bless Nicholson was a sign that the young Irishman had arrived. Torrey wrote the following in *The King's Business*, the magazine of the Institute:

> I have followed the work of William P. Nicholson for several years with great interest. I have heard him preach; and he has held a campaign in the Moody church in Chicago, of which I was formerly pastor. I have made many inquiries about him and his work there, and I find that everyone has nothing but good to say about him and his work. Mr. Nicholson is sound in his doctrine, careful in his methods, thorough in his work, and leaves a good impression upon a city after he has visited it.[21]

The same issue of the magazine, which Torrey edited, contained a small biographical sketch of the Rev. William P. Nicholson, introduced with an appreciation by a fellow Pennsylvanian, Rev. J. H. Souser, D. D.:

> Mr. Nicholson is a man of fine physique and strong personality. His tremendous earnestness, his ready Irish wit, his overflowing vitality, his stirring masculinity, appeal to all. His power of description is remarkably graphic, and everyone who hears him feels that here is an honest, self-sacrificing, godly man, who declares the whole counsel of God, and regards not the face of friend or foe. He has a message for men in the churches and out of the churches. His appeals are eloquent and impressive, and his attitude uncompromising as to what he believes to be wrong. Neither men nor devils can

turn him aside from his firm convictions of the right. As a preacher, he is a star of the first magnitude; as a prophet, of the first order—strong, forceful, eloquent and scriptural. His arguments, sustained by his invincible logic and thorough knowledge of the Word, are unanswerable.[22]

Even given the art of self-promotion of which the fundamentalist enterprise was sometimes prone, this is high praise for Nicholson. Now forty-two years of age and a seasoned campaigner on several continents, he could be declared a preaching star of the first magnitude, a forceful prophet and an unanswerable apologist. The career of Nicholson thus was launched into the premier league of evangelists in Los Angeles. He soon became a regular preacher at the Church of the Open Door and was conducting well-publicized and apparently well-received evangelistic missions in various parts of California.[23]

Before discussing the rhetoric of Nicholson in the pulpit, it is useful to look for a moment at the language used among fundamentalist Christians throughout the world. This common rhetorical pattern—of which Nicholson was a prime example—enabled fundamentalists to identify each other and to establish a group consciousness that escaped them in organizational terms. Virginia L. Brereton's study of the Bible School movement locates fundamentalist rhetoric in the educational nexus of which the Bible Institute of Los Angeles was, after Moody Bible Institute, the prime American example. Brereton recognizes, of course, that fundamentalist rhetoric has deep roots in two hundred years of American Protestant experience and that it changes over time. She also accepts that fundamentalist rhetoric was meant, by the speakers themselves, to be a vehicle of evangelistic zeal. But, in a world of shifting realities, a standard rhetoric was comforting insofar as it promoted group self-identity and solidarity. For example, a speaker using a construction like "standing on the promises of God," or "washed in the blood of the lamb," "located him or herself squarely in an identifiable theological and cultural camp (and outside other camps)."[24] The distinguished and well-educated R. A. Torrey chided fundamentalists for using too many latinate,

King James version sorts of constructions and for not using words of zeal like "the tinpail brigade, humble, hard-working men and women."[25]

Fidelity to certain truths, moreover, begat an attitude of watchfulness among fundamentalists, especially in the Bible schools, lest there be any deviation. They were wary about possible inroads of what they took to be modernist influences. At the Bible Institute of Los Angeles, the new central building of 1914 had blazoned across its front the following: "For ever, O Lord, Thy Word is settled in heaven." The building also had a sign outside inviting passersby to visit the Biola book room, where "reliable religious literature" could be examined.[26] This is another evidence that steadfastness in reality and appearances is a key to understanding fundamentalism. The collective mind of the Bible Institute was severely challenged in this respect by the fallout surrounding the "MacInnis Controversy" in 1927–1929. John Murdoch MacInnis was the handpicked successor to Torrey at Biola, and he assumed office in 1925. His book *Peter the Fisherman Philosopher: A Study in Higher Fundamentalism* (1927) caused a great commotion in fundamentalist circles. Daniel W. Draney's insightful work describes and decodes what was at stake in the controversy. MacInnis's book and his style of leadership at Biola can be called fundamentalist. His critics can also be called fundamentalist. The question was: what kind of fundamentalist? The historian Joel Carpenter, in another place, refers to two opposing tendencies within fundamentalism: "evangelical inclusivist" and "militant separatist." MacInnis believed that Christianity was intellectually credible, thus making the intellectual task at Biola an important calling; this went against the grain of premillennialism, which had largely given up on the world and would save as many souls as possible. Moreover, MacInnis wanted his fundamentalist students at Biola to find alliances with the mainline churches, not with those seceding from denominations. As Draney suggests, the "radical" fundamentalists (Carpenter's militant separatists) won out over the moderate MacInnis, who cherished his association with the Presbyterian Church.[27] The big guns of fundamentalism trained their sights on Biola and MacInnis: *Moody Monthly* gave the book a bad review, as did Arno

Gaebelein in *Our Hope*. The most damaging criticism came from Charles Trumbull in *The Sunday School Times* and from William B. Riley of the Christian Fundamentals Association. The Bible Institute held its ground for a while, and even the redoubtable G. Campbell Morgan sallied forth in public defense of MacInnis.[28] In the end, both because of financial stress and a need to shore up the confidence of the Institute's supporters, the Board forced the resignation of MacInnis. The newly appointed president of the Institute's Board of Directors, Charles E. Fuller, gave an assurance to all and sundry that the Institute now rejected the MacInnis book, and that all remaining copies, including the type-forms, had been destroyed. Moreover, Fuller announced that the new president of the Institute, William P. White, was a sound fundamentalist, "without a fad in his stand."[29] By 1929, then, the fundamentalist movement was increasingly becoming shrill, reductionist, and separatist in its militant determination to never yield another inch to (what the Irish poet William Butler Yeats called in another connection) "this filthy modern tide."[30]

Nicholson was clearly a partisan of the militant faction that would allow no association with what he and others would call the compromises of the likes of MacInnis in Los Angeles or J. E. Davey in Belfast. The high point of Nicholson's career would be the years 1921–26 when he successfully preached the gospel of "not an inch" of surrender throughout Ulster. The fact that this period was also one of protracted social and political crisis allowed Nicholson's message to be heard by Ulster Protestants on several levels of awareness. Finlay Holmes, as noted above, is correct in declining to answer directly whether or not fundamentalism—in the several meanings of the term—is native to Ulster or brought from America, especially if the example given is W. P. Nicholson. He surely drew upon his own Irish roots in his developing spirituality, but he also drew upon the holiness emphases of the Keswick movement and upon the more doctrinalist fundamentalism emerging in the United States. Nicholson was, in fact, a creature of that transatlantic movement among revivalist Protestants who, in the social crisis of Victorian culture, became militant in their opposition to modern culture in general and specifically to church and political leaders who might compromise the heritage. This populist movement was successful because the things it was defending were fairly vague, and more felt than known, thus allowing adherents to supply local specifics to the general idea that dark forces would conspire against them, requiring them to be vigilant. It was not possible to accuse people of paranoia when they said there was a conspiracy afoot if nearly the entire adult Protestant population believed there was a conspiracy, about which they asked their King for relief.

Nicholson brought his unique, bombastic style to a province already divided and he divided it still more. His message had a profound social function, that of aiding the development of a religiously based populist consciousness that had so much to do with Ulster Unionist identity. He came back from America in 1920 to have some much needed rest from his constant campaigning and also to see his aged mother. After the visit, he already had plans to conduct several missions in Scotland for which he had been given leave from the Bible Institute of Los Angeles. Through his first group of missions in Ireland he kept the folks back home in California fully informed of his news. Keeping the California connection was apparently important to Nicholson because, when the Irish crusades were completed, he returned to Southern California where he maintained his home for the rest of his life. His children would settle permanently in California, and one of his sons was to work at the Bible Institute of Los Angeles until 1967.

In Bangor during the late summer of 1920 Nicholson became reacquainted with S. G. Montgomery, a successful businessman in Bangor, the brother of Rev. Henry Montgomery of the Shankhill Road Mission in Belfast. Nicholson was asked to conduct an evangelistic mission in Bangor during October under the auspices of the Christian Workers Union. Ever since 1859, folks of evangelical persuasion in Ulster had been praying for a revival like that of '59. In 1920, a time of great uncertainty, they believed all the more that a revival would be the recipe for contentment and reorientation of life. Nicholson's work in Bangor during October was very successful. The word about it spread around Ulster, and rather quickly invitations from various towns were pouring in to Bangor. As one enthusiastic participant wrote,

Though a prophet in his own country, and to his own people, the reception he got was marvelous. The crowds attending the services overflowed the large hall, and sinners of all kinds were attracted, many of whom being won for Christ. A great work of grace was accomplished, and the society, which had so nobly stood in the breach for years, and fought a good fight, was quite transformed. Larger buildings had to be procured to accommodate the converts, as well as to provide for the growth of the work. As a result of the mission, too, Christian Endeavour and other meetings were started, and the whole religious life of the town was revived.[31]

For people pleading to God for a revival in their own time like in that of their parents, they looked eagerly to each sign of the hoped-for works of God, and asked themselves, "is this the beginning?" Many people apparently believed it was so, and invitations to Nicholson came in from many towns, mostly in the Protestant heartland areas of counties Down (Lurgan, Lisburn, and Donaghadee) and Antrim (Carrickfergus, Whitehead, and Ballymema), but also from county Tyrone (Omagh), county Armagh (Portadown), and county Londonderry (Coleraine and Derry city). A committee, headed by the Montgomery brothers, worked with a large, multidenominational group to coordinate the missions planned for Nicholson in 1921, once he had completed his obligations in Scotland during the winter months of 1920–21 under the auspices of the Glasgow United Evangelical Association.[32]

The spring of 1921 was a season of socioeconomic and especially political instability. There was a coal strike and a dock strike in Belfast, which prevented Nicholson's crossing from Glasgow. His first mission, in Portadown, had to be delayed for a week.[33] Of greater importance, however, is that an election was to be held for the first time under the auspices of the state of Northern Ireland. In an effort to contextualize the work of Nicholson, we offer the following example. Nicholson's first mission was to be in Portadown in county Armagh, to begin on May 8. Accordingly, the organizing committee took out a large advertisement in the *Portadown News*, giving the relevant details about the meetings to be lead by the Rev. W. P. Nicholson of Los Angeles, U.S.A.[34] Next to the

Nicholson notice is another, and longer, political advertisement taken out by James Craig, leader of the Ulster Unionists [the emphases are Craig's].

To the Loyalist Electors of Northern Ireland

In view of the near approach of the ELECTIONS FOR THE FIRST PARLIAMENT OF NORTHERN IRELAND, may I be allowed to offer a few words of encouragement and counsel to those loyal men and women of Ulster to whom I look confidently for support in the position of responsibility to which they have called me.

Those for whom I venture to speak place in the forefront of their ideals and aspirations, *devotion to the throne, close union with Great Britain, pride in the British Empire, and an earnest desire for peace throughout Ireland.*

I hope that the election will be fought with all the vigor and determination which have characterized our actions in the past, and that our people will realize how vital it is to *record every single vote in favour of all the candidates democratically and constitutionally selected by the various Unionist Parliamentary Associations.* This is doubly important by reason of the fact that the elections will be conducted under the system of Proportional Representation.

A serious responsibility rests with each individual. The fate of the Six Counties hangs in the balance, and with the Six Counties the interests of Loyalists in other parts of Ireland. The eyes both of friends through the Empire who wish us success and of enemies who desire our failure, will be watching our first proceedings. It is our duty therefore, not only *to lay aside minor issues,* and if need be, *to sacrifice personal interests,* but to work with whole-hearted energy and good will between now and the day of the poll in order to secure the election of these candidates alone who can be trusted worthily to represent the great cause which we all have at heart.

We have overcome many a crisis, weathered many a storm. Let us together win yet another victory and lay the foundation of a model Parliament of our own.

JAMES CRAIG[35]

The Nicholson mission in Portadown went on for a month, and over 2,000 people a day came to hear him in either the First Presbyterian Church or the Thomas Street Methodist Church. Mrs. Ellison Nicholson often took the leadership in the overflow service. A reporter on the scene wrote that "Mr. Nicholson gained the ear of the people in a marked degree and although uncompromising in his condemnation of smoking and dancing and the picture show, and presenting the bold alternative of "Christ or Hell," even those who disagreed with him came under his spell and were converted."[36] The reporter said that there were over 900 registered conversions, whereas Nicholson himself suggested the figure was higher; "Over one thousand have come out for Christ."[37] Protestants in Portadown, then, were asked in the spring of 1921 to consider several sets of alternatives for their lives: James Craig held up the traditions of Ulster versus the disaster of a Dublin dominance; William Nicholson contrasted Christ or Hell. Shades of different meanings between such stark alternatives were not allowed in these matters, since in both it was a time for decision. As the local newspaper reported, this is a "strong, virile and courageous" man from Los Angeles "and his message has gripped the community."[38]

Even though Nicholson and his committee had planned several more missions in Ulster for spring and summer, he did not want to lose his connections with the Bible Institute of Los Angeles. He wrote to Lyman Stewart, benefactor of the Institute and of many other fundamentalist causes. Stewart replied with his congratulations on Nicholson's good work in Ireland, but also added his own personal disappointment in not seeing the Irishman sooner. Stewart seemed delighted at the prospect of having Nicholson back at the Institute by the end of 1921.[39] To readers of *The King's Business*, Nicholson wrote a note, placed under his picture and those of three other Institute staff evangelists, that his mission in Portadown was "one of the finest old-fashioned revivals I have ever had. . . . Old folks say that they never saw the like even during the 1859 revival."[40] Nicholson was apparently at pains not to burn his bridge back to Los Angeles because the next month of *The King's Business* printed a telegram from S. G. Montgomery asking that Nicholson be allowed another year in Ulster. Since both Montgomery and the magazine's editors were aware that this concession to Nicholson would cause cancellation of already-planned missions in America, Montgomery wrote, "I trust you will pardon me for interfering in any way with what you have been planning for Mr. Nicholson, but this is his native land and native province, and never have we had any evangelist whom the Lord has so used in the awakening of the careless."[41] Nicholson himself added a bit of self-promotion in writing that although he "had twenty-two invitations from towns in the North of Ireland here for united missions, the council of men who have gathered around me have picked out eight, so that will keep me busy right up to next June." But as well as reporting his successes, Nicholson also disclosed something of his contentious, even provocative, style. For Ireland he prayed: "May the Lord set this dear land on fire and burn up the old pope and his dirty work;" about his opposition he went beyond the pope to Presbyterian clergy: "I know that you will be praying for me, for the old devil will not take this assault on his kingdom quietly. It is wonderful how many of the Presbyterian ministers he gets against me here. They are as dead as can be and as worldly."[42]

Missions flowed in rapid succession during 1921 and 1922, but the style, the attitude, and the expectations were fairly well established after the Portadown mission. The style was to ensure a broad acceptance among all Protestants, so emphasis was placed on interdenominational cooperation. The attitude of confrontation was also fairly well in place. It was to be a populist campaign, with attacks on the pope, liberal clergy generally, and the professors who corrupt the youth. The expectations, already high, increased with each campaign. The missions were intended, and hoped, to be a witness not merely to the locale, although surely that; the missions were meant to signal a revival throughout Ulster, possibly meeting or exceeding the standard of 1859, thus creating a link with the deep memory of Ulster exceptionalism, i.e., exceptional to the unfortunate history of the other three provinces of Ireland.

In Newtownards, in November of 1921, the local newspaper hailed the organizational skills of Nicholson's committee. By comparison to the celebrated missions of R. A. Torrey, Wilbur Chapman, and John McNeill, it was said that Nicholson's was better organized with follow-up to have a more long-range consequence.[43] A unique feature of Nicholson's missions that would characterize them later on also emerged in Newtownards. The number of men, especially the rough and tough sorts, who participated and who professed conversion, was uniquely high in the Nicholson mission. The newspaper noted this with apparent pleasure, commending the stability and good "masculine character" of the work being done.

> Often a supercilious and short sighted judgement wags its head and says regarding evangelistic work, "it is the usual turn for old women and children." No one can say that of the present movement in our town. The work began among men, continues to prevail among men, and is largely carried out by men.[44]

Nicholson's mission arrived in Lisburn in January 1922. That year was the most significant in Ulster's history for social strife. None of the more media-scrutinized years since 1969 can match 1922 for lacking social cohesion and for high levels of violence. The impact that Nicholson and his committee were trying to achieve was personal and religious, but that alone would not have been enough if lives and communities were not also renewed. It was in the Lisburn mission that this community transformation was first seen. The community context was well set by the local newspaper, which reported nearly verbatim the events of the mission's first night, including the broad spectrum of society represented in those giving the evangelist a warm welcome.[45] The editor went even further later in the mission in his acknowledgement of Nicholson's unorthodox methods (like teaching people to whistle newly learned songs) and not only assured readers that, in context, it was acceptable, but invited all readers to attend and hear for themselves the power of the message given.[46] Entire sermons were reprinted, especially a celebrated one that Nicholson gave elsewhere, "The Public House, The Human Slaughter House."[47] A report on the mission by the local Methodist minister spoke of the large number who heard Nicholson and the reported conversions in excess of 2,000. He went on:

> Powerfully as the numbers speak, the changed atmosphere of the town is an even more striking testimony. It is not too much to say that the entire community has been brought face to face with the question "What shall I do with Jesus?" In market and shop, in factory and workroom, in public house and club, in the villa and in the slum, in street and train, in fact everywhere the mission has been the constant subject of conversation. There have been some very practical illustrations of the effect of the mission. Business people have had debts, long since written off as irrecoverable, paid in full. Money wrongfully used has been returned. At the last petty sessions court there was only one case down for trial and the man concerned lives some miles out of Lisburn, a unique experience. There has been a great diversity in the types of character reached. Drunkards and gamblers have had the chains of their sins snapped. Formalists have been quickened into new life. A holy concern has gripped and changed the careless. Two classes have been roused to bitter anger—the Pharisees and the publicans—a sure sign the Holy Spirit is working.[48]

While Nicholson was to have considerable impact elsewhere, especially in Belfast, as we shall see, it is probably that his most significant impact on a community was in Lisburn, and that even months later reports of a renewed community life could still be noted with gratitude back in California.[49]

Belfast was the place where the Nicholson committee's hope to transform Ulster would be tested. We have no record of its deliberations as to why organizers chose smaller towns before coming to Belfast, but one can suppose the desire of Nicholson and his colleagues to get their team well organized before trying to tackle Belfast. In fact, they could not have planned better, for February

1922 possibly would be the least stable month in Belfast's history in the new state of Northern Ireland. It is unsurprising that Nicholson headed straight for the Protestant urban heartland, the Shankhill Road, and to the friendly confines of the Albert Hall at the Shankhill Road Mission, and to the support of his old friend and mentor, Henry Montgomery.

It might be well to recall the religious and political context into which the Nicholson team came when they approached Belfast. Recall the prior spring, when elections were held for the new parliament of the new state, and how James Craig had appealed to voters in the Portadown newspaper. In an important Belfast paper, the *Northern Whig and Belfast Post*, Craig had appealed to Protestant voters in even more sectarian terms. In his capacity not only as political leader of Ulster Unionists but specifically as Grand Master of the Orange Order in county Down, he joined the Grand Masters of the other five counties in Northern Ireland (Antrim, Armagh, Londonderry, Tyrone, and Fermanagh) in placing the largest advertisement that we've seen in a newspaper:

A Call to the Orange Orders in Northern Ireland

Hitherto on the shoulders of our representatives in the Imperial Parliament have rested the stress and strain of a protracted struggle against our submergence in a Dublin Parliament, and under Sir Edward Carson's leadership they have delivered us from such a calamity. Now, however, the obligation rests on us, as upon every Loyalist on the register, to see to it that the victory so far won is not turned into a defeat at the polls. Our opponents have combined against us on the single issue of "No Partition." Therefore, we on our part must, in the first instance, defeat that combination, and then rely upon our chosen representatives to carry on in the best traditions of our race by legislating wisely for the benefit of the whole community. The situation demands a supreme effort. Unity and courage will win the day—let not man stand apart.[50]

To complete the context of conjoining Unionism and Orange-oriented Protestantism, we refer to the same newspaper and to a news report of a speech given at the Albert Hall of the Shankhill Road Mission by Rev. Henry Montgomery. He encouraged his hearers "to discharge a sacred duty" by voting for the "supporters of law and order and of civil and religious freedom." They dare not turn their backs on the great heritage of Ulster, "and so, in the name of their Lord and Master, with good cheer and confidence, they should face the future, and the Divine blessing would rest on their earnest, united and persevering service."[51]

Nine months later, in February 1922, when the Nicholson team headed for the Shankhill Road, everything was in place to determine whether or not Nicholson would be able to bring the renewal to Ulster that would match or exceed the great movement of 1859. The leading newspaper in the city reported a prayer meeting on behalf of the mission held a few weeks prior to its start. The meeting was, of course, at the Albert Hall.[52] On Thursday, 9 February 1922, just three days before the Nicholson mission would begin, an event occurred that gripped all of Ulster. The Irish Republican Army (IRA) conducted a raid of spectacular daring across the border, capturing at least fifty men in border areas and taking them back across into the Irish Free State. The editor of the *Northern Whig* noted that hostage-taking was not murder and speculated that the raid was an attempt by the forces under Michael Collins to get James Craig and his Ulster colleagues back to the negotiations in the boundary commission.[53]

The atmosphere was heavy in Belfast, as many confrontations occurred between gunmen and security forces, and among the gunmen themselves. On the weekend before the mission would begin, it was announced that more than twenty clergy from all Protestant denominations would stand with Nicholson on Shankhill Road.[54] The same newspaper also reported that the political scene was worsening and very tense. It was confirmed that the number of men taken hostage across the border was now over 100. The government of Collins and Griffith in Dublin was apparently unable to control the situation, though they pledged their efforts to get the men returned. Craig was reported as grateful for the Collins statement but that if something was not done soon he would "carry out [his] own plans," presumably a military intervention in the Free State.[55]

The great day for which many had prayed—Sunday, 12 February 1922—came to a Belfast loaded with both fear and expectation. There were three meetings in several parts of the Protestant heartland of west Belfast: at the Townsend Street Presbyterian Church at 11:30 A.M., at the Agnes Street Methodist Church at 3:30 P.M., and at the Albert Hall, Shankhill Road at 7:30 P.M. During the week to come, all meetings would be in the evening and at the Albert Hall. The newspapers were careful to point out that while Mr. Nicholson had been ordained in America, he was indeed a Presbyterian clergyman and a native of Bangor, county Down.[56] The churches were reportedly full for both services on the first day, and the Albert Hall was said to be full to capacity at 2,500 people. Nicholson preached on Psalm 85:6, "Will Thou Not Revive Us Again?" In the course of the sermon he referred to the great work of personal and social transformation that had just recently gone on in Lisburn. He hoped and prayed that the same would happen in Belfast.[57] He intimated that it would be instructive if a delegation from Lisburn could come the following night to testify. As the Lisburn newspaper later recounted, many people responded with willingness to go, but "the tragic affrays in the City during the weekend made many reconsider their decision and stay at home." But about 250 people did go up to Belfast on the Monday night and filled a special section in the Albert Hall reserved for them. They formed a small choir to sing for their Belfast friends, and several people gave testimonies about the work that had gone on under Nicholson in Lisburn.[58]

The people who came from Lisburn that night, as well as the Belfast folk, came to the Albert Hall at some risk to their lives and limbs. Many of those present later recalled hearing the sound of rifle and machine-gun fire during the course of the meeting. Some who came on tram cars had been ordered to lie flat when passing certain crossings.[59] The Northern Whig, not a newspaper given to hysteria but to good reporting, had a leading story the following morning under the headline: "Black Day in Belfast." It reported the scenes of murder and mayhem in Belfast the previous night, with eleven people killed and forty wounded.[60] Yet, in another part of the same edition of the newspaper, the reporter at the Nicholson meeting told of a full house at the Albert Hall.[61] The first week of the Nicholson mission continued in like fashion, with people showing bravery and determination to come to the meeting on the Shankhill Road despite social strife verging on civil war. On Wednesday ten civilians were killed and twenty wounded, yet the Hall was full to hear Nicholson on "The Baptism of the Holy Spirit."[62] On Thursday another nine people died on the streets of Belfast and approximately twenty more were wounded.[63] On Friday the Northern Whig gave a great deal of coverage to the larger political scene. Especially noted was the second reading of the Government of Ireland Act that went through the House of Commons in London, over the amendments of James Craig.[64] The Nicholson mission was also reported in the same edition as being "unprecedented in solemnity and numbers."[65] The mission went on for another three weeks, with the same pattern of packed halls every night at the Albert Hall, and several services at various churches on the Sundays, concluding on Sunday March 12, with no less than five separate services. The Northern Whig's reporter told of the "deep impression in the community" that the mission had made.[66] The reporter for the Belfast Telegraph, however, was nearly enraptured by the final evening, when over 3,000 people crammed into the Albert Hall, a structure designed for an absolute maximum of 2,500. All the more impressive was the fact that some 2,200 of those in attendance were those who had, during the mission, gone to the inquiry room at the end of a service and had made, in their terms, "a decision for Christ." The gathering gave a thundering farewell to Mr. and Mrs. Nicholson, singing lustily the hymn "God Be with You till We Meet Again," while waving white handkerchiefs which, the reporter stated, "strongly resembled a heavy snowstorm." Mr. Nicholson replied and asked for the handkerchiefs to be raised again while he led them in "Shall We Gather at the River," in memory of the loved ones of those present who had died, or, as Nicholson's Victorian language had it, "who had passed beyond the veil."[67]

Nicholson gave several other missions in the Belfast area during 1922–23, with similar criticisms of his tactics, and moreover, similar results in terms of lives changed and communities transformed. One puckish version of the aftermath of a Nicholson mission has it that the mission was "the best debt collector Belfast had ever known."[68] He held the new converts to high ethical standards, and since the grog shop and the betting shop were now off limits to these working men, there was money to pay their bills. In a mission in East Belfast, near the shipyards, in an area known as Island Street, working men would march together from work to hear Nicholson, either to St. Patrick's (Church of Ireland) or the Newtownards Road Methodist Church. An unknown poet among the "Islandmen" wrote the following:

> What means the curious eager throng
> That line the streets and wait so long.
> And what went ye out for to see?
> The Island men in dongaree.
> Those are the men that have been won
> For Christ by Pastor Nicholson.
> Make way, make way, you hear the cry,
> And let the Islandmen pass by.
>
> They come, they come, you hear them sing,
> And loud their songs of praises ring.
> Ballymacarrett is glad to see
> Her sons from sin and bondage free.
> While shouts and praises fill the air,
> The devil leaves them in despair,
> And once again you hear the cry—
> The Islandmen are passing by.
>
> No bullets fly, no bombs explode,
> For Jesus leads them on the road,
> Peace is proclaimed and all is well,
> The devil has lost recruits for hell.
> Down in the dumps we'll let him go.
> And that's the place to keep him low;
> Make way, make way, you hear the cry,
> And let the Islandmen pass by.
>
> Oh, wondrous change, who can it be
> That moves the city mightily?

Give God the praise, for He alone
Can melt the heart that's hard as stone.
Oh, why will you procrastinate,
Tomorrow you may be too late,
Join up, join up, why will you die,
While Christ the Lord is passing by.[69]

Nicholson had a unique hold on the hearts and minds of Ulster working people. Every reporter, whether from a secular or a religious newspaper agreed that "the common people heard him gladly."[70] Back in Los Angeles it was celebrated in much the same way, that ordinary people were responding overwhelmingly to Nicholson.[71] Ever mindful of keeping up his links in California, Nicholson wrote back to the Bible Institute's magazine:

> We are just closing one of the biggest missions we have had here, in which twenty churches united. The church seats 3300 and both Dr. Torrey and Mr. Moody held meetings in it. Some nights we turn away more than would fill it twice. . . . There is a "breath of God" on this land at present and an ear for the Gospel. The crowds are tremendous. Think of ship-yard men arranging for their wives to meet them coming from work with their supper so that they can get to the meetings! If they took time to get home, they wouldn't be able to get into the church. Tell the Institute people that the Lord is working and the fire is burning. Glory to God![72]

Nicholson had indeed created a considerable stir in the religious lives of people in Ulster, and particularly in Belfast. Back at the Bible Institute of Los Angeles, *The King's Business* later reported with apparent pleasure and pride about the conclusion of Nicholson's work. The Institute, it said, had "loaned" Nicholson to the Irish committee in 1920 with the understanding that he would return to California in a year. Now it had been three years, and Nicholson was indeed returning to Biola. But by way of assessment, they reprinted some comments from a unnamed British newspaper. An officer in the constabulary remarked to the reporter, "This'll do what we couldn't do—settle Belfast." The reporter said that leaders in politics and business agreed with this sentiment that the religious revival had a calming effect on Ulster, and especially Belfast. "There are still a few barricades to be seen in Belfast, charred and bullet-marked. The police still carry revolvers openly, yet the need for barricades and guns has been (perhaps temporarily) swept away. . . . One can feel the revival in the air. It is everywhere, and if an armed policeman pulls up, more likely than not it is to inquire into the state of one's soul."[73] The same journal also reprinted, from the British magazine *The Life of Faith*, an article by J. Kennedy MacLean reflecting on the meaning of Nicholson's work in Ireland during 1920–23. Some 23,000 people in Ulster had made a public profession of their faith at Nicholson's meetings, and many others had been touched by the message who had kept their thoughts private. But MacLean, like many others, was not content to leave his analysis only in terms of individual salvation.

> It may not be altogether unprofitable to compare the Ulster of today with the Ulster of three years ago; then the gun was in the ascendant, and some parts of Belfast were miniature battlefields, literally raining bullets and running blood. Today the city is back to its normal state. It is not claimed that for this happy change the revival alone is responsible, but it is not too much to say that the faithful preaching of the Word and the vast numbers of redeemed lives have contributed in no small degree to this betterment, for the spirit of God cannot be abroad among men in Ireland, or anywhere else, without producing mighty rest.[74]

With Nicholson's good work in Ireland completed, the reporter agreed that despite more work to be done in Ireland, "America has claims of her own, and so the evangelist, who has stirred Ulster for God as has not been done since the memorable days of 1859, sails back to Los Angeles about the end of June."[75]

Nicholson, forever the wanderer, could not stay in one place for long, and, as the years went on, he increasingly could not work with people who formerly had been his allies. After a year back in California, he abruptly returned to Ireland and severed his links with the Bible Institute. While the record is curiously blank on this point, one can surmise that the new leadership at Biola was not playing on the same page as Nicholson. John Murdoch MacInnis assumed office as dean of the Bible Institute in 1925. He was a fundamentalist in spiritual and doctrinal terms, but he had a different attitude towards opposition. His policy would be to seek "the triumph of God's truth rather than the downing of an enemy."[76] That was not Nicholson's style, which was becoming increasingly censorious; this perhaps accounts for his precipitous departure from the Institute staff. It is otherwise difficult to explain his leaving the staff of the Institute whose favor he had curried during his three years in Ireland, and whose magazine so faithfully had reported his Irish missions. He did maintain a home in the Los Angeles suburb of Glendale until his death in 1959. The second Mrs. Nicholson (his first wife had died in 1928 during an Australian evangelistic campaign, where Nicholson met and married Fanny Elizabeth Collett) brought his body home to Bangor for burial. The last thirty years of Nicholson's ministry were a story of decline from the heights of influence he had achieved in Belfast in 1922. He would conduct missions in Ireland, Scotland, Australia, America, and South Africa during the years before his health began to fail in 1946, but his missions would never be the same again.

Nicholson arrived back in Ulster in 1925, thinking he would take up where he had left off in early 1923. There were still some requests for missions remaining from his earlier visit and new requests came in. As in 1921–23, in 1925 Nicholson gave missions in the Protestant rural heartland of counties Antrim (Magherafelt, Whitehead) and Down (Ballynahinch, Donaghadee) before returning to Belfast. This time, however, Nicholson did not return to his natural habitat of working-class west Belfast and the Shankhill Road Mission. Now he would bring the message of "Christ or Hell" to the city's center of political and religious power. He was not to have the success he had previously known. He preached in his characteristically rough-hewn manner, and in religious terms, his message had not substantially changed; the starkest contrasts were portrayed between the way of truth and light and the way of error and darkness. But the message Nicholson preached was couched in an even greater populist casing than before. He had always attacked hypocrisy and "spiritually-dead" clergy. However, he now mounted an offensive against "modernism," and even "apostasy" in the church. He named names and he attacked powerful people in the church as well as church institutions themselves. Always possessed of a sharp tongue towards authority, he now raised the level of the stakes in his populist theology.

Populist ideology often, but not always, sees truth as over against established order, and it questions the nature of that authority itself. The big Belfast meeting was held in the Assembly Hall in the Presbyterian Church office complex during August 1925. That building is within shouting distance of City Hall, so Nicholson had the sacred and secular authorities within his sights. On the first day, 2 August 1925, Nicholson was escorted to the platform by two well-known conservative Presbyterian ministers, Henry Montgomery and James Hunter. The two were from different parts of town (Shankhill is working class in West Belfast, whereas Hunter ministered in middle-class Knock, east of Belfast), and they ministered to different constituencies (Montgomery in social service to the poor, Hunter to the better educated and to the theology students). The tone of defensive populism was set in Montgomery's introduction. In standing with Nicholson, Montgomery said,

> I am here because I still love the Gospel he preaches and I rejoice infinitely in all that God has done by him and through him in this part of the world and indeed in many other parts of the world. . . . I am here further because I want to commend Mr. Nicholson to you as one who believes in the Word of God as we understand it. That means that he speaks to men and women of the substitutionary death of Jesus Christ, tells them of a full and free salvation, and lets them know of deliverance from the power of the enemy of Satan, and their call to serve God in righteousness and holiness without fear all the days of their lives. It is because Mr. Nicholson preaches all that with apostolic zeal that I am by his side today.[77]

The other platform colleague, James Hunter, had only recently been excoriating the Presbyterian theological college as a seedbed of rationalism and modernism. It was Hunter's attacking style of which Nicholson was a master; he would not disappoint the people who wanted an attack on the theological establishment that would "water-down" the gospel.

> A mutilated Saviour can never save or bring peace. If He is not God of every God, He is merely a fraud and a liar; in fact, the biggest fraud and liar the world has ever known, for He claimed to be God and lived and acted as God. No mere man, however perfect, or great, could save our soul and atone for our sin. These are days when many ministers preach a Christ who was born a bastard and lived a life of fraud and lies and died a coward's death and never rose again, and then they expect us to believe in Him, and if we do they wonder we can never find ease to our conscience and power to overcome sin. Why should they wonder? I grant you they do not express themselves in such clear and unthinkable terms. They are too "learned" for that, but any man or minister who doubts or denies the Virgin Birth, calls Mary a Jewish prostitute and Jesus a bastard. Any man or minister who tells us Jesus made mistakes, owing to His ignorance, is only calling Him a fraud and a liar. If He said God created man and we are told by them he was never created, he was evolved; if He tells us Moses was the author of the first five books of the Old Testament, and Jonah was swallowed by a great fish, and David wrote the 110th Psalm, just because He didn't know any better owing to ignorance, then He lied and we would be foolish to believe in Him. "If I have told you earthly things," (such as above) says Jesus, "and ye believe not, How shall ye believe if I tell you of heavenly things? Had ye believed Moses, ye would have believed Me, for he wrote of Me. But if ye believe not his writings, how shall ye believe My words?" We can't believe in Him if He lied about earthly things such as the above. It's impossible, no matter what Un-bloody Unitarianism and Modernism says.[78]

Nicholson associated himself with the group of clergy and lay leaders that was, in 1926, to found the Bible Standards League, an organization that was zealous, even relentless, in its attempt to combat the putative ills of the Presbyterian Church of Ireland. It was the League, with Hunter in the lead, that was to bring charges against Professor J. E. Davey and the Presbyterian College. By implication, of course, the charges were against the religious establishment. To complete the cycle of these comrades at arms against liberalism, the theological student, William J. Grier, whose notebook would be so prominent in the Davey heresy trial, had himself been converted at a Nicholson mission in Belfast, presumably in 1922.[79] He had gone to Princeton but was now back at the Presbyterian College for his final year of study. While there is no record of Grier attending the August 1925 Nicholson mission at the Assembly Hall, one supposes he would have eagerly attended a meeting in which his two mentors, Nicholson and Hunter, figured so prominently.

It has been said of Nicholson that he was a great evangelist but was hard on his mother, i.e., the church. John Barkley wrote that a climate of suspicion and distrust of religious authority was prevalent. Nicholson "helped fan the embers into a blaze" against the theological college in general and Professors Davey and Corkey in particular.[80] As detailed elsewhere in this book, the forces led by Hunter and Grier, aided by Nicholson and Montgomery, and organized in the Bible Standards League, were to be defeated in several General Assembly actions in the late 1920s. Hunter and Grier were to secede from the Presbyterian Church in Ireland to form the Irish Evangelical Church. When Nicholson returned to his home in Los Angeles in 1927, he accepted an appointment as a pastor of a Christian and Missionary Alliance Church, despite his ordination in the Presbyterian Church in the U.S.A.

Nicholson seemingly preached to the choir in 1925 and 1926 in Ulster. The halls were filled to be sure, but one wonders if those attending were repeaters from the earlier mission. This question is not a badgering but an honest one because the newspapers paid little attention to Nicholson, a marked contrast to his 1920–23 visit. Further, there are no reports of social changes like in the earlier mission. Things were different in 1925. The mission was no longer called a mission, but, American style, it became an "evangelistic crusade."[81] Nicholson railed against the secularity of the modern age, communism, and drink. But, this time, he could not even get away with saying that no "blood-sucking publican" be allowed membership in the church. He received a sharply-worded and witty reply from Mr. Job Stott, apparently the secretary of the Ulster Anti-Prohibition council. How could Montgomery's words about "the old gospel and the Word of God" be taken seriously, Stott asks, when Nicholson's attitudes about wine are so out of keeping with the Bible?[82] That letter launched a series of letters to the Northern Whig in which Stott took on various of Nicholson's supporters. One writer tried to patronize Stott even for daring to criticize a leading light of the evangelical world: "Nicholson towers head and shoulders above anything in the evangelical world that has hitherto reached our province."[83]

The next day Stott shot back a reply that must have stung the Nicholson entourage, cheered those in established authority, and undermined the bona fides of the evangelistic crusade at the Assembly Hall.

> It is no business of mine to assess Mr. Nicholson's standing in the "evangelical world," although it would appear that even the Presbyterian clergy, as a whole, are not unanimous about Mr. Nicholson's ministry. I know one leading minister in the city who tendered his resignation when it was proposed to bring Mr. Nicholson to his church. Even the Assembly Building authorities were divided on the question of hiring the buildings to him. I would, however, compliment on his skillful use of everything theatrical and emotional in his mission. . . . The only qualification Mr. Nicholson appears to lack is that which the greatest of the Apostles considered the most important, *viz.*, charity. As for Mr. Nicholson's skill in commercializing his evangelical abilities, I admit that in this he does "tower head and shoulders" above anyone else we have seen in this city.[84]

The respondent to whom Stott had replied, writing under the pen name "Sigma" fired another shot back at Stott. He quotes the Bible on wine and its uses and other matters of ad hominem against Stott, but Sigma's real ire came out in his populism:

> It is all to the good that the clergy are offended at, and some even opposed to, Mr. Nicholson. Their prototypes were the same with Jesus Himself, and this great opposition is not

from "the common people" but from "they who sat in Moses' seat." Mr. Nicholson has been instrumental in showing the people in the pews that clericalism and churchianity have been and are a shutter against the light and a consequent barrier to the knowledge of salvation.[85]

The editor of the Northern Whig allowed one more letter on this subject before announcing his closure of correspondence. He gave Job Stott the last word. Replying to "Sigma" again, he notes that his opponent is unable to use the Bible on behalf of prohibition. The Bible, he writes, does not condemn wine itself, just the abuse thereof.

> It may be, as "Sigma" quotes, that "drunkards shall not inherit the Kingdom of God," but I would remind him that there are drunkards other than those for who he specially reserves that term—for instance, those who are intoxicated with their own extreme fads and self-righteousness, and who launch out into intemperate vituperation of their fellow creatures, thus defying the stern injunction "Judge not that ye be not judged." I would suggest that the emotional evangelism of the type served out by Mr. Nicholson is as intoxicating as any wine or strong drink on the market.[86]

It is significant to note that, after the closure of the drink controversy in the Northern Whig, neither that newspaper nor the Belfast Newsletter reported further on the Nicholson crusade in the city center. The Nicholson team apparently left town without any further comment from the two major newspapers. This is at marked contrast to the celebratory descriptions of Nicholson's farewell meeting on the Shankhill Road some three years earlier. Nicholson and his work had, apparently, ceased to be news. He had struck a populist blow against the Protestant establishment in Belfast, but it was a less than mortal blow. His work in 1922 with the "common element" of the working class had been highly valued by religious and political authorities. Oral tradition in Ulster has it that no less than James Craig was aware of, and appreciative of, Nicholson's work on the Shankhill Road in West Belfast and among the shipyard workers in East Belfast. The historians S. E. Long and A. A.

Fulton hint at leading members of the Unionist government talking with Nicholson about both his efforts in keeping Protestant workingmen loyal and in not unnecessarily antagonizing the Catholic minority.[87] S. W. Murray, the historian most partial to Nicholson, acknowledges that the criticism of Nicholson had always been there, but his work during the period of grave political and social strife was valued enough to avert much criticism. By 1925 a relative peace had been restored and Nicholson himself had changed. Thus his work was not valued so much because it was not needed as much. Moreover his style, always pugnacious, had by 1925 risen to a shrill censoriousness. Even conservative Presbyterian lay leaders who had worked with him in 1922 found that Nicholson would not take well-meant advice from his friends. As Murray writes, "So thoroughly had he been imbued with the danger of compromise in his work that anything which savoured of it was anathema."[88]

What William P. Nicholson would have had a difficult time admitting is that "revivals" come and go; they wax and they wane. For one who believes that a revival is "a mighty work of God," the waning of a revival is hard to explain because one has already given the entire agency to God. Has God withdrawn his spirit? These are questions that historians cannot answer, but they surely vexed the people who had to explain a revised view of the world after the singing stopped.

By the end of the 1920s, attacks by militant fundamentalists like Nicholson seem to have been beaten back. Fundamentalism appeared defeated, or at least marginalized. However, as Joel Carpenter has insightfully observed, the genius of fundamentalism is that it is a popular movement.[89] Battles can be lost and leaders defeated. Yet, the structure of fundamentalism is not hierarchical and institutional but democratic and cellular. They establish their own networks away from the centers of power from which they have been spurned. But they never lose sight of the conjunction of religion and society in covenantal terms that more sophisticated members of the elite perhaps forget. Then, when the time is right, and their support is needed, fundamentalists in religion and politics re-emerge with new leaders preaching the old-time religion. In America, the rise to leadership of Jerry Falwell was as much unexpected as unwelcomed by established leadership. In Ulster the same can be said of Ian R. K. Paisley, whose populist power is as undoubted as it was unwelcomed in Church House (Presbyterian Church Headquarters), Stormont (Ulster's Parliament), and Westminster. In the 1920s, Nicholson and his populist religion had served the establishment of social order by encouraging the working class to remain loyal to the Union and by sacralizing the Union. Once the threats had been weathered, populist power was unwelcome because it was not easily controlled. It might be marginalized for a time, but populism would not die. Paisley did not create the religiopolitical fundamentalism of our time, as, one thinks, he would readily admit. Rather the return of a contested legitimacy in Ulster since 1969 has created conditions in which that sort of fundamentalist populism is useful, even necessary, to maintain the stability of society and state. When Ian Paisley speaks, one can hear echoes of W. P. Nicholson, who was present at the creation of the state in Northern Ireland, and who made a vital contribution to an evangelical Christian component in an Ulster Unionist identity.

Conclusion

The preceding chapters have congregated around a number of discrete but related debates in the culture of Ulster-American Presbyterianism in the late nineteenth and early twentieth centuries. These include controversies over the intellectual management of education, accommodation to post-Darwinian science, the maintenance of ecclesiastical control through heresy hunting, debates on how best to handle political and cultural threats to identity, and the wisdom of resorting to religious revivalism as a strategy for personal and corporate renewal. The moments we have chosen to elucidate the transatlantic nature of these discourses are not intended to be exhaustive, of course; rather they are illustrative. They are not so much diagnostic as emblematic. Their purpose has been to continue an inquiry recently begun on the transatlantic character of evangelical religion and to initiate a conversation on the intellectual trafficking between conservative Protestants of evangelical orientation in the north of Ireland and in the United States. In so doing, we hope to widen the common understanding of the associations between these two sides of the Atlantic and to enrich the connotations of the label "Irish-American." If anything of this ambition has been achieved, it is hoped that these essays will further contribute to the growing awareness of the value of comparative work in understanding the historically negotiated character of evangelical Protestantism. As Noll, Bebbington, and Rawlyk put it in the introduction to their volume of essays on the subject: "evangelicalism has never by any stretch of the imagination been a strictly national phenomenon. Important as transnational, and especially transatlantic, connections have always been for sustaining evangelicalism and explaining its development, however, relatively scant attention has been directed specifically to those connections."[1]

In interrogating these particular episodes we are fully aware that they are situated in a much deeper historical framework. Long-standing patterns of demographic and intellectual migration between Ulster and America are crystallized in the particular encounters and incidents that form the fabric of our investigations. In the educational and political arenas, we recall the formative influence of the Irish-born Francis Hutcheson whose brand of Scottish—or perhaps better Hiberno-Scottish—thinking so strongly influenced the cultural life of American intellectuals in the revolutionary period and the network of Ulster immigrants (mostly members of, or related to, the Tennent family) who played a large part in midcolony higher education all throughout the eighteenth century.[2] McCosh's later endeavors were thus in direct line of intellectual succession to this Enlightenment interchange. Again, the resort to revivalism exhibited in the later Victorian period, and even more recently in the campaigns conducted by W. P. Nicholson, continued an impulse in popular transatlantic Presbyterianism that had its roots in a much earlier period.[3] More recently yet, the fundamentalist vectors within conservative Protestantism are compound products of the forces molding society on both sides of the Atlantic. The episodes to which we attend, therefore, are to be seen as snapshots in a much longer historical narrative.

While the character of evangelical Protestantism is brought under greater scrutiny through the deployment of a comparative historical methodology, it would be mistaken to conclude that the enlightenment thereby gained exhausts its potential scope. Such a judgment would be to underestimate the extent to which more subtle treatments of religious sentiment and practice are real desiderata for coming to terms with the cultural politics of Ulster both past and present. For despite the palpable salience of religion in Northern Irish everyday life, there are reasons for suspecting that its complex and contested character has only begun to be plumbed to the depth it merits. The reasons for this absence are doubtless manifold, but two suggestions immediately present themselves.

First, in popular presentation and scholarly treatise alike, the so-called "two traditions" in Northern Ireland have been victims of a too convenient stereotyping that routinely reduces people to one of two religious communities—Protestant or Catholic—without any acknowledgment of their internal complexity and variation. To be sure there has been a range of key political issues on which Protestants and Catholics have remained diametrically opposed; on matters of national identity, political partisanship, and constitutional aspiration, the gap has long been wide indeed. However, to subsume every aspect of social life and cultural identity under the bipolar rubric of constitutional antithesis is to fall captive to a political reductionism whose status is highly contestable. Such ascriptions, of course, may be analytically convenient and politically expedient; but the rudimentary dualistic taxonomy they promote must ultimately fail for want of sensitivity to the facts of hard particularity.[4] By scrutinizing certain moments in the history of Ulster evangelical Protestantism and attending to its transatlantic connections we hope to have begun the task of historical retrieval by enriching the repertoire of categories upon which to draw. Even within the broad family of evangelical Protestantism we have detected differing attitudes to, for example, the role and meaning of scientific inquiry, the place of revival and its associated language within evangelical traditions, and the pursuance of supposed heterodoxy through the courts of established churches. Besides, we have uncovered a considerable range of style and nuance within Ulster-American conservative Protestantism, from intellectual elites dominating Victorian high culture on both sides of the Atlantic, to a rough-speaking evangelical populism suspicious of, if not downright hostile to, modern scholarship. Such revelations at once confirm that the episodes we have highlighted are part of a genuinely transatlantic genre, and that an immense variety of idiom and tone are subsumed under the rubric of "evangelical Presbyterianism."

Second, what has tended to reinforce interpretations trading in the language of bipolar antipathy is the array of narratives that have been woven, in one way or another, around the assumed precedence of social or political realities in cultural reproduction. Whatever their differences, traditional Irish nationalists, Marxists and socialists of various stripes, advocates of the two-nation thesis, and champions of the double minority model, all assume the reality of two distinct and highly homogeneous communities actually or potentially in conflict. Not only do such accounts tend to minimize internal variation within Northern Irish society, but they also diminish the significance of religion in the lives of many people. The consequence, moreover, is an all-too-frequent exasperation at the province's evident failure to comply with theoretical prescription when religious sentiment gets in the way of tidy political or economic readings. Either an over-straining of facts to fit theory, or a complete impasse, has regularly crippled such diagnoses, resulting in the traducing of the Northern Irish as the voice of illogicality, unreason, madness, or atavism.[5] Exasperation and vituperation have thus gone hand in hand with an evident, if remarkable, unwillingness to subject to analysis either the casual resort to the labels "Protestant" and "Catholic" or the propriety of relegating their theologies to the dubious status of mere symbolism.

The case studies we have presented are thus intended to open up something of the complexity of religious sentiment embodied in the tradition of Presbyterian evangelicalism. What they also display, we believe, is a pervasive interpenetration of Ulster and American conservative Protestant cultures in the decades around 1900 such that neither can be considered the local products of hermetically sealed regions. To be sure, this does not imply that each lacks religious or cultural distinctiveness—our argument is not that they are identical. What we find, rather, is a set of subtle mediations, mutually transforming, articulated through a shared conversation and domesticated to the needs and wants of local ideology. The specific items that have attracted our attention, while far from "the whole story," are nonetheless crucially significant episodes centering on incidents or events perceived as threatening to either the identity or integrity of evangelical Calvinism.

Consider the following. In James McCosh's case, the need for preserving the educational ideals of Scottish curricular culture as fundamental to Christian learning found expression both in his inaugural years at Queen's College and in his strenuous efforts to make Princeton into a great Christian university. These proposals, of course, were voiced in a day when Scottish Common Sense philosophy was rapidly fragmenting in the face of newer intellectual fashions. As George Marsden remarks, "In the age of Nietzsche and

Freud or even of James and Dewey, his was a voice that could be ignored."[6] In the long run, McCosh's strategy would do little to stem a cultural tide running too strongly against him, though it would only be fair to recall that more recent voices have been heard in favor of mounting a campaign aimed at retrieving the Scottish "generalist" model of learning in a day when the idea of the university is being rapidly—and radically—cut off from its historical roots.[7]

If, for McCosh, the inroads of curricular revision was the form that modernity's challenge to a Calvinist heritage assumed, then for Robert Watts—recently returned to Belfast from Princeton and thus traveling in the opposite direction—it was the specter of naturalistic science with all its deadening materialism that incarnated the self-same threat to vital religion. Like his Princeton mentor, Charles Hodge, Watts divined in Darwin and his henchmen a scientific imperative that would exterminate metaphysics and annihilate the spiritual. On this matter, strategies at Princeton and Belfast ultimately came to diverge, but the underlying motive forces were identical even if local events determined the operational shape of the tactics adopted. A generation later, the self-designated heirs of the Hodge-Watts coalition—James Hunter and W. J. Grier in Belfast, and J. Gresham Machen at Princeton—would perceive either in the inroads of the new biblical criticism promulgated (however so modestly) by J. E. Davey in Belfast, or in the moves towards ecclesiastical inclusiveness in the PCUSA, the very Trojan horse that would corrupt the entire fabric of genuine faith. What provided the intellectual engine power behind both campaigns were the lingering vestiges of the Scottish Common Sense philosophy championed by McCosh in both places a half-century earlier.

Concurrently, with the assault on the integrity of Northern Ireland as a viable—or justifiable—polity on the one hand, and the perceived crisis of traditional American culture in the aftermath of World War I on the other, a yet more militant fundamentalist mood crystallized, at least in part, to preserve conventional values in the teeth of seeming cultural dissolution. In such an environment, revivalism was welcomed as a favored and dependable mode of calling individuals and cultures back to basics, of reaffirming the reality of spiritual warfare at the highest and lowest levels, and of finding a secure identity in the face of obliteration. When confronted with the erosion of godly learning, the materialist savor of the new science, the weakening of biblical authority, and a decadent culture crying out for renovation, Ulster-American evangelical Protestants were mutually engaging in a struggle for the souls of men and women and for the souls of their own communities.

As we have been at pains to insist, the episodes that have come within our purview are not intended to be "representative" of Ulster-American culture in any simple sense. But in spaces where, as Hempton and Hill put it, "evangelical Protestants began to feel that history was working against them,"[8] figuring out the strategies they adopted at precise moments of crisis may throw light on the more general features of the *mentalité*. What they do confirm is that some of the key configurations that conservative Presbyterianism assumed in both Ulster and America were conditioned by experiences on the other side of the Atlantic, and that certain of its key architects were the products of a genuinely transatlantic religious culture. What they also show, we believe, is something of the ways in which shared belief systems, jointly-held theological convictions, and a common religious language are molded by the local circumstances within which their adherents are domesticated. To emphasize the continuities between Ulster and America is not to remove the Atlantic Ocean from the cultural map, but rather to draw attention to interdependent adjustment, situated encounters, and local response in the light of domestic affairs. Subjecting these to scrutiny, moreover, has the added advantage of providing clues to the different social arrangements into which beliefs and practices were launched. For it is precisely in the interplay of universality and particularity, of the shared and the specific, that the character of religious communities is shaped.

It has been said, no doubt somewhat tongue-in-cheek, that ideas in the British Isles move east-west, not north-south. If indeed this is so, then the western reaches of north British intellectual geography must be extended across the Atlantic to incorporate North America within the bounds of a single evangelical culture-zone.

Appendix

Irish Students at Princeton Seminary:
An Example of the Ulster-American Connection
Peter Wallace

On 26 September 1859, James Gibson was ordained by the Strabane Presbytery in Northern Ireland. For the next fourteen years he pastored the First Presbyterian Church in Strabane, before accepting a call to the Free West Church in Perth, Scotland, where he ministered until 1893. Gibson had graduated in the spring of 1859 from Princeton Theological Seminary. He had taken his bachelor's degree from the Queen's University, Belfast in 1855 and received a master's in 1857, while he also attended the General Assembly's Theological College (also known as the Presbyterian College) in Belfast. He only attended Princeton for a year before returning to his native Ireland.

Gibson was not the first Irish student to attend Princeton Seminary, but he was the first to return to pastoral ministry in Ireland. He was the first of more than a hundred Irish Presbyterians who would study for a brief time with Charles Hodge, Archibald Alexander Hodge, or Benjamin Breckinridge Warfield, as special theological preparation for ministry in Ireland.

Most seminaries in the nineteenth century attracted students from the particular region where it was located, or the denomination that supported it. Princeton was unique in this regard, attracting students from across regional and denominational boundaries. The international flavor of Princeton's student body is one of the most noticeable differences between Princeton and other nineteenth-century seminaries. While many seminaries attracted immigrants, Princeton was the seminary of choice for students who wished to study in America and then return to their native land. These students either came from countries where there was a significant Reformed or Presbyterian church, or where Presbyterian missions had been established. There were four "waves" of foreign students from four separate regions: the Canadians from the late 1860s through the end of the century; the British—especially the Northern Irish—from the late 1880s through the 1920s (though maintaining a significant immigrant presence ever since the founding of the seminary); the East Asians in the 1910s and 1920s; and the Central Europeans in the 1920s.

The Irish connection is the most significant. We are used to thinking of American students studying overseas in Germany or Britain during the nineteenth century, but the Irish came to Princeton. Over 350 Irish-born students attended Princeton Seminary between 1812 and 1932 (by which point, Princeton's changing reputation would lead to a different set of dynamics). Admittedly, most of these students were immigrants, but there were 117 who returned to Ireland—and another score or so who returned to Scotland.

The flood began after Robert Watts was called as professor of theology at Assembly's College in 1866. Born in Ireland, he had moved to America and attended Washington College in Virginia and Princeton Seminary, graduating in 1852. Ordained by the Presbytery of Philadelphia, he spent eleven years pastoring Westminster Presbyterian Church in Philadelphia before accepting an invitation to Gloucester Street Church in Dublin in 1863. After assuming his duties at Assembly's College, Watts encouraged Irish students to finish their education at Princeton. In the years of his teaching at Assembly's College (1866–1895), more than forty students attended both Assembly's College and Princeton—another fifty continued the trend between 1895 and 1929.

A number of Irish students became moderators of various General Assemblies:

Francis McFarland ('20)	PCUSA (Old School), 1856
Nicholas Murray ('29)	PCUSA (Old School), 1849
Stuart Robinson ('41)	PCUS, 1869
William Moore ('65)	Presbyterian Church of Canada, 1897
James Henry ('75)	Free Church of Scotland, 1906
John Macmillan ('78)	PCI, 1911

Robert Hanna ('97)	PCI, 1927
Robert H. Boyd ('06)	PCI, 1947–49
James Dunlop ('32)	PCI, 1964–65

1812–1859

Prior to the return of James Gibson, seventy Irish-born students had attended Princeton. Thirteen came straight from Belfast College, while three others had attended the University of Glasgow and two Queen's University. Gibson was the first student from Assembly's College to attend Princeton—but by no means the last. Most, however, were children of immigrants attending American colleges, such as the eight from the College of New Jersey (Princeton) and the nine from Lafayette College. None had ever returned to Britain in any professional capacity. All but nine became pastors; fifty-nine served in the PCUSA, spread out evenly between north and south, though largely Old School, while one ministered in the Dutch Reformed Church. A couple also pastored in Congregational or Dutch Reformed Churches in addition to their Presbyterian service. Edward John Hamilton ('58) returned briefly to Dromore, Ireland, in 1862, as an evangelist, before returning to the States where, like several of his countrymen, he taught philosophy and political science at various American colleges.

Three went on to become moderators of Presbyterian General Assemblies: Francis McFarland ('20) of Bethel, Virginia, who moderated the Old School Assembly in 1856; Nicholas Murray ('29) of Elizabethtown, New Jersey, who moderated the 1849 Assembly; and Stuart Robinson ('41), the prominent Kentucky pastor and author who moderated the Southern Presbyterian General Assembly in 1869. But the best-known Irishman in Presbyterian circles was Thomas Smyth ('31), pastor of Second Presbyterian Church in Charleston, South Carolina, from 1834–1873, and author of numerous articles and books on Presbyterian doctrine polity.

1860–1879

Forty-six students came from Ireland before the death of Charles Hodge. Ten returned to Ireland, eight as pastors. While a handful came from Irish universities (six from Queen's, Belfast), five came from Canadian schools, and most graduated from American colleges, with the College of New Jersey leading the way with eight.

Thomas Johnston ('63) and Robert John Orr Moore ('67) both completed their entire theological education at Princeton before returning to be ordained in the same presbytery, Bailieborough, and each pastored for over thirty years. Thomas McCrea and William Hunter Stuart (both '74) had remarkable tenures: McCrea pastored in Bellaghy from 1877–1927, while Stuart ministered in Dromore West from 1883–1921. But the most significant achievement belongs to James Henry ('75) who pastored thirty years in Cahans, Ireland, before accepting a call to the Free Church in Burghead, Scotland, and being elected moderator of the Free Church General Assembly in 1906.

The influence of Robert Watts appears the likely cause behind the increased flow of students from Ireland to Princeton and back again. All three Assembly's College students returned to Ireland. His first student to double cross the Atlantic was John Macmillan, who studied at Assembly's College in 1875–76, before finishing his theological education at Princeton. Ordained in Strabane Presbytery in 1879, he pastored Cooke Centenary Church in Belfast from 1892–1930, and moderated the Irish General Assembly in 1911. He also edited the *Irish Temperance League Journal* from 1893 to 1906. Two other Assembly's College students attended during this era: Andrew Chambers ('71) who was ordained in Ireland as a missionary pastor to Australia, where he served for thirty-five years; and George Benaugh ('72), who after twenty-five years of ministry in America, returned to Knockbracken Church in Belfast from 1898–1913.

Of the other thirty-six Irishmen, all but one became pastors (and he died within months of graduation). All but one Congregationalist served in Presbyterian churches, although one Irishman received a second ordination in the Episcopal Church. Whereas the antebellum Irish were geographically spread out, only three of the postwar generation spent any significant amount of time in the South—two in Maryland, and one who pastored both in Kentucky and Missouri. Four men pastored in Canada, and five became foreign missionaries: two in China, one each in West Africa,

Chile, and India. William Moore ('65), who had moved to Canada during his youth, pastored for thirty-six years in Ottawa, serving as moderator for the Canadian General Assembly in 1897.

1880–1889

In the last couple of years of Charles Hodge's life—and especially after his death—there was a four-year hiatus when no new Irish students came to Princeton. But after 1880 the numbers started to pick up again. Whereas thirty-three Irish students had attended in the 1870s, only twenty-one attended during the 1880s. Only after Warfield came to Princeton did the Irish start to pour across the Atlantic. At least fifteen were educated in Ireland, with seven from Queen's University and another five from Magee College. Ten did theological training in Robert Watts's Assembly's College, half of whom returned to Ireland. Three others also returned, but two returned to join the Episcopal Church. A total of four Irishmen in the decade joined the Episcopal Church, and another one even converted to Catholicism. All became pastors, except two who died young. Of the eight who returned to Ireland, Wilfred Shaw ('82) was ordained as a missionary and went to China before pastoring in America, Alexander Hall ('84) pastored in Drogheda for forty-seven years, and Arthur Torrens pastored in Dungannon, Edinburgh, and Australia.

1890–1899

During the 1890s, Irish students comprised nearly 10 percent of Princeton's student body. Particularly interesting was the overwhelming predominance of Assembly's College students during the heyday of Robert Watts's tenure. Starting in 1888 hordes of Irishmen poured across the Atlantic. Of the eighty-five Irish students who attended during the 1890s, twenty-eight did their undergraduate work at Queen's University, thirteen at Magee College, and thirteen more at Royal College, Dublin. Thirty-five had attended Assembly's College. But Watts's personal influence cannot explain everything. The 400 percent increase in Irish enrollment suggests that other factors were at work. Twenty returned for ordination in the Presbyterian Church of Ireland, and another seven returned to Ireland later. Factoring in the half dozen or so who ministered in England and Scotland, around 40 percent of these students returned to Britain. Seventeen of these returnees were graduates of Assembly's College. So while half of Assembly's College graduates returned to Ireland, only 20 percent of other students did so.

Of those Assembly's College students who returned to Ireland, Joseph Moorhead ('90), after studying in Edinburgh, Gottingen, and Berlin, pastored the First and Second Presbyterian churches in Anaghlone, Banbridge, from 1905–1937; Thomas John Harrison ('93) the Second Presbyterian Church of Rathfriland from 1895–1931; Samuel Currie ('96) in Clones from 1897–1924; Samuel Clarke ('97) in Ballycairn from 1908–1931; Thomas Jones in Killymurris Church in Belfast from 1898–1912; along with Frank Martin ('97) in Perth and St. Matthew's in Edinburgh, Scotland from 1900–1933. After ministering for sixteen years in Whiteabbey, and in the midst of his thirty-three year tenure at Adelaide Road Church in Dublin (1914–1947), Robert Kennedy Hanna ('97) was elected moderator of the Irish General Assembly in 1927, simultaneously being honored with a doctor of divinity degree from the University of Glasgow. Samuel Killen ('91), another Assembly's graduate, entered the educational field, rising to Master of Eaton in Hull from 1918–1920. Of the thirteen non-Assembly's College students who returned, John Stevenson ('94) spent twenty-five years as a missionary in India, while his classmate, Hugh McMullan, pastored in Wexford from 1905–1925. The rest either left the ministry or only spent a few years in Ireland either at the beginning or end of their careers. Of those who stayed in the States, Joseph Hunter ('97) served as the Stated Clerk of the PCUSA from 1928–1956, as well as president of Bloomington Theological Seminary from 1931–1945. Hunter was something of an anomaly among the Irish. Whereas 10–15 percent of all Princeton Seminary graduates became college and seminary professors or presidents at some point in their lifetimes, Hunter was the only Irishman to do so of all the graduates between 1865 and 1903.

Fifty-seven Irish students attended Princeton, and twenty-three returned to Ireland. Royal College, Dublin (14), surpassed Queen's (8) and Magee (9) as the leading undergraduate supplier of Irish students to Princeton. Twenty were ordained in the Presbyterian Church of Ireland, the other three ministered in the United States for a while before returning to their native land. Continuing the pattern of previous decades, of the twenty-three who had attended Assembly's College, sixteen returned to Ireland (70 percent return rate compared to 21 percent of all others). Besides those who attended Assembly's College, there were seventeen who attended other Irish colleges and universities. Only six (35 percent) ever returned to minister in their native land.

All entered the ministry, though one died while still a licentiate. All were Presbyterians, though one became Congregational. While most served either the PCI or the PCUSA, others represented the Church of Scotland, Free Church of Scotland, Presbyterian Church of Canada, United Church of Canada, Reformed Presbyterian, United Presbyterian, Southern Presbyterian, Australian Presbyterian, Presbyterian Church of South Africa, Presbyterian Church of England, and RCA. Of the thirty-two who ministered in the United States at some point, twenty-three remained in the north and east. Four served some time in the midwest, four on the west coast, and only one in the south.

Of the Assembly's College students, Robert H. Boyd ('06) served as a missionary in India for more than a decade before returning to Ireland to serve as the convener of Foreign Missions from 1921–1954 and moderator of the Irish General Assembly from 1947–1949, while William Megaw ('09), the editor of *Daybreak*, pastored Trinity Church in Ahoghill for twenty years and then St. John's, Belfast, from 1929–1953. Most served in parishes scattered throughout Northern Ireland.

Of those Assembly's students who did not return to Ireland, John Gilmour ('01) was ordained in the United Free Church of Scotland and pastored in Fife for a decade and at Holyrood Abbey Church in Edinburgh from 1929–1950; John Edgar Park ('03) moved from the PCUSA to the Congregational fold, pastoring in Andover and West Newton, Massachusetts, for twenty-two years before becoming president of Wheaton College, Norton, Massachusetts, from 1926–1944 and presiding over the American Congregational Association in 1948.

There were others of note among the Irish students: Samuel Angus ('06), a graduate of the Royal University, Dublin, went on to study in Marburg, Berlin, and Edinburgh, before becoming professor of New Testament in St. Andrew's College of the University of Sydney, Australia, from 1914–1943. He served as a visiting professor at Yale and Columbia during the 1920s and received honorary doctorates from Princeton University, Queen's, and Glasgow. Walter Montgomery ('09), a Queen's graduate, was ordained in the Presbyterian Church of Canada as a missionary to Formosa from 1909–1949 and acted as principal of Tainan Theological College from 1926–1949.

1910–1919

Forty-three Irishmen attended Princeton, while twenty-two returned during this period. More than thirty graduated from Irish colleges, including eight from Queen's, seven from Trinity, Dublin, six from Magee, and four from Royal College, Dublin. Only fifteen came from Assembly's College, of whom ten returned (67 percent compared to 43 percent of all others, and 55 percent of other students from Irish colleges). In other words, the Assembly's College connection was starting to fade.

Six of these men did not enter the ministry—four of whom died during World War I. Of those who did, the diversity of callings increased. One entered the Baptist Church of Canada, and another received Anglican orders in the Episcopal Church of Ireland. Most, however, served in the Presbyterian Churches of Ireland, Canada, and the U.S.

Magee College graduate Moses Thompson ('11) returned to Belfast to pastor Killymurris Church before moving across town to Mountpottinger Church where he served for nearly thirty years. Robert Knox Lyle ('13), who attended Assembly's College after returning from the States, served as a missionary to China for several years before returning to pastor churches in the counties of Wexford and Wicklow. His classmate from Trinity, Dublin, and Princeton, James McCammon, remained in China from 1915–1942. Another student who went to Assembly's College after returning from Princeton was William John Harrison ('16), who pastored fifteen years in Ballyeaston before being called to Crumlin Road Church in Belfast from 1931–1951.

1920–1932

Thirty-three Irishmen attended Princeton during the last years before the reorganization (the class of '32 would have been accepted to Princeton prior to the reorganization of 1929, and Princeton's reputation probably would not have been immediately altered). Twenty-three returned to Ireland, and five migrated to Canada. Immigration was drying up. All sixteen Assembly's College students returned to Ireland (100 percent compared to 41 percent of all others, and 67 percent of other Irish-educated students). Twelve studied at Trinity College, Dublin, while ten came from Queen's University, Belfast.

While all but four entered the Presbyterian ministry at some point in their lives, one served as a Baptist minister, another was ordained in the Reformed Episcopal Church, while two more entered the United Church of Canada. Only four ministered for any length of time in the United States. One of these, Joseph Francis Mathews ('22), had served for thirteen years as a Roman Catholic priest in Ireland and America before attending Princeton. He spent the last decade of his life as a Presbyterian minister in Oregon and California.

Of those who returned to Ireland, Alfred Eric Scott ('21) pastored from 1923–1967 in Ramelton, receiving an honorary doctorate from Assembly's College; Austin Alfred Fulton ('27) served as a missionary in Manchuria for over a decade before returning to Belfast as a pastor and later convener and secretary of Foreign Missions from 1954–1967. Samuel Young ('27), after pastoring in Belfast, moved to Adelaide Road Church in Dublin from 1947–1967, replacing fellow Assembly's College and Princeton graduate, Robert Hanna. James McFarland ('28) pastored in county Antrim, at the

Sinclair Seamen's Church in Belfast, and in Castlerock Church, Londonderry, for over fifteen years apiece. He received an honorary doctorate from Assembly's College in 1974. Topping the list is James Dunlop ('32), who pastored Oldpark Church in Belfast from 1933–1973, serving as moderator of the Irish General Assembly from 1964–65. In addition, George Walker ('26) was ordained in the Presbyterian Church of England, ministering in St. Andrew's Church in Nottingham from 1936–1974. William James Martin ('29) studied in Berlin and Leipzig before accepting a post as head of the department of Hebrew and Ancient Semitic Languages at the University of Liverpool from 1937–1971.

While Irish enrollment continued at its earlier pace through 1934, the last five years of the decade saw only nine Irish students—two of whom were graduates of American colleges who never returned to Ireland. Occasionally Irishmen would continue to study at Princeton, but the overwhelming numbers of the turn of the century would never again be equaled.

Table. Irish Students at Princeton Seminary

Decade	All Irish Students	Assembly's College Students	Other Irish Schools*	All Others**
1812–1819	1 (0)	0	0	1 (0)
1820–1829	6 (0)	0	0	6 (0)
1830–1839	14 (0)	0	6 (0)	8 (0)
1840–1849	16 (0)	0	3 (0)	13 (0)
1850–1859	33 (2)	1 (1)	9 (0)	23 (1)
1860–1869	25 (4)	0	4 (4)	21 (0)
1870–1879	21 (6)	3 (3)	6 (3)	12 (0)
1880–1889	21 (8)	10 (5)	6 (3)	6 (0)
1890–1899	85 (27)	35 (17)	32 (6)	18 (4)
1900–1909	57 (23)	23 (16)	17 (6)	17 (1)
1910–1919	43 (22)	15 (10)	14 (9)	14 (3)
1920–1932	33 (23)	16 (16)	13 (7)	4 (0)
Total	355 (117)	103 (68)	120 (38)	132 (9)

(Number in parentheses refers to how many returned to Ireland)
*Includes Scottish schools
**Include those who were educated in Canada or the U.S.

Notes

INTRODUCTION

1. "The Comparability of American History," in *The Comparative Approach to American History,* C. V. Woodward, ed., (New York: Basic Books, 1968), 3. Ian Tyrrell, "American Exceptionalism in an Age of International History," *American Historical Review* 96 (1991): 1031–55.

2. H. C. Allen and Roger Thompson, eds., *Contrast and Connection: Bicentennial Essays in Anglo-American History* (Athens, Ohio: Ohio University Press, 1976). Daniel Snowman, *Britain and America: An Interpretation of Their Culture, 1945–1975* (New York: Harper and Row, 1977).

3. David B. Davis, *The Problem of Slavery in Western Culture* (Ithaca, N.Y.: Cornell University Press, 1966); Carl Degler, *Neither Black Nor White: Slavery and Race Relations in Brazil and the United States* (New York: Macmillan, 1971); George M. Fredrickson, *White Supremacy: A Comparative Study in American and South African History* (New York: Oxford University Press, 1981).

4. James Axtell, *After Columbus: Essays in the Ethnohistory of Colonial North America* (New York: Oxford University Press, 1988); Gary B. Nash, *Red, White and Black: The Peoples of Early America* (Englewood Cliffs, N.J.: Prentice-Hall, 1994); Mario Materassi and Maria Irene Ramalho de Sousa Santos, eds., *The American Columbiad: "Discovering" America, Inventing the United States* (Amsterdam: VU Press, 1996).

5. Jack P. Greene, *Peripheries and Center: Constitutional Developments in the Extended Politics of the British Empire and the United States* (Athens, Ga.: University of Georgia Press, 1986); Edmund S. Morgan, *Inventing the People: The Rise of Popular Sovereignty in England and America* (New York: Norton, 1988); Bernard Bailyn and Philip D. Morgan, eds., *Strangers Within the Realm: Cultural Margins of the First British Empire* (Chapel Hill, N.C.: University of North Carolina Press, 1991).

6. Ernest R. Sandeen, *The Roots of Fundamentalism: British and American Millenarianism, 1800–1930* (Chicago: University of Chicago Press, 1970);

Richard Carwardine, *Transatlantic Revivalism: Popular Evangelicalism in Britain and America, 1790–1865* (Westport, Conn.: Greenwood Press, 1978); Susan Durden O'Brien, "A Transatlantic Community of Saints: The Great Awakening and the First Evangelical Networks, 1735–1755," *American Historical Review* 91 (October 1986): 811–32; Harry S. Stout, *The Divine Dramatist: George Whitefield and the Rise of Modern Evangelicalism* (Grand Rapids, Mich.: Eerdmans, 1991); Mark A. Noll and George A. Rawlyk, eds., *Amazing Grace: Evangelicalism in Australia, Britain, Canada and the United States* (Grand Rapids, Mich.: Baker Books, 1993); David W. Bebbington, Mark A. Noll, George A. Rawlyk, eds., *Evangelicalism: Comparative Studies of Popular Protestantism in North America, the British Isles, and Beyond, 1700–1990* (New York: Oxford, 1994).

7. Peter Gould and Rodney White, *Mental Maps* (London and New York: Penguin, 1974).

8. Anthony P. Cohen, ed., *Belonging: Identity and Social Organization in British Rural Cultures* (St. John's, Newfoundland: Institute of Social and Economic Research, 1982); Anthony P. Cohen, ed., *Symbolizing Boundaries: Identity and Diversity in British Cultures* (Manchester: Manchester University Press, 1987).

One   CULTURE AND CURRICULUM

1. See Mark A. Noll, *The Princeton Theology, 1812–1921: Scripture, Science and Theological Method from Archibald Alexander to Benjamin Warfield* (Grand Rapids, Mich.: Baker, 1983).

2. Archibald Alexander, "Presbyterian Church in Ireland," *The Biblical Repertory and Princeton Review* 16 (1844): 199–229, on 200. This essay was an extended review of *The History of the Presbyterian Church in Ireland* by James Seaton Reid.

3. J. Addison Alexander, "Presbyterian Church in Ireland," *The Biblical Repertory and Princeton Review* 31 (1859): 717–33, on 718. This too was an essay review of a range of historical accounts of Irish Presbyterianism.

4. Robert Allen, *The Presbyterian College Belfast, 1853–1953* (Belfast: William Mullan, 1954), 101.

5. Allen, *Presbyterian College,* 179.

6. Peter Wallace and Mark Noll, "The Students of Princeton Semi-

nary, 1812–1929: A Research Note," *American Presbyterians* 72 (1994): 203–15, on 210. See also the appendix, pp. 145–154.

7. John Macmillan, "Irish and American Presbyterianism," in *The Centennial Celebration of the Theological Seminary of the Presbyterian Church in the United States of America at Princeton* (Princeton, N.J.: Princeton Theological Seminary, 1912), 499–525, on 518, 525, 518.

8. See W. T. Blackstone, *Francis Hutcheson and Contemporary Ethical Theory* (Athens, Ga.: University of Georgia Press, 1965); T. D. Campbell, "Francis Hutcheson: 'Father' of the Scottish Enlightenment," in R. H. Campbell and Andrew S. Skinner, eds., *Origins and Nature of the Scottish Enlightenment*, (Edinburgh: John Donald, 1982), 165–85.

9. See Mark A. Noll, *Princeton and the Republic, 1768–1822. The Search for a Christian Enlightenment in the Era of Samuel Stanhope Smith* (Princeton, N.J.: Princeton University Press, 1989). A useful brief assessment of Hutcheson's moral and political influence in pre-Revolutionary America is provided in David Fate Norton, "Salus Populi Suprema Lex," *Fortnight*, Supplement 308 (July/August 1992), 14–17.

10. Norman Fiering, *Moral Philosophy at Seventeenth-Century Harvard: A Discipline in Transition* (Chapel Hill, N.C.: University of North Carolina Press, 1981), 300.

11. On the deployment of Hutcheson in the cause of rebellion, see Caroline Robbins, "'When It Is That Colonies May Turn Independent': An Analysis of the Environment and Politics of Francis Hutcheson," *William and Mary Quarterly* 11 (1954): 214–51.

12. J. M. Barkley, "Francis Hutcheson (1694–1746)," *Bulletin of the Presbyterian Historical Society of Ireland* 14 (March 1985): 12. On Allison and his influence, see also Ian McBride, "The School of Virtue: Francis Hutcheson, Irish Presbyterians and the Scottish Enlightenment," in D. George Boyce, Robert Eccleshall, and Vincent Geoghegan, eds., *Political Thought in Ireland since the Seventeenth Century* (London and New York: Routledge, 1993), 73–99.

13. McBride, "The School of Virtue," 74.

14. Mark A. Noll, "Common Sense Traditions and American Evangelical Thought," *American Quarterly* 37 (1985): 216–38. This essay contains a very useful taxonomy of the various Common Sense traditions. See also Mark A. Noll, *The Scandal of the Evangelical Mind* (Grand Rapids, Mich.: Eerdmans, 1994), chap. 4; Michael Gauvreau, "The Empire of Evangelicalism: Varieties of Common

Sense in Scotland, Canada, and the United States," in Mark A. Noll, David W. Bebbington, and George A. Rawlyk, eds., *Evangelicalism: Comparative Protestantism in North America, the British Isles, and Beyond* (Oxford: Oxford University Press, 1994), 219–52.

15. See Marilyn J. Westerkamp, *Triumph of the Laity: Scots-Irish Piety and the Great Awakening* (New York: Oxford University Press, 1988); Leigh E. Schmidt, *Holy Fairs: Scottish Communions and American Revivals in the Early Modern Period* (Princeton, N.J.: Princeton University Press, 1990); Richard Carwardine, *Trans-Atlantic Revivalism: Popular Evangelicalism in Britain and America, 1790–1865* (Westport, Conn.: Greenwood Press, 1978).

16. Stewart J. Brown, "Presbyterian Communities, Transatlantic Visions and the Ulster Revival of 1859," in James P. Mackey, ed., *The Cultures of Europe: The Irish Contribution* (Belfast: Institute of Irish Studies, 1994), 87–105, on 91–92.

17. For various perspectives on the 1859 revival, see John T. Carson, *God's River in Spate: The Story of the Religious Awakening of Ulster in 1859* (Belfast: Presbyterian Historical Society, 1958); Peter Gibbon, *The Origins of Ulster Unionism: The Formation of Popular Protestant Politics and Ideology in Nineteenth-Century Ireland* (Manchester: Manchester University Press, 1975); Myrtle Hill, "Ulster Awakened: The '59 Revival Reconsidered," *Journal of Ecclesiastical History* 41 (1990): 443–62; David Hempton and Myrtle Hill, *Evangelical Protestantism in Ulster Society, 1740–1890* (London: Routledge, 1992).

18. Peter Brooke, *Ulster Presbyterianism: The Historical Perspective, 1610–1970* (Belfast: Athol Books, 1994), 158.

19. George M. Marsden, *The Soul of the American University: From Protestant Establishment to Established Nonbelief* (New York: Oxford University Press, 1994), 196.

20. The key biographical source is J. David Hoeveler, Jr., *James McCosh and the Scottish Intellectual Tradition, from Glasgow to Princeton* (Princeton, N.J.: Princeton University Press, 1981). See also William Milligan Sloane, ed., *The Life of James McCosh: A Record Chiefly Autobiographical* (Edinburgh: T. & T. Clark, 1896).

21. Sloane, *Life of James McCosh*, 133–34, 151.

22. Marsden, *Soul of the American University*, 198.

23. Ibid., 199.

24. Quoted ibid., 200.

25. McCosh's perspective on evolution is discussed in James R. Moore, *The Post-Darwinian Controversies: A Study of the Protestant Struggle to Come to Terms with Darwin in the United States and Great Britain, 1870–1900* (Cambridge: Cambridge University Press, 1979), and David N. Livingstone, *Darwin's Forgotten Defenders: The Encounter between Evangelical Theology and Evolutionary Thought* (Grand Rapids and Edinburgh: Eerdmans and Scottish Academic Press, 1987). The most thorough investigation of the Princeton response to evolution is Bradley John Gundlach, "The Evolution Question at Princeton, 1845–1929" (Ph.D. diss., University of Rochester, New York, 1995).

26. See Marsden, *Soul of the American University*, 211–13.

27. Ibid., 196.

28. See T. W. Moody, "The Irish University Question in the Nineteenth Century," *History* 43 (1958): 90–109.

29. T. Hamilton, *History of the Irish Presbyterian Church* (Edinburgh: T. & T. Clark, 1887).

30. Moody, "The Irish University Question," 98.

31. On the history of Queen's, see T. W. Moody and J. C. Beckett, *Queen's, Belfast, 1845–1949: The History of a University*, 2 vols. (London: Faber & Faber, 1959); Brian Walker and Alf McCreary, *Degrees of Excellence: The Story of Queen's, Belfast, 1845–1995* (Belfast: Institute of Irish Studies, 1994).

32. The standard biographical treatments are J. L. Porter, *The Life and Times of Henry Cooke, D.D., LL.D.* (London, 1871); R. Finlay Holmes, *Henry Cooke* (Belfast: Christian Journals Limited, 1981).

33. Moody and Beckett, *Queen's Belfast*, vol. 1, 78.

34. Ibid., 116.

35. Ibid., 164.

36. The various factors surrounding the appointment are discussed in William Donald Patton, "James McCosh: The Making of a Reputation. A Study of the Life and Work of the Rev. Dr. James McCosh in Ireland, from his Appointment as Professor of Logic and Metaphysics in Queen's College, Belfast, 1851, to his Appointment as President of Princeton College, New Jersey, and Professor of Philosophy, in 1888" (Ph.D. diss., Queen's University of Belfast, 1993).

37. Hoeveler, *James McCosh*, 116.

38. Cited in J. Gresham Machen, *The Christian View of Man* (1937; reprint, London: Banner of Truth, 1965), 86.

39. George Elder Davie, *The Democratic Intellect: Scotland and Her Universities in the Nineteenth Century* (Edinburgh: Edinburgh University Press, 1961).

40. This extract and those preceding it come from the report of McCosh's lecture in the *Belfast Newsletter*, Wednesday, 14 January 1852.

41. Gauvreau, "The Empire of Evangelicalism"; see also Roger L. Emerson, "Science and Moral Philosophy in the Scottish Enlightenment," in M. A. Stewart, ed., *Studies in the Philosophy of the Scottish Enlightenment* (Oxford: Clarendon Press, 1990).

42. James McCosh, *The Scottish Philosophy, Biographical, Expository, Critical, from Hutcheson to Hamilton* (New York, 1875), 299.

43. *Belfast Newsletter*, Wednesday, 24 January 1852.

44. An insightful analysis along these lines is provided in Allen C. Guelzo, "Moral Philosophy as Science," in David N. Livingstone, D. G. Hart, and Mark A. Noll, eds., *Evangelicals and Science in Historical Perspective* (New York: Oxford University Press, 1999).

45. James McCosh, *The Method of the Divine Government, Physical and Moral* (Edinburgh: Sutherland and Knox, 1851), 197.

46. Graham Richards, *Mental Machinery, Part One: 1600–1850* (London: Athlone Press, 1992); and Graham Richards, "'To Know Our Fellow Men to Do Them Good': American Psychology's Enduring Moral Project," *History of the Human Sciences* 8 (1995): 1–24. See also Robert J. Richards, *Darwin and the Emergence of Evolutionary Theories of Mind and Behavior* (Chicago: University of Chicago Press, 1987).

47. Richards, "'To Know Our Fellow Men,'" 13.

48. Hall, for example, was severely critical of McCosh on several scores. See Dorothy Ross, *G. Stanley Hall: The Psychologist as Prophet* (Chicago: University of Chicago Press, 1972).

49. James McCosh, "The Place of Religion in Colleges," in George D. Mathews, ed., *Alliance of the Reformed Churches Holding the Presbyterian System. Minutes and Proceedings of the Third General Council,* Belfast 1884 (Belfast: Assembly's Offices, 1884), 465–80, on 467.

50. This is discussed in Patton, "James McCosh: The Making of a Reputation."

51. Sloane, *Life of James McCosh*, 128.

52. Details of this episode are also discussed in Patton, "James McCosh: The Making of a Reputation."

53. Hoeveler, *James McCosh*, 114.

54. James McCosh, *The Mental Sciences and the Queen's University in Ireland; Being a Letter to the Secretary of the Queen's University* (Belfast, 1860), 7.

55. Ibid. The same concerns were also evident in Newman's educational project in Dublin. See David N. Livingstone, "The Idea of a University: Interventions from Ireland" (forthcoming).

56. William Nesbitt, *A Reply to the Strictures of Rev. Dr. McCosh on the Recent Ordinance of the Senate of the Queen's University in Ireland* (Dublin, 1860), 7.

57. Cited in Thomas Jefferson Wertenbaker, *Princeton: 1746–1896* (Princeton, N.J.: Princeton University Press, 1946), 293.

58. Current critics of specialization continue to call upon the intellectual resources of the Scottish educational tradition. See, for example, Alasdair MacIntyre, *Whose Justice? Which Rationality?* (Notre Dame, Ind.: University of Notre Dame Press, 1988); Andrew Lockhart Walker, *The Revival of the Democratic Intellect* (Edinburgh: Polygon, 1994).

59. Cited in Hoeveler, *James McCosh*, 255.

60. These events are recorded ibid., 256.

61. Nathan O. Hatch, *The Democratization of American Christianity* (New Haven: Yale University Press, 1989), 196.

62. James Gerald Donat, "British Medicine and the Ulster Revival of 1859" (Ph.D. diss., University of London, 1986), 13.

63. Hempton and Hill, *Evangelical Protestantism in Ulster Society*, 150.

64. W. T. Latimer, *A History of the Irish Presbyterians*, 2d ed. (Belfast, 1902), 492.

65. William Gibson, *The Year of Grace* (Belfast, 1860), 250.

66. Isaac Nelson, *The Year of Delusion: A Review of 'The Year of Grace'* (Belfast, 1860), 165, 180.

67. J. Addison Alexander, "Presbyterian Church in Ireland," *The Biblical Repertory and Princeton Review* 31 (1859): 717–33, on 717, 732.

68. *The Banner of Ulster*, for example, reprinted, from one of the Pittsburgh newspapers, a report on the enthusiastic reception Edgar received at the Synod of Pittsburgh. See *The Banner of Ulster*, 12 November 1859.

69. Allen, *The Presbyterian College*, 95.

70. I am grateful to Donald Patton for providing these details from his reading of early issues of the Evangelical Alliance's serial, *Evangelical Christendom*.

71. See Hempton and Hill, *Evangelical Protestantism in Ulster Society*, 122–28.

72. *The Banner of Ulster*, Saturday, 24 September 1859.

73. William M'Ilwaine, *Revivalism Reviewed* (Belfast: T. M'Ilroy, 1859), 15, 9.

74. William M'Ilwaine, *The 'Revival Movement' Examined* (Belfast: Wheatcroft & Henry, 1859).

75. M'Ilwaine, *Revivalism Reviewed*, 12.

76. *The Banner of Ulster*, Saturday, 24 September 1859.

77. James McCosh, *The Ulster Revival and Its Physiological Accidents. A Paper Read Before the Evangelical Alliance, September 22, 1859*. (Belfast: C. Aitchison, 1859).

78. *The Banner of Ulster*, Saturday, 24 September 1859.

79. See John Rogerson, *Old Testament Criticism in the Nineteenth Century: England and Germany* (Philadelphia: Fortress Press, 1984). For evangelical responses see the discussion in Mark A. Noll, *Between Faith and Criticism: Evangelicals, Scholarship, and the Bible in America* (San Francisco: Harper & Row, 1986), 64–67.

80. James McCosh, *The Supernatural in Relation to the Natural* (Cambridge and London, 1862), 142.

81. See Patton, "James McCosh: The Making of a Reputation," 67. Cooke's lectures on *Essays and Reviews* delivered in April 1862 received comment in *The Weekly Review*, 3 May 1861; James G. Murphy was the author of *The Nineteen Alleged Impossibilities of Part I of Colenso on the Pentateuch Shown to Be Possible with a Critique on Part II* (Belfast: McComb and C. Aitchison, 1863).

82. A summary is provided in Patton, "James McCosh: The Making of a Reputation," 70–73.

83. See Moore, *The Post-Darwinian Controversies*; Livingstone, *Darwin's Forgotten Defenders*; Hoeveler, *James McCosh*; Frederick Gregory, "The Impact of Darwinian Evolution on Protestant Theology in the Nineteenth Century" in David C. Lindberg and Ronald L. Numbers, eds., *God and Nature: Historical Essays on the Encounter between Christianity and Science* (Berkeley, Calif.: University of California Press, 1986),

369–90; Jon Roberts, *Darwinism and the Divine in America: Protestant Intellectuals and Organic Evolution, 1859–1900* (Madison, Wisc.: University of Wisconsin Press, 1988).

84. James McCosh, "Religious Aspects of the Doctrine of Development," in S. Irenaeus Prime, ed., *History, Orations, and Other Documents of the Sixth General Conference of the Evangelical Alliance* (New York: Harper, 1874), 264–71.

85. James McCosh, *The Religious Aspect of Evolution* (New York: Scribner's, 1890), 113. McCosh's social optimism (entirely in keeping with his postmillennial eschatology) is emphasized in Boyd Hilton, *The Age of Atonement: The Influence of Evangelicalism on Social and Economic Thought, 1785–1865* (Oxford: Oxford University Press, 1988), 363.

86. Ernst Benz, *Evolution and Christian Hope: Man's Concept of the Future from the Early Fathers to Teilhard de Chardin*, trans. Heinz G. Frank (New York: Doubleday, 1966), 134. See also David N. Livingstone, "Evolution and Eschatology," *Themelios* 22 (1996): 26–36.

87. McCosh had written to Argyll in 1867 and received a reply in which Argyll noted that it was a "great pleasure to find that on the whole our agreement is so great on the questions raised respecting 'Law in the Realm of Mind'. I think we are substantially at one." Letter, Duke of Argyll to Dr. McCosh, 21 September 1867 (General Mss. [misc.] C0140, Firestone Library, Princeton University). (It is worth noting that Argyll was a staunch opponent of Irish Home Rule.) That Benz locates Henry Drummond's evolutionary theology and what might be called the Darwinian Calvinism of George Frederick Wright in the self-same conceptual frame is also entirely predictable. See the discussion of Drummond's views in James R. Moore, "Evangelicals and Evolution: Henry Drummond, Herbert Spencer, and the Naturalization of the Spiritual World," *Scottish Journal of Theology* 38 (1985): 383–417. Wright is discussed in Ronald L. Numbers, "George Frederick Wright: From Christian Darwinist to Fundamentalist," *Isis* 79 (1988): 624–45.

88. See the discussion in Livingstone, *Darwin's Forgotten Defenders*, 107; also David N. Livingstone, "The Idea of Design: The Vicissitudes of a Key Concept in the Princeton Response to Darwin," *Scottish Journal of Theology* 37 (1984): 329–57.

89. On transcendental morphology in general and Owen's work in particular, see Philip F. Rehbock, *The Philosophical Naturalists: Themes in Early Nineteenth-Century British Biology* (Madison, Wisc.: University

of Wisconsin Press, 1983); Nicolaas A. Rupke, *Richard Owen, Victorian Naturalist* (New Haven, Conn.: Yale University Press, 1994).

90. This is the term used by Bowler. See Peter J. Bowler, "Darwinism and the Argument from Design: Suggestions for a Re-evaluation," *Journal of the History of Biology* 10 (1977): 29–43.

91. See Adrian Desmond, *The Politics of Evolution: Morphology, Medicine, and Reform in Radical London* (Chicago and London: University of Chicago Press, 1989).

92. Hoeveler, *James McCosh,* 191–92. James McCosh, "Some Remarks on the Plant Morphologically Considered," *Transactions of the Edinburgh Botanical Society* 4 (1853).

93. James McCosh, "Typical Forms," *North British Review* 15 (1851): 389–418.

94. James McCosh and George Dickie, *Typical Forms and Special Ends in Creation* (Edinburgh: Thomas Constable, 1856), 5, 27.

95. James McCosh, *Christianity and Positivism: A Series of Lectures to the Times on Natural Theology and Christian Apologetics* (London: Macmillan, 1871), 90–92.

96. Hilton, *Age of Atonement,* 304.

Two SCIENCE AND SCRIPTURE

1. The general outlines of the response of Protestant intellectuals to evolution is, by now, fairly well known. See, for example, James R. Moore, *The Post-Darwinian Controversies: A Study of the Protestant Struggle to Come to Terms with Darwin in the United States and Great Britain, 1870–1900* (Cambridge: Cambridge University Press, 1979); David N. Livingstone, *Darwin's Forgotten Defenders: The Encounter between Evangelical Theology and Evolutionary Thought* (Grand Rapids and Edinburgh: Eerdmans and Scottish Academic Press, 1987); Frederick Gregory, "The Impact of Darwinian Evolution on Protestant Theology in the Nineteenth Century" in David C. Lindberg and Ronald L. Numbers, eds., *God and Nature: Historical Essays on the Encounter between Christianity and Science* (Berkeley, Calif.: University of California Press 1986), 369–90; Jon Roberts, *Darwinism and the Divine in America: Protestant Intellectuals and Organic Evolution, 1859–1900* (Madison, Wisc.: University of Wisconsin Press, 1988).

2. This incident and other biographical details are surveyed in

Robert E. L. Rodgers, "The Life and Principal Writings of Robert Watts, D.D., LL.D. An Historico/Theological Examination of the Life and Principal Writings of Robert Watts with Particular Reference to the Doctrine of the Verbal Inspiration of Holy Scripture" (Th.D. thesis, Faculté Libre de Théologie Réformée, Aix-en-Provence, 1984). See also R. E. L. Rodgers, *The Life and Work of Robert Watts* (Houston, Tex.: Christian Focus Publications 1989).

3. Robert Allen, *The Presbyterian College Belfast, 1853–1953* (Belfast: William Mullan, 1954), 179.

4. In the *Presbyterian Review*, for example, he published "Agnosticism," 6 (1885): 77–90, and "A Short Answer to Some Objections to the Protestant Doctrine of the Canon of Scripture Urged by Romanists," 6 (1885): 328–30.

5. The following works represent some of these polemics: *Essays Theological and Scientific: An Outline of the Calvinistic System with a Defence of Its Fundamental Doctrine and Principles against Barnes, Bushnell and Others* (Edinburgh: T. & T. Clark, 1866); *Prelatic Departures from Protestant Principles* (Edinburgh: T. & T. Clark, 1871); *Arminian Departures from Reformation Principles* (Edinburgh: T. & T. Clark, 1871); some of his tracts on scientific philosophy were reprinted in *The Reign of Causality: A Vindication of the Scientific Principle of Telic Causal Efficiency* (Edinburgh: T. & T. Clark, 1888). He also engaged in a transatlantic altercation with G. W. Northrup, criticizing in the pages of the *Western Recorder* the argument Northrup had advanced in the *Standard*. These pieces were drawn together into a volume by Northrup and Watts, with each other's rejoinders and replies, entitled *Sovereignty of God* (Louisville, Ky.: Baptist Book Concerns, 1894).

6. These were published as *The Rule of Faith and the Doctrine of Inspiration* (London: Hodder & Stoughton, 1885); see also *The New Apologetic and Its Claims to Scriptural Authority* (Edinburgh: T. & T. Clark, 1890).

7. Cited in Allen, *The Presbyterian College Belfast*, 182.

8. *The Northern Whig*, 19 August 1874.

9. Adrian Desmond and James Moore, *Darwin* (London: Michael Joseph, 1991), 611.

10. John Tyndall, *Address Delivered before the British Association Assembled at Belfast, with Addition* (London: Longmans, Green, and Co., 1874). See the discussion in Ruth Barton, "John Tyndall, Pantheist. A Rereading of the Belfast Address." *Osiris* 2d series, 3 (1987): 111–34.

11. The paper, "An Irenicum: Or, a Plea of Peace and Co-operation between Science and Theology," was reprinted in Watts's *The Reign of Causality*. The rejection is noted in *The Witness*, 9 October 1874.

12. Robert Watts, "Atomism—An Examination of Professor Tyndall's Opening Address before the British Association, 1874," in *The Reign of Causality*.

13. Hodge's letter is reproduced in full in *The Witness*, 6 November 1874, and in [Robert] Watts, *Atomism: Dr. Tyndall's Atomic Theory of the Universe Examined and Refuted. To Which Are Added, Humanitarianism Accepts, Provisionally, Tyndall's Impersonal Atomic Deity; and A Letter to the Presbytery of Belfast; Containing a Note from the Rev. Dr. Hodge, and a Critique on Tyndall's Recent Manchester Recantation, Together with Strictures on the Late Manifesto of the Roman Catholic Hierarchy of Ireland in Reference to the Sphere of Science* (Belfast: William Mullan, 1875), 34. Later in a letter to A. A. Hodge in 1881 thanking him for sending a copy of the biography of his father, Watts wrote: "Precious indeed it is to me and mine. We feel towards it as if it were the history of one of our own kith and kin." Letter, Robert Watts to A. A. Hodge, 1 January 1881 (Archives, Speer Library, Princeton Theological Seminary). Earlier in 1879 he had supplied A. A. Hodge with copies of letters from Charles Hodge to Principal Cunningham. Letter, Robert Watts to A. A. Hodge, 2 December 1879 (Archives, Speer Library, Princeton Theological Seminary).

14. In time these addresses would be drawn together into a book, distributed on both sides of the Atlantic, under the title *Science and Revelation: A Series of Lectures in Reply to the Theories of Tyndall, Huxley, Darwin, Spencer, Etc.* The volume was announced, for example, in *The Presbyterian Quarterly and Princeton Review* 5 (1876): 17.

15. J. G. C., "Darwinism," *Irish Ecclesiastical Record* 9 (1873): 337–61.

16. "Pastoral Address of the Archbishops and Bishops of Ireland." *Irish Ecclesiastical Record* 11 (November 1874).

17. Robert Watts, *Atomism*, 34, 38, 39.

18. Letter, Robert Watts to A. A. Hodge, 1 January 1881 (Archives, Speer Library, Princeton Theological Seminary).

19. Letter, Robert Watts to B. B. Warfield, 18 June 1890 (Warfield Papers, Archives, Speer Library, Princeton Theological Seminary). The widespread character of this disillusioning shock among Ulster Presbyterians is noted in Graham Walker, "Empire, Religion and Nationality in Scotland and Ulster before the First World

War," in Ian S. Wood, ed., *Scotland and Ulster* (Edinburgh: Mercat Press, 1994), 97–115; and Graham Walker, *Intimate Strangers: Political and Cultural Interaction between Scotland and Ulster in Modern Times* (Edinburgh: John Donald, 1995). The political culture of Ulster Protestantism in this period is admirably elucidated in David Hempton, "Ulster Protestantism: The Religious Foundations of Rebellious Loyalism," chap. 5 in *Religion and Political Culture in Britain and Ireland: From the Glorious Revolution to the Decline of Empire* (Cambridge: Cambridge University Press, 1996).

20. Watts, "Evolution and Natural History," in *The Reign of Causality*, 316–17. This review had originally appeared in the April 1887 issue of the *British and Foreign Evangelical Review*.

21. Robert Watts, "Natural Law in the Spiritual World," *British and Foreign Evangelical Review* (1885), reprinted in Watts, *The Reign of Causality*. See also Robert Watts, *Professor Drummond's 'Ascent of Man', and Principal Fairbairn's 'Place of Christ in Modern Theology', Examined in the Light of Science and Revelation* (Edinburgh: R. W. Hunter, n.d., c. 1894).

22. The Princetonians, of course, were keeping a keen eye on the machinations in Scotland. See, for example, Francis L. Patton, "Rationalism in the Free Church of Scotland," *The Princeton Review* 56 (1880): 105–24.

23. Letter, Robert Watts to B. B. Warfield, 23 September 1889 (Warfield Papers, Archives, Speer Library, Princeton Theological Seminary).

24. Ibid., 5 October 1893.

25. Ibid., 18 June 1890.

26. In a postcard to Warfield dated 11 February 1891, he reported to Warfield that "Spurgeon's 'Sword and Trowel', 'Expository Times', 'United Pres. Mag.' & 'The Theological Monthly' have all given most flattering reviews of my 'New Apologetic &c.'"

27. Letter, Robert Watts to B. B. Warfield, 13 October 1890 (Warfield Papers, Archives, Speer Library, Princeton Theological Seminary). These same sentiments were also expressed in a letter of 31 May, the following year. Of course he dreaded no less the inroads biblical criticism was making in the United States too and chose to provide a detailed critique of Briggs's biblical theology in his opening address to the Assembly's College in November 1891. See letter, Robert Watts to B. B. Warfield, 22 July 1891 (Warfield Papers, Speer Library, Princeton Theological Seminary).

28. Greene was inaugurated in 1892. See William K. Selden, *Princeton Theological Seminary: A Narrative History, 1812–1992* (Princeton: Princeton University Press, 1992), 56.

29. Letter, Robert Watts to B. B. Warfield, 20 February 1894 (Warfield Papers, Archives, Speer Library, Princeton Theological Seminary).

30. A. A. Hodge, review of *Natural Law in the Spiritual World* by Henry Drummond, *Presbyterian Review* 4 (1883): 872–73.

31. The full title of the work was *The Newer Criticism and the Analogy of the Faith. A Reply to Lectures by W. Robertson Smith, M.A., on the Old Testament in the Jewish Church* (Edinburgh: T. & T. Clark, 1882).

32. W. H. Green, review of *The Newer Criticism and the Analogy of the Faith* by Robert Watts, *Presbyterian Review* 3 (1882): 411–12. We should note, however, that A. A. Hodge had reacted very favorably to Watts's *The Rule of Faith*. See Hodge's review in the *Presbyterian Review* 7 (1886); 183–84.

33. This is recorded in a manuscript by George Macloskie entitled "Biographical Sketch" housed in the Macloskie Papers (CO498, Carton 4, Firestone Library, Princeton University).

34. Quoted in Edwin G. Conklin, "Biology at Princeton," *Bios* 19 (1948): 151–71, on 157.

35. Bradley John Gundlach, "The Evolution Question at Princeton, 1845–1929," (Ph.D. diss., University of Rochester, New York, 1995), 167.

36. Gundlach, "The Evolution Question at Princeton," 171.

37. These letters are extant in the Macloskie Papers (CO498, Carton 4, Firestone Library, Princeton University).

38. Letter, James McCosh to Rev. George Macloskie, 29 August 1871 (McCosh Correspondence, General Mss. [misc.] CO140, Firestone Library, Princeton University).

39. G. Macloskie, "The natural history of man," *The Ulster Magazine* 3 (1863): 230.

40. Miscellaneous Zoology Notes (n.d., Macloskie Papers, CO498, Box 1, Firestone Library, Princeton University).

41. G. Macloskie, review of *The Problem of Human Life* by A. Wilford Hall, *Presbyterian Review* 12 (1882): 798–99.

42. George Macloskie, "The Silicified Wood of Lough Neagh, with

Notes on the Structure of Coniferous Wood," *Proceedings of the Belfast Natural History and Philosophical Society* (14 Feb. 1872): 51–74.

43. Macloskie's 1880 transcription and introduction were republished by the New Jersey Historical Records Survey Project in 1941 under the title, *Transcriptions of Early Church Records of New Jersey: John Brainerd's Journal* (Newark, N.J.: The Historical Records Survey, 1941).

44. "Biographical Sketch" (Macloskie Papers, CO498, Carton 4, Firestone Library, Princeton University).

45. George Macloskie, "The Drift of Modern Science" (Mss. in Notebook, Macloskie Papers, CO498, Carton 1, Firestone Library, Princeton University).

46. George Macloskie, ibid., 9.

47. Scrapbook (Macloskie Papers, CO498, Carton 2, Firestone Library, Princeton University).

48. George Macloskie, "The Scotch-Irish, Their Services in Education" (Notebook, Macloskie Papers, CO498, Carton 2, Firestone Library, Princeton University).

49. He had, for example, written to the *Northern Whig* on 26 August during the Tyndall furore insisting that there was no desire in Belfast "to stifle free scientific inquiry," 27 August 1874, 8.

50. *The Examination of the Rev. James Woodrow, D.D., by the Charleston Presbytery* (Charleston, S.C.: Lucas & Richardson Co., 1890).

51. See the discussion in George M. Marsden, *The Soul of the American University: From Protestant Establishment to Established Nonbelief* (New York: Oxford University Press, 1994), 196–218.

52. I have surveyed these key publications in *Darwin's Forgotten Defenders*, 92–96.

53. George Macloskie, "Scientific Speculation," *Presbyterian Review* 8 (1887): 617–25, on 618.

54. George Macloskie, "Concessions to Science," *Presbyterian Review* 10 (1889): 220–28, on 220, 222.

55. Macloskie, "Scientific Speculation," 620.

56. Ibid., 625.

57. Macloskie, "Concessions to Science," 227.

58. George Macloskie, "The Testimony of Nature," *Presbyterian and Reformed Review* 1 (1890): 587–97, on 587.

59. Hutchinson published *Moses' Principia* in a determined effort to provide a Christian gloss on Newton's *Principia*. Macloskie referred to Hutchinson's efforts on several occasions. Hutchinson's views are discussed in John Hedley Brooke, *Science and Religion: Some Historical Perspectives* (Cambridge: Cambridge University Press, 1991).

60. For example, George Macloskie, "The Outlook of Science and Faith," *Princeton Theological Review* 1 (1903): 597–615; George Macloskie, "Mosaism and Darwinism," *Princeton Theological Review* 2 (1904): 425–41.

61. George Macloskie, Review of *Life and Letters of Charles Darwin* by Francis Darwin, *Presbyterian Review* 9 (1888): 519–22, on 522.

62. George Macloskie, "Theistic Evolution," *The Presbyterian and Reformed Review* 33 (1898): 1–22, on 21.

63. George Macloskie, "The Origin of New Species and of Man," *Bibliotheca Sacra*, 60 (1903): 261–75, on 273.

64. For example, Macloskie, "Mosaism and Darwinism," 427.

65. George Macloskie, "The Outlook of Science and Faith," 602.

66. Quoted in William Milligan Sloane, ed., *The Life of James McCosh: A Record Chiefly Autobiographical* (Edinburgh: T. & T. Clark, 1896), 117–24. I (David N. Livingstone) have discussed this in "Darwinism and Calvinism: The Belfast-Princeton Connection," *Isis* 83 (1992): 408–28.

67. George Macloskie, "Preliminary Talks on Science and Faith" (Notebook, Macloskie Papers, CO498, Carton 3, Firestone Library, Princeton University).

Three   CONTENDING FOR THE FAITH

1. Willa Cather, *Not under Forty* (New York: Alfred Knopf, 1936 [1988]).

2. Robert T. Handy, *A Christian America: Protestant Hopes and Historical Realities* (New York: Oxford University Press, 1984), 185–210.

3. Paul Carter, *The Spiritual Crisis of the Gilded Age* (DeKalb, Ill.: Northern Illinois University Press, 1971).

4. R. F. G. Holmes, *Our Irish Presbyterian Heritage* (Belfast: Presbyterian Church in Ireland, 1985), 152–53.

5. George M. Marsden, *The Evangelical Mind and the New School Presbyterian Experience* (New Haven, Conn.: Yale University Press, 1970); *Fundamentalism and American Culture* (New York: Oxford University Press,

1980); *Reforming Fundamentalism: Fuller Seminary and the New Evangelicalism* (Grand Rapids, Mich.: William B. Eerdmans, 1986); *Understanding Fundamentalism and Evangelicalism* (Grand Rapids, Mich.: William B. Eerdmans, 1991).

6. George M. Marsden, "Fundamentalism as an American Phenomenon: A Comparison with English Evangelicalism," *Church History* 56 (June 1977): 215–32.

7. Steve Bruce, *God Save Ulster: The Religion and Politics of Paisleyism* (Oxford: Oxford University Press, 1989). Lefferts A. Loetscher, *The Broadening Church: A Study of Theological Issues in the Presbyterian Church since 1869* (Philadelphia: University of Pennsylvania Press, 1957). Bradley Longfield, *The Presbyterian Controversies* (New York: Oxford University Press, 1991).

8. William J. Weston, *Presbyterian Pluralism: Competition in a Protestant House* (Knoxville: University of Tennessee Press, 1997).

9. J. Edwin Orr, *The Fervent Prayer: The Worldwide Impact of the Great Awakening of 1858* (Chicago: Moody Press, 1974). Richard Carwardine, *Trans-Atlantic Revivalism: Popular Evangelicalism in Britain and America, 1790–1865* (Westport, Conn.: Greenwood Press, 1978).

10. *The Year of Grace: A History of the Revival in Ireland, A.D. 1859* (Boston: Gould and Lincoln, 1860).

11. *The Year of Delusion* (Belfast, 1859).

12. The best revisionist discussion of the revival of 1859 is Myrtle Hill, "Ulster Awakened: The '59 Revival Reconsidered," *Journal of Ecclesiastical History* 41 (1990): 443–62.

13. S. W. Murray, *W. P. Nicholson: Flame for God in Ulster* (Belfast: The Presbyterian Fellowship, 1973). J. A. Gamble, *From Civil War to Revival Victory: A Souvenir of the Remarkable Evangelistic Campaigns in Ulster from 1921 to December 1925* (Belfast: Emerald Isle Books, 1976).

14. Loetscher, *Broadening Church*, 9–18.

15. A. A. Fulton, "The Church in Tension—In the Twentieth Century—Mainly," in *Challenge and Conflict: Essays in Irish Presbyterian History and Doctrine* (Antrim, Northern Ireland: W. and G. Baird, 1981), 152.

16. George M. Marsden, "The New School Heritage and Presbyterian Fundamentalism," in Charles G. Dennison and Richard C. Gamble, eds., *Pressing toward the Mark: Essays Commemorating Fifty Years*

of the *Orthodox Presbyterian Church* (Philadelphia: Orthodox Presbyterian Church, 1986), 169–82.

17. Loetscher, *Broadening Church*, 93.

18. Ibid., 98.

19. Fulton, "The Church in Tension," 156; Holmes, *Presbyterian Heritage*, 125.

20. Fulton, "The Church in Tension," 157.

21. Robert Allen, *The Presbyterian College, Belfast: 1853–1953* (Belfast: William Mullan and Son, 1954), 224.

22. Fulton, "The Church in Tension," 157.

23. Quoted in Allen, *Presbyterian College*, 225.

24. Quoted in Loetscher, *Broadening Church*, 104.

25. Randall Balmer and John R. Fitzmier, "A Poultice for the Bite of the Cobra: The Hocking Report and Presbyterian Missions in the Middle Decades of the Twentieth Century," *Diversity and Discipleship: Presbyterians and Twentieth Century Christian Witness*, Milton Coalter, et al., eds., (Louisville, Ky.: Westminster/John Knox Press, 1991), 109–11.

26. Ibid., 149–52.

27. Allen, *Presbyterian College*, 256; Holmes, *Presbyterian Heritage*, 163.

28. Quoted in Fulton, "The Church in Tension," 164.

29. *Minutes of the General Assembly*, PCI (1926), 18.

30. John M. Barkley, St. Enoch's Congregation, 1872–1972. *An Account of Presbyterianism in Belfast through the Life of a Congregation* (Belfast: Presbyterian Bookshop, 1973).

31. Ibid., 107.

32. A. A. Fulton, *J. Ernest Davey* (Belfast: Presbyterian Church of Ireland, 1970).

33. Ibid., 3.

34. Ibid., 37.

35. Ibid., 73.

36. Ibid., 74.

37. The trial of Davey by the Presbytery of Belfast was recorded, verbatim, and later printed by the presbytery. It is an extraordinarily

valuable historical document. *The Trial of Professor Davey by the Presbytery of Belfast* (Belfast, 1927), hereinafter *The Trial*.

38. *The Trial*, 112.

39. Ibid.

40. Ibid., 113.

41. Ibid., 88–91.

42. Ibid., 120.

43. Ibid., 119.

44. *Minutes of the General Assembly*, PCI (1927), 43.

45. *The Origin and Witness of the Irish Evangelical Church* (Belfast: Evangelical Bookshop, 1945), 63–64.

46. *Minutes of the General Assembly*, PCUSA (1925), 88.

47. Loetscher, *The Broadening Church*, 125–55; Weston, *Presbyterian Pluralism*; Longfield, *Presbyterian Controversies*.

48. Loetscher, *Broadening Church*, 135.

49. John M. Mulder and Lee A. Wyatt, "The Predicament of Pluralism: The Study of Theology in Presbyterian Seminaries since the 1920s," in *The Pluralistic Vision: Presbyterians and Mainstream Protestant Education and Leadership*, Milton J. Coalter, et al., eds., (Louisville, Ky.: Westminster/John Knox, 1992), 42.

50. Quoted in *The Broadening Church*, 139.

51. Quoted, ibid., 141.

52. Quoted, ibid., 143.

53. Ibid., 148; George M. Marsden, "Perspective on the Division of 1937," in *Pressing Toward the Mark*, eds. Dennison and Gamble, 295.

54. Longfield, *The Presbyterian Controversies*, 51, 124.

55. D. G. Hart, *Defending the Faith: J. Gresham Machen and the Crisis of Conservative Protestantism in Modern America* (Baltimore, Md.: Johns Hopkins University Press, 1994), 8.

56. Ibid., 37.

57. *Christianity and Liberalism* (Grand Rapids, Mich.: Eerdmans, 1992), 1.

58. Hart, *Defending the Faith*, 60.

59. Quoted, ibid.

60. Ibid., 85.

61. Loetscher, *Broadening Church*, 155.

62. Allen, *Presbyterian College*, 259.

63. Holmes, *Presbyterian Heritage*, 155.

64. *The Trial*, 193.

65. Allen, *Presbyterian College*, 260.

66. For example, Richard Hofstadter, *Anti-Intellectualism in American Life* (New York: Alfred Knopf, 1962).

67. *What Is Faith?* (New York: Macmillan, 1925), 249.

68. For a full explication of the relationship of history to truth in this context, see George M. Marsden, "J. Gresham Machen, History and Truth," *Westminster Theological Journal* 42 (1979): 157–75. The argument herein is drawn from that article and from Marsden's later piece, "Understanding J. Gresham Machen," in *Understanding Fundamentalism and Evangelicalism*, 182–201.

69. Loetscher, *Broadening Church*, 146.

70. Ibid., 105.

Four   KEEPING THE COVENANT

1. Richard Rose, *Governing Without Consensus* (London: Faber, 1971).

2. The best single book on this subject is the magisterial work of the late John Whyte, *Interpreting Northern Ireland* (Oxford: Clarendon, 1990), to which we shall refer again in the discussion to follow. I have discussed some of these issues in a similar way elsewhere: "Protestant Ideology and the Irish Conflict: Comparing Ulster Protestantism and American Evangelicalism," *Fides et Historia* 23 (fall 1993): 3–17.

3. Duncan Morrow, *The Churches and Inter-Community Relationships* (Coleraine: Centre for the Study of Conflict, University of Ulster, 1991), 2.

4. Liam DePaor, *Divided Ulster* (Hardmondsworth: Penguin, 1970).

5. Michael Farrell, *Northern Ireland: The Orange State* (London: Pluto, 1976).

6. Paul Bew, Peter Gibbon, Henry Patterson, *The State in Northern Ireland, 1921–72* (Manchester: Manchester University Press, 1979).

7. Peter Gibbon, *The Origins of Ulster Unionism* (Manchester University Press, 1975); Henry Patterson, *Class Conflict and Sectarianism: The Protestant Working Class and the Belfast Labour Movement* (Belfast: Blackstaff, 1980).

8. Whyte, *Interpreting Northern Ireland*, 187.

9. Richard Jenkins, "Northern Ireland: In What Sense Religion in Conflict?" in *The Sectarian Divide in Northern Ireland Today*, Richard Jenkins, Hastings Donnan and Graham McFarlane (London: Royal Anthropological Institute, occasional paper no. 41, 1986), 4–5. While Jenkins does not mention the following work, it fits his concerns well: an egregious example of social scientific work that largely misses the point by insisting that class and status, rather than culture and religion, are vital is, Cecilia A. Karch, "Anglo-Saxon Ethnocentrism: Its Roots and Consequences in Northern Ireland and the Southern United States," in *Taking State Power: The Sources and Consequences of Political Challenge*, John C. Leggett, ed. (New York: Harper and Row, 1973), 419–33.

10. Frank Gallagher, *The Indivisible Island: The History of the Partition of Ireland* (London: Gollancz, 1957).

11. Especially Donal Barrington, *Uniting Ireland* (Dublin: Tnairim, 1959), who wrote in conscious opposition to Gallagher.

12. Garret Fitzgerald, *Towards a New Ireland* (London: Charles Knight, 1972); Conor Cruise O'Brien, *States of Ireland* (London: Hutchinson, 1972).

13. M. W. Heslinga, *The Irish Border as a Cultural Divide* (Assen, the Netherlands, van Gorcum, 1962).

14. A. T. Q. Stewart, *The Narrow Ground: The Roots of Conflict in Ulster* (London: Faber and Faber, 1977), 180.

15. Ibid.

16. Fred Boal, John A. Campbell and David N. Livingstone, "The Protestant Mosaic: A Majority of Minorities," in *The Northern Ireland Question: Myth and Reality*, Patrick J. Roche and Brian Barton, eds., (Aldershot, England: Avebury, 1991), 99–129.

17. John Hickey, *Religion and the Northern Ireland Problem* (Dublin: Gill and Macmillan, 1984), 80.

18. Ibid., (emphasis is Hickey's).

19. Ibid., 87.

20. David Hempton and Myrtle Hill, *Evangelical Protestantism in Ulster Society, 1740–1890* (London: Routledge, 1992), 81.

21. The comparison between Calvinism and political ideology in Ulster and South Africa is suggested in Robert C. Crawford, *Loyal to*

King Billy: A Portrait of the Ulster Protestants (New York: St. Martin's Press, 1987), 106–17. A more highly developed and well-articulated rendering of this comparison, and on the idea of religiosocial covenant, to which we shall return, is Donald Harman Akenson, *God's People: Covenant and Land in South Africa, Israel and Ulster* (Ithaca, N.Y., and London: Cornell University Press, 1992).

22. Quoted in Hickey, *Religion and the Northern Ireland Problem*, 88.

23. Whyte, *Interpreting Northern Ireland*, 104.

24. Ibid., 105.

25. Jenkins, "Northern Ireland: In What Sense Religion in Conflict?" 9.

26. Frank Wright, "Protestant Ideology and Politics in Ulster," *European Journal of Sociology* 14 (1974): 213.

27. Owen Dudley Edwards, *The Sins of Our Fathers* (Dublin: Gill and Macmillan, 1970), 64.

28. Tom Gallagher, "Religion, Reaction and Revolt in Northern Ireland: The Impact of Paisleyism in Ulster," *Journal of Church and State* 23 (Autumn 1981): 423–44.

29. The book by Steve Bruce, *God Save Ulster*, noted above, is a model of careful yet diffident scholarship on this controversial leader.

30. From *The Protestant Telegraph*, 28 May 1966, quoted in Wright, "Protestant Ideology," 224.

31. Ibid., 223.

32. Especially John Whyte, *Interpreting Northern Ireland*, 108; and Ian McAllister, "The Devil, Miracles and the Afterlife: The Political Sociology of Religion in Northern Ireland," *British Journal of Sociology* 33 (1982): 330–47; "Political Attitudes, Partisanship and Social Structures in Northern Ireland," *Economic and Social Review* 14 (1983): 185–202.

33. David Taylor, "Ian Paisley and the Ideology of Ulster Protestantism," in *Culture and Ideology in Ireland*, Chris Curtain, Mary Kelley, and Liam O'Dowd, eds., (Galway: Galway University Press, 1984), 59–78; "The Lord's Battle: Paisleyism in Northern Ireland," in *Religious Movements*, Rodney Stark, ed., (New York: Paragon House, 1985), 241–78. Martha Abele MacIver, "A Clash of Symbols in Northern Ireland: Divisions between Extremist and Moderate Protestant Elites," *Review of Religious Research* 30 (1989): 360–74.

34. The most outstanding scholarly interpreter of fundamentalism in the United States is George M. Marsden, whose *Fundamentalism and American Culture* (New York, Oxford University Press, 1981) is the definitive study.

35. "Fundamentalism as an American Phenomenon: A Comparison with English Evangelicalism," *Church History* 46 (June 1977): 215–32.

36. I have explored some of the perpectival issues surrounding the claim of American exceptionalism in "Viewing America: A Christian Perspective," *Fides et Historia* 17 (1984): 56–67.

37. Robert Bellah, "Civil Religion in America," *Daedalus* 96 (winter 1967): 1–21.

38. The fruits of the new work have been discussed with care and insight by Leonard J. Sweet, "Wise as Serpents, Innocent as Doves: The New Evangelical Historiography," *Journal of the American Academy of Religion* 56 (1988): 397–416; and by Douglas A. Sweeney, "The Essential Dialectic: The Historiography of the Early Neo-Evangelical Movement and the Observer-Participant Dilemma," *Church History* 60 (March 1991): 70–84.

39. Richard Hofstadter's *Anti-Intellectualism in American Life* (New York: Alfred Knopf, 1963) is a notable example.

40. *The Roots of Fundamentalism: British and American Millenarianism, 1800–1930* (Chicago: University of Chicago Press, 1970), xix.

41. George M. Marsden, "Defining Fundamentalism," *Christian Scholar's Review* 1 (winter 1971): 141–51; Ernest R. Sandeen, "Defining Fundamentalism: A Reply to Professor Marsden," *Christian Scholar's Review* 1 (spring 1972): 227–32 (to which Marsden added a short reply, 232–33).

42. These interpretive possibilities are carefully laid out in *Fundamentalism and American Culture*, 199–228.

43. "Fundamentalism and American Identity," *Annals of the American Academy of Political and Social Sciences*," 387 (January 1970): 65.

44. R. F. G. Holmes, *Our Irish Presbyterian Heritage* (Belfast: Presbyterian Church in Ireland, 1985), 152–53.

45. G. M. Marsden, "Fundamentalism as an American Phenomenon," 216.

46. Peter Brooke, *Ulster Presbyterianism: The Historical Perspective* (New York: St. Martin's Press, 1987).

47. Best articulated, e.g., in Ernest Tuveson, *Redeemer Nation* (Chicago: University of Chicago Press, 1968).

48. Bernard Bailyn, *The Ideological Origins of the American Revolution* (Cambridge: Harvard University Press, 1967); Nathan O. Hatch, *The Sacred Cause of Liberty: Republican Thought and the Millennium in Revolutionary New England* (New Haven: Yale University Press, 1977).

49. Quoted in Bruce, *God Save Ulster*, 269–70.

50. Akenson, *God's People*, 185–89.

51. Ibid., 186. On the same point, see also R. F. G. Holmes, "Ulster Presbyterians and Irish Nationalism," in *Religion and National Identity*, Stuart Mews, ed., (Oxford: Basil Blackwell, 1982), 535–48.

52. Alvin Jackson, "Unionist Myths, 1912–1985," *Past and Present*, 136 (1992): 164–185.

53. Marsden, *Fundamentalism and American Culture*, 11–21; and more fully developed in the same author's *Understanding Fundamentalism and Evangelicalism* (Grand Rapids, Mich.: William B. Eerdmans, 1991), 9–61.

54. Paul Johnson, *A Shopkeeper's Millennium: Society and Revivals in Rochester, New York, 1815–1837* (New York: Hill and Wang, 1978).

55. Marsden, *Understanding Fundamentalism*, 1.

56. David Miller, *Queen's Rebels* (Dublin: Gill and Macmillan, 1978), 5.

57. Steve Bruce, *The Edge of the Union: The Ulster Loyalist Political Vision* (Oxford: Oxford University Press, 1994), 122–53.

58. Arthur Aughey, *Under Siege: Ulster Unionism and the Anglo-Irish Agreement* (New York: St. Martin's Press, 1989), 21.

Five   POPULIST IDEOLOGY AND REVIVALISM

1. The argument here is drawn from Bew, Gibbon, and Patterson, *The State in Northern Ireland*, 44–74.

2. Ibid., 49.

3. Patrick Buckland, *A History of Northern Ireland* (New York: Homes and Meier, 1981), 38–46; Jonathan Bardon, *A History of Ulster* (Belfast: Blackstaff Press, 1992), 474–79; Steve Bruce, *The Red Hand: Protestant Paramilitaries in Northern Ireland* (Oxford: Oxford University Press, 1992), 10–13.

4. Quoted in Bardon, *History of Ulster*, 476.

5. Alvin Jackson, *Colonel Edward Saunderson: Land and Loyalty in Victorian Ireland* (Oxford: Oxford University Press, 1995).

6. Hempton and Hill, *Evangelical Protestantism in Ulster Society*, (London and New York: Routledge, 1992). See a reprise of some of the same themes in David Hempton's Cadbury Lectures at the University of Birmingham: *Religion and Political Culture in Britain and Ireland* (Cambridge: Cambridge University Press, 1996), 93–116.

7. Hempton and Hill, *Evangelical Protestantism*, 165.

8. Ibid., 180.

9. Ibid., 187.

10. James Loughlin, *Ulster Unionism and British National Identity since 1885* (London: Pinter, 1995), esp. 50–97.

11. S. W. Murray, *W. P. Nicholson: Flame for God in Ulster* (Belfast, 1976); S. E. Long, *W. P. Nicholson: The Rude Evangelist* (Cromara, co. Down, Ireland: The Slieve Croob Press, 1983); *W. P. Nicholson: Tornado of the Pulpit*, I. R. K. Paisley, ed., (Belfast: Martyrs Memorial Productions, 1982).

12. Paisley, *Tornado*, 131.

13. Long, *Rude Evangelist*, 5.

14. Murray, *Flame for God*, 8.

15. Long, *Rude Evangelist*, 5.

16. Quoted in Murray, *Flame for God*, 9.

17. W. P. Nicholson, "Riot and Revival in Lanarkshire," *The Alliance News* 32 (June 1957), 2.

18. W. P. Nicholson, "A Year in Glasgow, Then Back to the U.S.A.," *The Alliance News* 32 (October 1957), 2.

19. Ibid., and letter from Nicholson's daughter, Jessie Ryder to S. W. Murray, 16 April 1976 (copy in authors' possession).

20. Nicholson, "A Year in Glasgow," 3.

21. "Our New Evangelist," *The King's Business* 9 (February 1918), 11.

22. Ibid., 108.

23. "Evangelist Nicholson," *The King's Business* 9 (April 1918), 386.

24. Virginia L. Brereton, *Training God's Army: The American Bible School, 1880–1940* (Bloomington, Ind.: Indiana University Press, 1990), 24.

25. Quoted, ibid., 177, n. 21.

26. Robert Williams and Marilyn Miller, *Chartered for His Glory: Biola University, 1908–1983* (La Mirada, Calif.: Biola University, 1983), 27. For a good discussion of the growing conservatism in southern California Protestantism during 1900–1930, see Eldon G. Ernst and Douglas F. Anderson, *Protestant Progression: The Protestant Experience in California* (Santa Barbara, Calif.: Fithian Press, 1993), 83–92.

27. Daniel W. Draney, "John Murdoch MacInnis and the Crisis of Authority in American Protestant Fundamentalism, 1925–29" (Ph.D. diss., Fuller Theological Seminary, 1996); Joel Carpenter, "The Fundamentalist Leaven and the Rise of an Evangelical United Front," in *The Evangelical Tradition in America*, Leonard Sweet, ed. (Macon, Ga.: Mercer University Press, 1984), 286.

28. Williams and Miller, *Chartered for His Glory*, 48–50; Daniel P. Fuller, *Give the Wind a Mighty Voice: The Story of Charles E. Fuller* (Waco, Tex.: Word Books, 1972), 68–74.

29. Quoted in Fuller, *Give the Wind*, 72–73.

30. W. B. Yeats, "The Statues," *The Variorum Edition of the Poems of W. B. Yeats*, Peter Allt and Russell Alspach, eds. (New York: Macmillan, 1957).

31. *A Souvenir of the Remarkable Evangelistic Campaigns in Ulster from 1921 till December, 1925, Conducted by Rev. W. P. Nicholson* (Belfast: Emerald Isle Books, 1976), 3, (hereinafter *Souvenir*).

32. Long, *Rude Evangelist*, 8.

33. Murray, *Flame for God*, 12.

34. *Portadown News*, 30 April 1921, 4.

35. Ibid. (emphases are Craig's).

36. Quoted in Murray, *Flame for God*, 12.

37. Ibid., *The King's Business* 12 (September 1921), 900.

38. *Portadown News*, 11 June 1921, 3.

39. Lyman Stewart to W. P. Nicholson, 28 October 1921. Stewart Papers, Biola University Library; see also a notice in *The King's Business* that T. C. Horton, Director of Extension at the Institute, would accept invitations for a Nicholson mission in America after the fall, 1921. *The King's Business* 12 (September 1921), 901.

40. *The King's Business* 12 (September 1921), 901.

41. *The King's Business* 12 (October 1921), 998.

42. *The King's Business* 12 (November 1921), 1103.

43. *The Newtownards Chronicle and County Down Observer*, 29 October 1921, 5.

44. Ibid., 19 November 1921, 7.

45. *The Lisburn Standard*, 6 January 1922, 2.

46. Ibid., 13 January 1922, 5.

47. Ibid., 20 January 1922, 6.

48. Quoted in Murray, *Flame for God*, 14.

49. *The King's Business* 13 (October 1922), 1023–24.

50. *The Northern Whig and Belfast Post*, 11 May 1921, 5, (hereinafter *Northern Whig*).

51. *Northern Whig*, 16 May 1921, 7.

52. Ibid., 20 January 1922, 6.

53. Ibid., 9 February 1922, 5.

54. Ibid., 10 February 1922, 6.

55. Ibid., 11 February 1922, 5.

56. Ibid., 10 February 1922, 6.

57. Ibid., 13 February 1922, 7.

58. *The Lisburn Standard*, 17 February 1922, 8.

59. *Souvenir*, 5.

60. *Northern Whig*, 14 February 1922, 5.

61. Ibid., 8.

62. Ibid., 15 February 1922, 5 and 8.

63. Ibid., 16 February 1922, 5.

64. Ibid., 20 February 1922, 4–5.

65. Ibid., 7.

66. Ibid., 14 March 1922, 7.

67. *Belfast Telegraph*, 13 March 1922, 5.

68. Quoted in Long, *Rude Evangelist*, 9.

69. Quoted in Murray, *Flame for God*, 21–22.

70. *The Witness*, 27 April 1923, 8.

71. *The King's Business* 14 (February 1923), 148–49.

72. Ibid. 14 (April 1923), 374.

73. Ibid. 14 (June 1922), 603.

74. Ibid. 14 (June 1923), 920–21.

75. Ibid., 1921.

76. Quoted in Fuller, *Give the Wind*, 68.

77. Quoted in Murray, *Flame for God*, 30.

78. Paisley, *Tornado*, 10.

79. "Home Call of Rev. Wm. P. Nicholson," *The Alliance News* 35 (January 1960), 4.

80. John M. Barkley, *St. Enoch's Congregation, 1872–1972: An Account of Presbyterianism in Belfast through the Life of a Congregation* (Belfast: Presbyterian Bookshop, 1973), 131.

81. *Belfast Newsletter*, 1 August 1925, 6.

82. *Northern Whig*, 5 August 1925, 10.

83. Ibid., 6 August 1925, 10.

84. Ibid., 7 August 1925, 10.

85. Ibid., 8 August 1925, 10.

86. Ibid., 11 August 1925, 10.

87. Long, *Rude Evangelist*, 1.

88. Murray, *Flame for God*, 34–35.

89. Joel A. Carpenter, "Fundamentalist Movements and the Rise of Evangelical Protestantism, 1929–1942," *Church History* 81 (1980): 62–75.

CONCLUSION

1. "Introduction," Mark A. Noll, David W. Bebbington, and George Rawlyk, eds., *Evangelicalism: Comparative Studies of Popular Protestantism in North America, the British Isles, and Beyond, 1700–1990* (New York: Oxford University Press, 1994), p. 6.

2. See the various essays in Richard B. Sher and Jeffrey R. Smitten, eds., *Scotland and America in the Age of Enlightenment* (Edinburgh: Edinburgh University Press, 1990); see also Mark A. Noll, *Princeton and the Republic, 1768–1822: The Search for a Christian Enlightenment in the Era of Samuel Stanhope Smith* (Princeton: Princeton University Press, 1989).

3. Besides the sources quoted in chapter 1, see also Leigh Eric Schmidt, "Sacramental Occasions and the Scottish Context of Presbyterian Revivalism in America," in Sher and Smitten, eds., *Scotland and America*, 65–80.

4. For the contemporary relevance of this claim, see Frederick W. Boal, Margaret C. Keane, and David N. Livingstone, *Them and Us: Attitudinal Variation among Belfast Churchgoers* (Belfast: Institute of Irish Studies, 1997); and David N. Livingstone, Frederick W. Boal, and Margaret C. Keane, "Space for Religion: A Belfast Case Study," *Political Geography* 17 (1998): 145–70.

5. For example, Geoffrey Bell, *The Protestants of Ulster* (London: Pluto Press, 1976); Tom Nairn, *The Break-Up of Britain: Crisis and Neo-Nationalism* (London: NLB, 1977); Michael Hechter, *Internal Colonialism: The Celtic Fringe in British National Development, 1536–1966* (London: Routledge and Kegan Paul, 1975).

6. George M. Marsden, *The Soul of the American University: From Protestant Establishment to Established Nonbelief* (New York: Oxford University Press, 1994), 213.

7. See, for example, George Elder Davie, *The Democratic Intellect: Scotland and Her Universities in the Nineteenth Century* (Edinburgh: Edinburgh University Press, 1961); Alasdair MacIntyre, *Whose Justice? Which Rationality?* (Notre Dame, Ind.: University of Notre Dame Press, 1988); Andrew Lockhart Walker, *The Revival of the Democratic Intellect* (Edinburgh: Polygon, 1994); Craig Beveridge and Ronnie Turnbull, *Scotland after Enlightenment: Image and Tradition in Modern Scottish Culture* (Edinburgh: Polygon, 1997).

8. David Hempton and Myrtle Hill, *Evangelical Protestantism in Ulster Society, 1740–1890* (London: Routledge, 1992), 189.

Select Bibliography

Akenson, Donald Harman. *God's People: Covenant and Land in South Africa, Israel and Ulster*. Ithaca and London: Cornell University Press, 1992.

Allen, H. C., and Roger Thompson, eds. *Contrast and Connection: Bicentennial Essays in Anglo-American History*. Athens, Ohio: Ohio University Press, 1976.

Allen, Robert. *The Presbyterian College Belfast, 1853–1953*. Belfast: William Mullan, 1954.

Aughey, Arthur. *Under Siege: Ulster Unionism and the Anglo-Irish Agreement*. New York: St. Martin's Press, 1989.

Axtell, James. *After Columbus: Essays in the Ethnohistory of Colonial North America*. New York: Oxford University Press, 1988.

Bailyn, Bernard. *The Ideological Origins of the American Revolution*. Cambridge: Harvard University Press, 1967.

Bailyn, Bernard, and Philip D. Morgan, eds. *Strangers within the Realm: Cultural Margins of the First British Empire*. Chapel Hill, N. C.: University of North Carolina Press, 1991.

Balmer, Randall, and John R. Fitzmier. "A Poultice for the Bite of the Cobra: The Hocking Report and Presbyterian Missions in the Middle Decades of the Twentieth Century." In *Diversity and Discipleship: Presbyterians and Twentieth-Century Christian Witness*, ed. Milton Coalter, et. al. Louisville, Ky.: Westminster John Knox Press, 1991.

Bardon, Jonathan. *A History of Ulster*. Belfast: Blackstaff Press, 1992.

Barkley, John M. *St. Enoch's Congregation, 1872–1972: An Account of Presbyterianism in Belfast through the Life of a Congregation*. Belfast: Presbyterian Bookshop, 1973.

———. "Francis Hutcheson (1694–1746)." *Bulletin of the Presbyterian Historical Society of Ireland* 14 (March 1985): 12.

Barrington, Donal. *Uniting Ireland*. Dublin: Tnairim, 1959.

Bebbington, David W., Mark A. Noll, and George A. Rawlyk, eds. *Evangelicalism: Comparative Studies of Popular Protestantism in North America, the British Isles, and Beyond, 1700–1990*. New York: Oxford, 1994.

Bellah, Robert. "Civil Religion in America." *Daedalus* 96 (winter 1967): 1–21.

Bew, Paul, Peter Gibbon, and Henry Patterson. *The State in Northern Ireland,* *1921–72.* Manchester: Manchester University Press, 1979.

Blackstone, W. T. *Francis Hutcheson and Contemporary Ethical Theory.* Athens, Ga.: University of Georgia Press, 1965.

Boal, Fred, John A. Campbell, and David N. Livingstone. "The Protestant Mosaic: A Majority of Minorities." In *The Northern Ireland Question: Myth and Reality,* eds. Patrick J. Roche and Brian Barton. Aldershot, England: Avebury, 1991.

Bowler, Peter J. "Darwinism and the Argument from Design: Suggestions for a Re-evaluation." *Journal of the History of Biology* 10 (1977): 29–43.

Brooke, Peter. *Ulster Presbyterianism: The Historical Perspective, 1610–1970.* Belfast: Athol Books, 1994.

Brown, Stewart J. "Presbyterian Communities, Transatlantic Visions and the Ulster Revival of 1859." In *The Cultures of Europe: The Irish Contribution,* ed. James P. Mackey. Belfast: Institute of Irish Studies, 1994.

Bruce, Steve. *God Save Ulster: The Religion and Politics of Paisleyism.* Oxford: Oxford University Press, 1989.

———. *The Red Hand: Protestant Paramilitaries in Northern Ireland.* Oxford: Oxford University Press, 1992.

———. *The Edge of the Union: The Ulster Loyalist Political Vision.* Oxford: Oxford University Press, 1994.

Buckland, Patrick. *A History of Northern Ireland.* New York: Homes and Meier, 1981.

Campbell, T. D. "Francis Hutcheson: 'Father' of the Scottish Enlightenment." In *Origins and Nature of the Scottish Enlightenment,* ed. R. H. Campbell and Andrew S. Skinner. Edinburgh: John Donald, 1982.

Carpenter, Joel. "The Fundamentalist Leaven and the Rise of an Evangelical United Front." In *The Evangelical Tradition in America,* ed. Leonard Sweet. Macon, Ga.: Mercer University Press, 1984.

Carter, Paul. *The Spiritual Crisis of the Gilded Age.* DeKalb, Ill.: Northern Illinois University Press, 1971.

Carwardine, Richard. *Transatlantic Revivalism: Popular Evangelicalism in Britain and America, 1790–1865.* Westport, Conn.: Greenwood Press, 1978.

Cather, Willa. *Not Under Forty.* New York: Alfred Knopf, 1936, [1988].

Cohen, Anthony P., ed. *Belonging: Identity and Social Organization in British Rural Cultures.* St. John's, Newfoundland: Institute of Social and Economic Research, 1982.

———. *Symbolizing Boundaries: Identity and Diversity in British Cultures.* Manchester: Manchester University Press, 1987.

Crawford, Robert C. *Loyal to King Billy: A Portrait of the Ulster Protestants.* New York: St. Martin's Press, 1987.

Davie, George Elder. *The Democratic Intellect: Scotland and Her Universities in the Nineteenth Century.* Edinburgh: Edinburgh University Press, 1961.

Davis, David B. *The Problem of Slavery in Western Culture.* Ithaca, N.Y.: Cornell University Press, 1966.

Degler, Carl. *Neither Black Nor White: Slavery and Race Relations in Brazil and the United States.* New York: Macmillan, 1971.

DePaor, Liam. *Divided Ulster.* Hardmondsworth: Penguin, 1970.

Desmond, Adrian. *The Politics of Evolution: Morphology, Medicine, and Reform in Radical London.* Chicago and London: University of Chicago Press, 1989.

Edwards, Owen Dudley. *The Sins of Our Fathers.* Dublin: Gill and Macmillan, 1970.

Ernst, Eldon G., and Douglas F. Anderson. *Protestant Progression: The Protestant Experience in California.* Santa Barbara, Calif.: Fithian Press, 1993.

Farrell, Michael. *Northern Ireland: The Orange State.* London: Pluto, 1976.

Fiering, Norman. *Moral Philosophy at Seventeenth-Century Harvard: A Discipline in Transition.* Chapel Hill: University of North Carolina Press, 1981.

Fitzgerald, Garret. *Towards a New Ireland.* London: Charles Knight, 1972.

Fredrickson, George M. *White Supremacy: A Comparative Study in American and South African History.* New York: Oxford University Press, 1981.

Gallagher, Frank. *The Indivisible Island: The History of the Partition of Ireland.* London: Gollancz, 1957.

Gallagher, Tom. "Religion, Reaction and Revolt in Northern Ireland: The Impact of Paisleyism in Ulster." *Journal of Church and State* 23 (autumn 1981): 423–44.

Gibbon, Peter. *The Origins of Ulster Unionism: The Formation of Popular Protestant Politics and Ideology in Nineteenth-Century Ireland.* Manchester: Manchester University Press, 1975.

Gould, Peter, and Rodney White. *Mental Maps.* London and New York: Penguin, 1974.

Greene, Jack P. *Peripheries and Center: Constitutional Developments in the Extended Politics of the British Empire and the United States.* Athens, Ga.: University of Georgia Press, 1986.

Handy, Robert T. *A Christian America: Protestant Hopes and Historical Realities.* New York: Oxford University Press, 1984.

Hart, D. G. *Defending the Faith: J. Gresham Machen and the Crisis of Conservative Protestantism in Modern America.* Baltimore, Md.: Johns Hopkins University Press, 1994.

Hatch, Nathan O. *The Sacred Cause of Liberty: Republican Thought and the Millen-*

nium in *Revolutionary New England*. New Haven, Conn.: Yale University Press, 1977.

——. *The Democratization of American Christianity*. New Haven, Conn.: Yale University Press, 1989.

Hechter, Michael. *Internal Colonialism: The Celtic Fringe in British National Development, 1536–1966*. London: Routledge and Kegan Paul, 1975.

Hempton, David. *Religion and Political Culture in Britain and Ireland: From the Glorious Revolution to the Decline of Empire*. Cambridge: Cambridge University Press, 1996.

Hempton, David, and Myrtle Hill. *Evangelical Protestantism in Ulster Society, 1740–1890*. London: Routledge, 1992.

Heslinga, M. W. *The Irish Border As a Cultural Divide*. Assen, the Netherlands: van Gorcum, 1962.

Hickey, John. *Religion and the Northern Ireland Problem*. Dublin: Gill and Macmillan, 1984.

Hill, Myrtle. "Ulster Awakened: The '59 Revival Reconsidered." *Journal of Ecclesiastical History* 41 (1990): 443–62.

Hilton, Boyd. *The Age of Atonement: The Influence of Evangelicalism on Social and Economic Thought, 1785–1865*. Oxford: Oxford University Press, 1988.

Hoeveler, David J., Jr. *James McCosh and the Scottish Intellectual Tradition, from Glasgow to Princeton*. Princeton, N.J.: Princeton University Press, 1981.

Hofstadter, Richard. *Anti-Intellectualism in American Life*. New York: Alfred Knopf, 1962.

Holmes, R. F. G. "Ulster Presbyterians and Irish Nationalism." In *Religion and National Identity*, ed. Stuart Mews. Oxford: Basil Blackwell, 1982.

——. *Our Irish Presbyterian Heritage*. Belfast: Presbyterian Church in Ireland, 1985.

Jackson, Alvin. "Unionist Myths, 1912–1985." *Past and Present* 136 (1992): 164–85.

——. *Colonel Edward Saunderson: Land and Loyalty in Victorian Ireland*. Oxford: Oxford University Press, 1995.

Jenkins, Richard. "Northern Ireland: In What Sense Religion in Conflict?" In *The Sectarian Divide in Northern Ireland Today*, ed. Richard Jenkins, Hastings Donnan, and Graham McFarlane. London: Royal Anthropological Institute, occasional paper no. 41, 1986.

Johnson, Paul. *A Shopkeeper's Millennium: Society and Revivals in Rochester, New York, 1815–1837*. New York: Hill and Wang, 1978.

Lindberg, David C., and Ronald L. Numbers, eds. *God and Nature: Historical Essays on the Encounter between Christianity and Science*. Berkeley: University of California Press, 1986.

Livingstone, David N. "The Idea of Design: The Vicissitudes of a Key Concept in the Princeton Response to Darwin." *Scottish Journal of Theology* 37 (1984): 329–57.

———. *Darwin's Forgotten Defenders: The Encounter between Evangelical Theology and Evolutionary Thought*. Grand Rapids, Mich. and Edinburgh: Eerdmans and Scottish Academic Press, 1987.

Loetscher, Lefferts A. *The Broadening Church: A Study of Theological Issues in the Presbyterian Church since 1869*. Philadelphia: University of Pennsylvania Press, 1957.

Longfield, Bradley. *The Presbyterian Controversies*. New York: Oxford University Press, 1991.

Loughlin, James. *Ulster Unionism and British National Identity since 1885*. London: Pinter, 1995.

MacIntyre, Alasdair. *Whose Justice? Which Rationality?* Notre Dame, Ind.: University of Notre Dame Press, 1988.

MacIver, Martha Abele. "A Clash of Symbols in Northern Ireland: Divisions between Extremist and Moderate Protestant Elites." *Review of Religious Research* 30 (1989): 360–74.

Marsden, George M. *The Evangelical Mind and the New School Presbyterian Experience*. New Haven, Conn.: Yale University Press, 1970.

———. "Defining Fundamentalism." *Christian Scholar's Review* 1 (winter 1971): 141–51.

———. "Fundamentalism as an American Phenomenon: A Comparison with English Evangelicalism." *Church History* 56 (June 1977): 215–32.

———. "J. Gresham Machen, History and Truth." *Westminster Theological Journal* 42 (1979): 157–75.

———. *Fundamentalism and American Culture*. New York: Oxford University Press, 1980.

———. "The New School Heritage and Presbyterian Fundamentalism." In *Pressing toward the Mark: Essays Commemorating Fifty Years of the Orthodox Presbyterian Church*, ed. Charles G. Dennison and Richard C. Gamble. Philadelphia: Orthodox Presbyterian Church, 1986.

———. *Reforming Fundamentalism: Fuller Seminary and the New Evangelicalism*. Grand Rapids, Mich.: Eerdmans, 1986.

———. *Understanding Fundamentalism and Evangelicalism*. Grand Rapids, Mich.: Eerdmans, 1991.

———. *The Soul of the American University: From Protestant Establishment to Established Nonbelief*. New York: Oxford University Press, 1994.

Materassi, Mario, and Maria Irene Ramalho de Sousa Sanntos, eds. *The American Columbiad: "Discovering" America, Inventing the United States*. Amsterdam: VU Press, 1996.

McAllister, Ian. "The Devil, Miracles and the Afterlife: The Political Sociology of Religion in Northern Ireland." *British Journal of Sociology* 33 (1982) 330–47.

———. "Political Attitudes, Partisanship and Social Structures in Northern Ireland." *Economic and Social Review* 14 (1983): 185–202.

Miller, David. *Queen's Rebels*. Dublin: Gill and Macmillan, 1978.

Moody, T. W., and J. C. Beckett. *Queen's, Belfast, 1845–1949. The History of a University*. 2 vols. London: Faber & Faber, 1959.

Moore, James R. *The Post-Darwinian Controversies: A Study of the Protestant Struggle to Come to Terms with Darwin in the United States and Great Britain, 1870–1900*. Cambridge: Cambridge University Press, 1979.

———. "Evangelicals and Evolution: Henry Drummond, Herbert Spencer, and the Naturalization of the Spiritual World." *Scottish Journal of Theology* 38 (1985): 383–417.

Morgan, Edmund S. *Inventing the People: The Rise of Popular Sovereignty in England and America*. New York: Norton, 1988.

Morrow, Duncan. *The Churches and Inter-Community Relationships*. Coleraine: Centre for the Study of Conflict, University of Ulster, 1991.

Mulder, John M., and Lee A Wyatt. "The Predicament of Pluralism: The Study of Theology in Presbyterian Seminaries since the 1920s." In *The Pluralistic Vision: Presbyterians and Mainstream Protestant Education and Leadership*, ed. Milton J. Coalter, et. al. Louisville, Ky.: Westminster John Knox Press, 1992.

Murray, S. W. *W. P. Nicholson: Flame for God in Ulster*. Belfast: The Presbyterian Fellowship, 1973.

Nash, Gary B. *Red, White and Black: The Peoples of Early America*. Englewood Cliffs, N.J.: Prentice-Hall, 1994.

Noll, Mark A. *The Princeton Theology, 1812–1921: Scripture, Science and Theological Method from Archibald Alexander to Benjamin Warfield*. Grand Rapids, Mich.: Baker, 1983.

———. "Common Sense Traditions and American Evangelical Thought." *American Quarterly*, 37 (1985): 216–38.

———. *Princeton and the Republic, 1768–1822. The Search for a Christian Enlightenment in the Era of Samuel Stanhope Smith*. Princeton, N.J.: Princeton University Press, 1989.

———. *The Scandal of the Evangelical Mind*. Grand Rapids, Mich.: Eerdmans, 1994.

Noll, Mark A., and George A. Rawlyk, eds. *Amazing Grace: Evangelicalism in Australia, Britain, Canada and the United States*. Grand Rapids, Mich.: Baker Books, 1993.

Numbers, Ronald L. "George Frederick Wright: From Christian Darwinist to Fundamentalist." *Isis* 79 (1988): 624–45.

O'Brien, Conor Cruise. *States of Ireland*. London: Hutchinson, 1972.

O'Brien, Susan Durden. "A Transatlantic Community of Saints: The Great Awakening and the First Evangelical Networks, 1735–1755." *American Historical Review* 91 (October 1986): 811–32.

Orr, J. Edwin. *The Fervent Prayer: The Worldwide Impact of the Great Awakening of 1858*. Chicago: Moody Press, 1974.

Patterson, Henry. *Class Conflict and Sectarianism: The Protestant Working Class and the Belfast Labour Movement*. Belfast: Blackstaff, 1980.

Rehbock, Philip F. *The Philosophical Naturalists: Themes in Early Nineteenth-Century British Biology*. Madison, Wisc.: University of Wisconsin Press, 1983.

Robbins, Caroline. "'When It Is That Colonies May Turn Independent': An Analysis of the Environment and the Politics of Francis Hutcheson." *William and Mary Quarterly* 11 (1954): 214–51.

Roberts, Jon. *Darwinism and the Divine in America: Protestant Intellectuals and Organic Evolution, 1859–1900*. Madison, Wisc.: University of Wisconsin Press, 1988.

Rose, Richard. *Governing without Consensus*. London: Faber, 1971.

Ross, Dorothy. *G. Stanley Hall: The Psychologist as Prophet*. Chicago: University of Chicago Press, 1972.

Rupke, Nicolaas A. *Richard Owen, Victorian Naturalist*. New Haven, Conn.: Yale University Press, 1994.

Sandeen, Ernest R. *The Roots of Fundamentalism: British and American Millenarianism, 1800–1930*. Chicago: University of Chicago Press, 1970.

———. "Defining Fundamentalism: A Reply to Professor Marsden." *Christian Scholar's Review* 1 (spring 1972): 227–32.

Schmidt, Leigh E. *Holy Fairs: Scottish Communions and American Revivals in the Early Modern Period*. Princeton, N.J.: Princeton University Press, 1990.

Selden, William K. *Princeton Theological Seminary: A Narrative History, 1812–1992*. Princeton, N.J.: Princeton University Press, 1992.

Sher, Richard B., and Jeffrey R. Smitten, eds. *Scotland and America in the Age of Enlightenment*. Edinburgh: Edinburgh University Press, 1990.

Snowman, Daniel. *Britain and America: An Interpretation of Their Culture, 1945–1975*. New York: Harper and Row, 1977.

Stewart, A. T. Q. *The Narrow Ground: The Roots of Conflict in Ulster*. London: Faber and Faber, 1977.

Stout, Harry S. *The Divine Dramatist: George Whitefield and the Rise of Modern Evangelicalism*. Grand Rapids, Mich.: Eerdmans, 1991.

Sweeney, Douglas A. "The Essential Dialectic: The Historiography of the Early Neo-Evangelical Movement and the Observer-Participant Dilemma." *Church History* 60 (March, 1991): 70–84.

Sweet, Leonard J. "Wise as Serpents, Innocent as Doves: The New Evangelical Historiography." *Journal of the American Academy of Religion* 56 (1988): 397–416.

Taylor, David. "Ian Paisley and the Ideology of Ulster Protestantism." In *Culture and Ideology in Ireland*, ed. Chris Curtain, Mary Kelley, and Liam O'Dowd. Galway: Galway University Press, 1984.

——. "The Lord's Battle: Paisleyism in Northern Ireland." In *Religious Movements: Genesis, Exodus, and Numbers*, ed. Rodney Stark. New York: Paragon House, 1985.

Turnbull, Ronnie. *Scotland after Enlightenment: Image and Tradition in Modern Scottish Culture*. Edinburgh: Polygon, 1997.

Tuveson, Ernest. *Redeemer Nation*. Chicago: University of Chicago Press, 1968.

Tyrrell, Ian. "American Exceptionalism in an Age of International History." *American Historical Review* 96 (1991): 1031–55.

Walker, Andrew Lockhart. *The Revival of the Democratic Intellect*. Edinburgh: Polygon, 1994.

Walker, Brian, and Alf McCreary. *Degrees of Excellence: The Story of Queen's, Belfast, 1845–1995*. Belfast: Institute of Irish Studies, 1994.

Wells, Ronald A. "Protestant Ideology and the Irish Conflict: Comparing Ulster Protestantism and American Evangelicalism." *Fides et Historia* 23 (Fall, 1993): 3–17.

——. "Viewing America: A Christian Perspective." *Fides et Historia* 17 (1984): 56–67.

Westerkamp, Marilyn J. *Triumph of the Laity: Scots-Irish Piety and the Great Awakening*. New York: Oxford University Press, 1988.

Weston, William J. *Presbyterian Pluralism: Competition in a Protestant House*. Knoxville, Tenn.: University of Tennessee Press, 1997.

Whyte, John. *Interpreting Northern Ireland*. Oxford: Clarendon, 1990.

Woodward, C. Vann. "The Comparability of American History." In *The Comparative Approach to American History*, ed. C. V. Woodward. New York: Basic Books, 1968.

Wright, Frank. "Protestant Ideology and Politics in Ulster." *European Journal of Sociology* 14 (1974): 213.

Index

Government of Ireland Act, 126
Gray, Asa, 45, 47
Great Britain. *See* Britain
Green, W. H., 8, 32, 39–40, 47
Greene, Jack P., 3
Greene, William Brenton, 38–39
Grier, William J., 66, 68–69, 77–78, 133, 143
Griffith, Arthur, 124
Gundlach, Bradley, 41
Guyot, Arnold, 40

Hall, G. Stanley, 17
Hamill, Thomas, 57
Hamilton, William, 15, 16
Handy, Robert T., 51
Hanna, Samuel, 66
Hart, D. G., 74
Hartt, Charles Frederick, 41
Hatch, Nathan O., 21, 97
Heilsgeschichte, 27
Hemmings, Raymond, 111
Hempton, David, 90, 105–6
heresy, trial of Davey, 62–68, 76
Heslinga, M. W., 87
Hickey, John, 89–90, 91
higher education
    curricular philosophies, 10–20, 142–43
    in Ireland, 12–16
    McCosh's ideals, 142
Hill, Myrtle, 90, 105–6
Hilton, Boyd, 30
History of Scottish Philosophy (McCosh), 16
History of the Philosophy of Mind (Blakey), 14
Hocking, William, 60
Hodge, A. A., 36, 39, 66–67
Hodge, Charles
    and Gibson, 22
    and McCosh, 11, 41
    and Macloskie, 45
    and MacMillan, 8
    mentioned, 66
    Systematic Theology, 8, 57
    and Watts, 32, 33, 34–35, 57, 143
    What Is Darwinism?, 40
Hoeveler, J. David, Jr., 15, 19
Holmes, R. Finlay G., 52, 76, 96–97, 115
Holy Spirit, in doctrinal standards, 56, 57
Home Rule issue, 98, 101, 105
Hooker, J. D., 34
hostage taking, 124
Hunter, James
    and biblical criticism, 77–79, 143
    and Davey, 64–65
    and Irish Evangelical Church, 68–69, 76

mentioned, 5
    and Nicholson, 131–33
    and O'Neill, 60–62
Hutcheson, Francis, 8–9, 140
Hutchinsonianism, 47
Huxley, Thomas Henry, 31, 34, 47

idealism, 41
inclusivist-exclusivist controversy, 69–70, 72, 75–76
Independent Board of Presbyterian Foreign Missions, 60, 73
The Indivisible Island (Gallagher), 86
inductive philosophy, 15–16
internal-conflict interpretation, of Northern Ireland, 87–88
interpretation, biblical, 78, 143
Intuitions of the Mind (McCosh), 15
Ireland
    Anglo-Irish agreement, 81, 97
    constitution, 86
    fundamentalist-modernist controversy, 76–77
    higher education, 12–16
    missionary controversy, 60–61
    modernism, 60–62
    nationalist and unionist views, 86
    national system of intermediate education, 18
    Presbyterian Church rift with America, 51–57
    revivalism, 21–26
The Irish Border As a Cultural Divide (Heslinga), 87
Irish Evangelical Church, 68, 76, 133
Irish Republican Army (IRA), 124

Jackson, Alvin, 99–100
James, William, 17
Jefferson, Thomas, 92
Jenkins, Richard, 85, 91
Jesus Christ, 47, 56
John C. Green School of Science, 40–42, 43–44

Lanarkshire Christian Union, 110
language
    of bipolar antipathy, 114–15
    of fundamentalism, 113–14
Latimer, W. T., 22
Leitch, Matthew, 57–58
liberalism
    cultural modernists, *vs.* Protestant liberals, 74–75